How Great Leaders Think, Act and Communicate

Mental Systems, Models and Habits of the World´s Richest Businessmen – Upgrade Your Mental Capabilities and Productivity with Stoicism, Emotional Intelligence & Decision Making Techniques

R. Stevens

© **Copyright 2019 - All rights reserved.**

The content contained within this book may not be reproduced, duplicated or transmitted without direct written permission from the author or the publisher.

Under no circumstances will any blame or legal responsibility be held against the publisher, or author, for any damages, reparation, or monetary loss due to the information contained within this book, either directly or indirectly.

Legal Notice:

This book is copyright protected. It is only for personal use. You cannot amend, distribute, sell, use, quote or paraphrase any part, or the content within this book, without the consent of the author or publisher.

Disclaimer Notice:

Please note the information contained within this document is for educational and entertainment purposes only. All effort has been executed to present accurate, up to date, reliable, complete information. No warranties of any kind are declared or implied. Readers acknowledge that the author is not engaged in the rendering of legal, financial, medical or professional advice. The content within this book has been derived from various sources. Please consult a licensed professional before attempting any techniques outlined in this book.

By reading this document, the reader agrees that under no circumstances is the author responsible for any losses, direct or indirect, that are incurred as a result of the use of information contained within this document, including, but not limited to, errors, omissions, or inaccuracies.

Hello,

You live in a stressful and fast-paced business world.

When reading, everything seems logical and clear, but when you´re at work, you tend to forget quickly and move on as usual.

You forget things, because you have to process a lot of new information every single day and you don´t actively repeat the lessons you have learned.

I have found a practical solution for you. One which doesn´t require any mental energy.

Based on the contents of the book you will get access to 4 different programs and summaries:

- Summary of 29 mental models, some used by presidents, billionaires and other successful business people.

- ´The 30-Day Emotional Intelligence Booster Program´ in PDF format

- The stoic quotes in a easy to print format

- 3-Month-Self-Evaluation-Journal

If you want to think, act and behave like a great leader:

- Go to:
  http://greatleadersthink.businessleadershipplatform.com/

  OR Scan the QR Code below

- Get the programs and summary
- print the one you want to work on first
- start reading and initiate the desired change

Tip: **Work on 1 program at the time**

Enjoy the book.

R. Stevens

Business Leadership Platform

www.businessleadershipplatform.

Table of Contents

BILLIONAIRE THOUGHT MODELS IN BUSINESS — 9

- Introduction — 11
- Chapter 1: Introduction to Mental Models — 17
- Chapter 2: The Way You See the World — 33
- Chapter 3: The Thought Patterns of Successful Managers — 53
- Chapter 4: Systemize for Productivity — 75
- Chapter 5: Negotiation—How to Make It a Win-Win — 95
- Conclusion — 115

EMOTIONAL INTELLIGENCE IN BUSINESS — 119

- Introduction — 121
- Chapter 1: Human Emotions — 129
- Chapter 2: 3 EQ Models Every Business Leader Needs to Know — 147
- Chapter 3: Introspection — 165
- Chapter 4: ´Extrospection´ — 183
- Chapter 5: 30-Day Emotional Intelligence Booster Program — 199
- Conclusion — 233

STOICISM FOR BUSINESS — 235

- Introduction: The Basics of Stoicism — 239
- Chapter 1: Introspection: Know Thyself — 251
- Chapter 2: Productivity — 269
- Chapter 3: Motivation and Discipline — 287
- Chapter 4: Adjusting to the Outside — 303
- Chapter 5: Stoicism in the Business World — 319
- Chapter 6: Stoicism in the Real World — 339
- Conclusion — 369

REFERENCES — 373

Billionaire Thought Models in Business

Replicate the thinking systems, mental capabilities and mindset of the Richest and Most Influential Businessmen to Earn More by Working Less

Introduction

Every employee dreams of the day they will be promoted from regular member of staff to a managerial position. For most people, being stuck in one position for a long time is the most demoralizing thing to go through. However, the managerial position comes with its own share of challenges. The responsibilities of a manager—even at the lowest level—are without a doubt greater than those of a regular employee. The skills you require to be considered for a managerial position, as well as those you will have to use to succeed in your new position, call for you to attain a superior mental model.

Among other things, you will have to coordinate a team, oversee work processes, and answer to the higher-ups about the performance of your division. Make no mistake about it; management is a giant leap for any employee. Apart from learning to resist sticking it to your peers about your newfound success, you will need another skill above all else. This is the skill of decision-making. As a manager, a lot of what you will be doing will be making decisions. If you do not change your mental model from employee to manager, things could quickly turn awry for you.

The greatest adjustment you will have to make as a new manager, however, is having people answering to you. Even if you move from one managerial level to another, there will be more people answering to you that before. Every decision you make in your new job will be more important, and if you are not careful, the very prospect could create massive anxiety issues that will hinder your delivery. Anxiety can be especially debilitating because it robs from you the self-belief and confidence to deliver on your new job. This is the last thing you want to do; you were obviously promoted because your bosses saw something in you. Stagnation is the best-case scenario for people who under-deliver in junior managerial positions. Demotion happens to be the worst, and your career might never recover from that.

Another thing that new managers struggle with is doing their old job, sometimes on top of your new responsibilities. Because the old job got you your new position, it is highly likely that your mind will gravitate toward it as a safe and proven alternative to the new and unproven world of team leadership. The only problem with this is that you will not have the energy to do your new job to the best of your abilities. When you suddenly find yourself leading a team, you will be tempted to think that performing your old job will prove to your team that you are the kind of leader who leads from the front. The only problem is that you will not be leading from the front; you will be working from the front. As a manager, your leadership comes more from plotting the path that your team will follow into the future than working on the day-to-day issues.

A managerial position comes with some authority and power. For some new managers, they cannot resist using their newfound power to shove their subordinates around. Sometimes you move into your new office and have to fire someone soon thereafter for valid reasons. You should not hold back just so you do not seem to be flexing your muscles. In fact, some of the most effective managers tend to be those who make some dramatic power move soon after being promoted. However, you should avoid doing so to flex your muscles because, for one, your seniors will not appreciate that.

Another area where most new managers struggle at is in determining just how much you need to work. Does moving up the ladder mean that you can start working fewer hours, or does the increased responsibility mean that you should work weekends and give yourself over to your job? If there is one area where the phrase "Work smart, not hard" applies best, then it is in managerial positions. That is not to say that the managers who work overtime and weekends even after being promoted are doing it wrong, but often you will find that they struggle to delegate or they are trying to justify their promotion by working harder than ever. The flip side is to delegate all the paperwork and focus more on strategic planning for your division. Your bosses will always be appreciative of a manager who comes to them with a plan on how the company can optimize a certain aspect of their business. After all, that is why they promoted you in the first place; they saw some potential in you.

Whether you are in a managerial position or hoping to be promoted to one, you need to learn how to make better decisions. This means that not only should your decision-making process be optimized, but it should also result in higher-quality decisions. People tend to waste a lot of their time and energy in the decision-making process because their approach to the issues on which they need to decide is wrong.

Biases also affect decision-making and lead to the wrong decisions altogether. When you make the wrong decisions in your personal life, you will waste a few thousand dollars at most, maybe get your heart broken, or waste a few months or years of your life. When you are a manager, the wrong decision will lose the company time and resources and bring the stakeholders down on your boss. Your bosses cannot afford to have that happen, so they will usually try to weed out possible letdowns before it comes to that. The one thing you will realize about managerial positions is that there is a very tiny margin of error. One mistake and you are out, with a good recommendation letter possibly being your only consolation.

The bottom line is that you cannot afford to make mistakes when you are a manager. Every decision has to be right or at least be mostly right—a higher-quality decision. You need to approach every problem in the right perspective, be aware of all your biases, and weed out any distractions. In turn, you will get more confident, lead better, and command greater respect from subordinates and superiors alike.

In this book, we will address the issue of decision-making in positions of leadership. Our focus will be on the mental models through which managers and team leaders arrive at their decisions. Mental models inform everything—from the way managers process information to the kind of questions they ask when faced with a conundrum and the way they answer questions. If you address the mental model you use to make your decisions, then your suitability to a position of leadership will be granted. If your bosses have not seen it yet, they will soon identify you as an employee who deserves a promotion.

Nothing works better in inspiring people than the story of other people who have made it before them. In this book, we will lean heavily on the stories of successful people like Elon Musk, Jeff Bezos, Ray Dalio, Warren Buffett, Walt Disney, and Bill Gates, to name a few. These men established some of the world's most successful businesses and outdid themselves as inspirational managers leading thousands of employees. Their stories, especially how they prevailed in the face of challenges and continued to press forward even after encountering bitter failure, leave a lot to be desired and teach some very important lessons. The inspirational stories of these men will be weaved into the book as a practical guide to show you that men have achieved that which you most desire—success.

The theories on how to attain a managerial mindset or crush it in your new job as manager will be brought to you in a narrative style, infused with practical lessons from the aforementioned super achievers. In the end, you should be able to apply decision-making to enhance your work process, increase your efficiency, and get more done in less time and with fewer resources. This may sound like a pitch for some Ponzi scheme, but it is the sort of improvement possible in your professional life if you follow the mental models of Charlie Munger and Warren Buffett. These two men have managed to build an investment fund 20,000-fold in just four decades. The mental models they use will feature prominently in the first chapter of this book.

In the second chapter, we will touch on destructive mental models, including framing, confirmation bias, selective perception, and ideology. After helping you identify the negative thinking styles that have been sabotaging your decision-making, we will introduce the positive models of thinking for better decision-making. They include Bayesian thinking, reverse thinking, the Pareto principle, KISS, and the minimum viable product. Finally, we will address the one area of a managerial career where you must exercise your power—negotiations. In the end, you should be perfectly capable of moving into that new office and impressing both your subordinates and your seniors. If you are already in that office, you can adapt these lessons to improve your job performance and further your career.

Chapter 1: Introduction to Mental Models

Every one of us has our own way of looking at and understanding the world around us. These strategies of interacting with our environment are called *mental models*. They influence not just our thinking but also our perception of challenges and opportunities. A person with a positive mental model will see opportunities in challenges while others perceive hardship. In trying to understand people and their behavior, mental models can paint a very distinct picture of how their brain works. This is because each one of us uses mental models to break down complex issues. As such, everything we do can be traced back to the mental models under whose influence we did it.

Technical professionals are trained to look at the world in terms of systems while social scientists think by looking at the incentives behind every word and every action. The sciences teach us to look at the world from the perspective of evolution, while religions examine everything through the eyes of higher powers. Using any one discipline alone will leave you with a massive blind spot, which can be detrimental to effective thinking. Only by combining all existing disciplines can you form a rational and well-rounded opinion about a subject and, ultimately, make the right decision.

With mental models, we attempt to create a latticework of theories in our minds and put them together in a practical model. Mental models are formed from education, both formal and that which comes from experience. The more educated you have about a subject, the better you will be about tackling issues in that particular area. The lessons you receive on a variety of topics ultimately creates your mental model.

Another way to illustrate mental models as a latticework of lessons and experiences is the nail-and-hammer analogy. To a person who walks around with a hammer, everything looks like a nail that deserves nothing than to be thumped hard. The more diverse and flexible your mental model is, the better you will be at a varied number of things.

When you don't have a mental model to fit a situation, human psychology is such that you will torture the reality you encounter to fit into the most relevant of your models, which is rather boggling. You would think that it is easier to stretch the models you have to fit the situation rather than going the other way round, but for most people, this is not the reality. Unless you train your brain to adjust to new encounters through a *mental model*, you will invariably twist situations instead of seeing them for what they are. A perfect example is a manager who has an insecure mental model. Everything around them will be viewed as a threat, including the well-meaning employee who comes to them with an idea to improve the efficiency of the division.

Mental models come in two basic types—simple generalizations and complex theories. In most cases, a simple generalization comes from thought patterns that have not been examined or lazy thinking. Simple generalization breeds stereotypical thinking because the person would rather judge at first sight than examine something further. When someone says that people from such and such place are rude or untrustworthy, they are essentially grouping everyone into one category based on their experience with a small portion of the whole. Simple generalizations breed such flawed thinking as sexism, racism, and other forms of discrimination.

Complex theories are thinking models that are arrived at

through a process of detailed evaluation. Mental models based on complex theories include the scientific method and critical thinking, among others. Complex theories also inform our thinking and, most notably, best illustrate the nail-and-hammer principle. If you do not know how to think critically, you will use whatever mental model you have, whether complex or generalized, in situations that require critical thinking. Understanding the mental model needed in every situation is thus very important because it informs our decisions.

The most important conclusion from this is that your views on the world will affect your decisions and their outcomes. Success in your chosen career will depend, in many ways, on the mental model through which you make decisions. If you use the right model, your decisions will result in more success and money than you could ever dream of because you will be able to manage your time in a gainful manner and enhance your overall efficiency in life.

Characteristics of Mental Models

Some of the most pertinent things to keep in mind about mental models include their limitations, flexibility, and reliance on information.

Limitations

Mental models inform the way we interpret information and events around us. We usually form mental models based on our experiences or learn them from various sources, such as books or other people. A mental model covers a very minute aspect of our lives compared to the complexities that exist in it. There are only a few areas of your life where you can apply a particular mental model. Luckily, there are just as many mental models as there are life situations. You can always find a mental model that is better suited to your specific situation within your personality. For example, if you have developed a fighter mentality and do not believe in giving up, you can always adopt a different mental model if the one you have been using to pursue a certain goal proves to be ineffective. Another limitation is that situations might come to you in such a way that all mental models you have developed do not quite cover it.

Flexibility

Luckily, mental models are usually flexible regardless of how we formed them in the first place. Mental models learned from early life experiences will often be unlearned as we go along meeting new people and learning new things. The decision to keep holding on to a mental model is one we make every day. If a mental model has been working well for you over time, it is totally expected that you will keep on holding it for as long as it continues working. This explains why Charlie Munger and Warren Buffett have held on to their mental models of value investing for such a long time.

However, when a mental model proves inefficient in a particular situation, it is entirely possible for you to adjust it. This is a healthier strategy than warping your interpretation of a situation to match your mental model. As much as you might feel like you have no fixed personality because you deviate from your chosen mental model when faced by different situations, you will make better decisions when you recognize that a one-size-fits-all mental model is not just impossible, but it is also impractical.

Reliance on Information

The decision to use one type of mental model over another relies on your ability to receive, interpret, and act on information. Mental models depend on information to develop and apply. For example, when Charlie Munger receives an investment opportunity, he must find out more about the opportunity before deciding whether it presents him with a chance for value investing. As much as we need to develop mental models, their effectiveness in streamlining our work or personal lives depends entirely on how efficiently we apply them. The only efficient way to apply a mental model is after evaluating all available information.

To become an efficient manager, you must, therefore, question every fact and every opportunity you encounter. Without proper questioning, you will never identify the opportunity that comes cloaked as a challenge or the problem that comes disguised as an opportunity. Therefore, the most reliable mental model to adopt is to question thoroughly everything that comes your way before acting.

Effects of Mental Models

Mental models affect every area of our lives. The way we view our world is as distinct to each one of us as the fingerprint. That is why one person sees an opportunity where others see a challenge. It is also why people react differently to different stimuli. In this section, we look at the effects of your worldviews on your decision-making capabilities. Specifically, we will look at how worldview affects your chances of time management, efficient work, success, and making money.

Time Management

As a manager, you will discover that a lot of the work you will be doing will be making decisions. You will also have to live with the fact that your decisions will have a greater impact on a larger number of people. As a manager, you will be part of the leadership of the company, responsible to the shareholders on financial output and business strategies. The long-term strategies that the senior management formulates will rely on the supervision of junior managers like you who are accountable for the company's grassroots. Therefore, your decisions will carry greater weight as a junior manager, and you cannot afford to make the wrong ones. This means that your worldview must be correct in every decision-making situation.

It is also for this reason that mental models are so indispensable to managers. They simplify our decision-making process by teaching us to look at specific aspects of an argument presented to us. Mental models are formed from years of experience or simply by reading about them from people who have been through a similar experience. In this book, we will teach you mental models gained from experience and critical observation of some of the world's best managers and thought leaders. By applying the correct mental model to a complex situation, you can always arrive at a quick solution and avoid spending too much time trying to disprove a theory and instead work on it. One reason why it is important to manage your time well, especially in relation to decision-making, is that you will be called on to make decisions at critical moments, like deciding whether to follow through on an opportunity. If you waste too much time deciding whether to explore an opportunity, you might wake up to find it gone.

In fact, a mental model exists for this very purpose. It is called the Occam's razor, and it posits that the simple explanation to a complex scenario is most likely to be the most accurate one. People who understand this mental model will make their decisions based on whatever explanation is the least complicated. Moreover, when the explanation does not seem to satisfy you, there is always the delayed judgment mental model. Here, you should never make decisions immediately if you can delay them to a later day. Alternatively, there is the suspended judgment in which you make your decision but still leave room for changes that might necessitate you changing it.

Efficiency

The most successful businesses are those that manage to create the most utility from limited resources. This is called efficiency, and it is critical for every part of life. However, in business, efficiency is even more important because it affects the business' ability to compete and make the maximum from minimum resources. The more effective you can make your department, the greater the profits you will be able to generate for your employer. A high ratio of output divided versus input means that you have a greater ability to make money. This increases your chances of getting a promotion into higher office up the corporate ladder.

Mental models streamline your decision-making process—meaning that the time between receiving an opportunity and the time at which you decide to either act on it or not will be lesser. Furthermore, mental models can be used to increase your effectiveness. For example, the subtraction model allows you to cut out any extras from every decision and every plan you make, increasing your efficiency. The better you are at subtracting, the more efficient you will be at cutting out the unnecessary parts of every process in your department, and the more efficient you will be overall as a manager. Interestingly, your ability to create an efficient system relies on your ability to create a system to determine the efficiency of every aspect of your work. This includes staff number, resource allocation, and collaboration, among other aspects.

Success

Your success at your new job will rely very heavily on your ability to manage time and work efficiently to deliver on the objectives you set for yourself. Your success as a manager will depend on your ability to deal with complex issues that will arise from your job day after day. If you can handle complex situations and make the best of them, then your success will be all but assured. Failure to command control will most probably leave you burdened by unwinnable situations. According to experts, the best way to command a situation is by building an effective mental model to simplify the decision-making process.

A mental model allows you to make sense of numerous data points and identify the connections between ideas that will come to you every single day at the workplace. With no definitive way of assessing all the information you receive, the sheer volume of thinking needed every day would paralyze you. But with the right mental model in every situation, you can know (just like a pilot knows how to operate the sophisticated dashboard in the cockpit and fly an airplane) how to make sense of complex information by isolating the most relevant points and acting on them.

Just like every other system, you should update your mental models to keep them current at all times. You can do this by using the models you currently possess in a fluid, deliberate, and strategic manner. By doing this, you will create a system of thinking through, which your managerial career will thrive but also one that will be self-sustaining enough to assure you of success in the long run.

Money

As much as money is associated with success, these two can exist in two different planes. When dealing with money, the only thing in question is the handling of personal finances. It is a relatively narrow field but one that is just as important, if not a little more so. Your financial endowment determines, in a huge way, your capacity to own the comforts you need to be able to do your job well. Whatever mental model you use in managing your personal finances will have a huge effect on the kind of lifestyle you can maintain over a long time and, in turn, your capacity to deliver year after year in your managerial position.

As far as mental models for money management go, the most effective is the rule of compounding. As you think about a retirement investment, compounding will grow any money you save exponentially.

Common Mental Models

As an introduction to mental models, we shall look at some of the most effective mental models out there. They include success by subtraction, the outlier algorithm, and the protégé effect.

Success by Subtraction

Success by subtraction is a mental model whereby you extricate from your life or work all the negative aspects, simplifying everything and thus being able to move ahead into greater success. This mental model has been referred to in various ways, including the "Less is more" slogan of world-renowned architect Ludwig Mies van der Rohe. In critical thinking, subtraction allows you to remove all the noise from a concept and look at the underlying idea for greater clarity. When making some strategic decision, subtraction allows you to shed off the extra baggage and improve your chances of winning. Depending on the strength of your ideas and character, you can use subtraction even in times when it might look to the world like a terrible idea.

The actions of the Arizona Women's Softball team coach in 2007 best illustrate this idea. With his team set to start participating in the Women's College World Series the next day, the star pitcher broke a team rule that warranted a suspension from the team. Most coaches and business leaders for that matter would cut their star performer some slack "for the greater good." However, Mike Candrea was cut from a different cloth, and he decided to drop her from the team. He reasoned that she was a huge distraction from the team because she had broken the rules of being a team. If he allowed her to come along by overlooking a major infraction, he would be sending a subliminal message that she was better than the team or that the team relied on her to function.

His actions boosted the team spirit and prompted each player in the team to work extra hard as they came together and annihilated the rest of the roster, including their greatest opponent, UCLA, to lift the Women's College World Series. It requires great courage and convictions to be able to do something like this. For most people, they would rather keep the wildcard in the team than take a risk on a more reliable player.

This concept applies to most things in life. Even at the workplace, sometimes it is necessary to cut off a work process that everyone has been using for ages. If by your critical evaluation something does not add to the good of the team, removing it will tilt the odds back in your favor. It is basic mathematics—two negative signs equal a positive sign, and positive and negative equate negative. Removing that which takes away from you adds to your value while leaving it in means that you will always be lacking something.

Subtraction works in every area of management. Do you want to start by outlining a list of your priorities for the team you have been appointed to lead? Subtract the priorities from ten to five, from five to three, and from three to one. With fewer priorities, you will focus your efforts on a few of the most promising goals and increase your chances of attaining them, and while you should not go around firing people, consider the story of Jack Welch, General Electric chairman and CEO from 1981 to 2001 and the man who steered the company through a growth period of about 4,000% in two decades.

When Jack Welch started at General Electric, it was an old company, staid in its ways and bloated by inefficiencies of age. Having been an employee of GE all through his career, he understood that the bureaucratic nature of its operations was discouraging to the hardworking employees. A firm believer in the concept of success by subtraction, he enforced a policy whereby he would fire every employee in the bottom 10% of every department in the company. GE improved drastically as a result.

The law of subtraction has been proven to work in other areas of life, too, because in an ineffective system, the things we spend most of our time on turn out to be the least profitable. By adopting the subtraction mental model, you will improve not just your job performance at the office but other areas of your life as well. You will dedicate your time to the most important things, improve your overall efficiency, and bring greater success to every aspect of your life. And because your personal life will always bleed into your work life, subtracting the harmful from your life will actively enhance your work life as a prospective or new manager.

The Outlier Algorithm

An outlier is a data point that varies in a significant way from other data points in a cluster. Outliers are a subjective statistical phenomenon that may result from a range of anomalous causes. However, it is a mathematically established fact that every 1 in 22 data points will be different by as much as twice the value of the standard deviation in a dataset. With a sample of 1,000 data points, the outliers could vary by as much as three times. But how exactly does this highly mathematical phenomenon apply to mental models?

People with an outlier mental model are adept at identifying the things that everyone else misses that have the best chance of bringing them success. Someone with an outlier mentality will set themselves apart from everyone else by "thinking outside the box" to come up with unique solutions to common problems, making themselves indispensable to the whole.

One of the most popular (but unsung) uses of the outlier mental model was the formation of Airbnb by roommates Brian Chesky and Joe Gebbia. The two former classmates came up with a multibillion-dollar idea by thinking outside the box and combining accommodation and residence.

By learning to look outside the box, you can improve your efficiency in solving problems, coming up with new ideas, and executing common business functions. And as usual, differentiating yourself from the crowd is granted to give you greater recognition and success in terms of career advancement and monetary rewards.

The Protégé Effect

Roman philosopher Seneca once said that people learn while they teach. This saying is as true today as it was 2,000 years ago. While you apply yourself to teaching others, you learn almost as much or more than them. This is because student teachers have to work twice as hard as their students do in order to be able to teach them. As a result, students who also tutor other students have been shown to perform significantly better than those who only study for themselves.

As you teach your coworkers the ropes of your workplace, you will automatically get better at it and post outstanding results in your own work. As an employee aspiring to one day become a manager, this is one mental model you could adopt to attract the attention of your superiors. As a young manager, you will be more effective in your job if you undertake the task of teaching new concepts you introduce to the workplace by yourself. The best thing about a protégé mindset is that it allows you to learn not just as you teach others but also from yourself. The mistakes you make in your quest for excellence will become great teachers and enable you to improve constantly upon the foundation you have established for yourself.

In a constantly changing world, information is the most effective tool for self-empowerment. Your success as a manager will rely, in a way, on your ability to learn, process, and apply new information. Similarly, your efficiency in your new position will be influenced in a huge way by your ability to learn and improve. In business, the protégé effect is best observed in mentorship. While you teach a promising new hire the ropes of making it in the job, you will improve your own ability to perform your job. What's more, mentorship is an inherently ego-inflating experience. You feel good to know that someone else is looking up to you, so you will pursue success more purposefully.

The capper on having a protégé mindset is that as you improve and move up the ladder to senior management, you will leave behind a great employee to continue the good work you started. And whether you like it or not, the performance of the department you left to take up your new position in a more senior position will be used to judge your mettle as a manager. Even the most successful CEOs will be considered less successful if the company they used to lead goes into a tailspin of poor performance after their departure. Jack Welch is one manager whose standing has taken a beating after leaving his last position because General Electric fell in market value after his exit.

Few other mental models work better than the protégé effect in inspiring personal improvement. This is because while you face competition from the peers who feel (probably quite justly) that they deserved the promotion just as much as you did, the people you mentor as part of your protégé mental model will prove to be an indispensable support network to prop your career.

The Story of Charlie Munger

Charlie Munger is currently among the most outstanding investors in America. He is the highly decorated right-hand man to the world's richest investor, Warren Buffett, at Berkshire Hathaway. However, Charlie Munger has always been his own man. Warren Buffett has been quoted asserting that Charlie has always danced to his own music. The two Omaha natives share a cordial relationship and investment strategies—a bond that makes them a very formidable team. Charlie has been working with Warren Buffett in the investment industry since the 1970s and has accumulated a fortune worth over $1 billion in the process.

What most people do not know is that he had tried his hand in investing long before Warren Buffett and Berkshire Hathaway. Between 1962 and 1975, he ran Wheeler, Munger, and Co. investing in the Pacific Coast Stock Exchange. This operation was a terrible loss-making venture. It made losses of 32% and 31% in 1974 and 1975 respectively. When he joined Berkshire Hathaway, Munger joined a company that was run on the principles of value investing. Buffett introduced him to the mental models of compounding, which enabled him to turn his investment career around and start making money, rising up the ranks to vice-chair today. A simple change in mental models was enough to turn Munger's investment career around and steer it toward profitability.

Chapter 2: The Way You See the World

As a manager, you will be responsible for the interpretation of complex information and data sets for your company. It is imperative that you interpret all the information you receive in the most accurate way possible. You must treat information as a separate entity from you and ensure that you understand the data as it is, rather than as you want it to be. This requirement for a high level of accuracy calls for a high level of awareness on the personal biases we hold that may warp our understanding of information. In this chapter, we shall look at the most common and debilitating personal biases. We shall evaluate the ways through which they affect our interpretation of evidence and how you can retrain your mind to think in the context of your corporate life.

Confirmation Bias

Confirmation bias is a phenomenon through which people select the information that confirms their own beliefs from a piece of evidence. Confirmation bias is especially common when we have invested ideologically or emotionally in a belief. In these instances, being proven wrong feels like a hit on our self-worth. Usually, people fight hardest to avoid having their self-worth invalidated. As a result, they will pick out tiny pieces of evidence from a pool of information supporting their views and hang on to them stubbornly regardless of the evidence to the contrary.

In confirmation bias, we act like financial criminals covering the paper trail to avoid being caught. We are already wrong, but instead of confronting the mistakes of our past, we gloss over it with tiny bits of truth from whatever sources we can get them. It indicates that we hold personal pride higher than truth and knowledge. The underside to confirmation bias is that it often leads to spectacular failures when we cannot recognize past wrongs and learn from them.

Warren Buffett describes confirmation bias as a human phenomenon whereby we interpret every new piece of information we receive in such a manner that any previous conclusions we have made are not challenged. But in a world where nothing is assured, change is the only thing you can count on. So to hold fast to beliefs formed in the past, even in the face of new information, is grossly erroneous. In fact, it is by being ever willing to be proven wrong that we can challenge ourselves first to vet any belief we have thoroughly before adopting it. Moreover, keep evaluating it from time to time to be sure of its validity, and finally, be flexible enough to change any time we receive evidence to the contrary.

The cost of confirmation bias in business is wrong decisions, faulty projects, and losses. As a manager, you should be aware of exactly how confirmation bias affects your personal and professional beliefs. Essentially, personal confirmation bias leads to you only looking at and accepting the information that confirms your beliefs. It makes you a poor manager but does not necessarily affect your employer—for example, your views on gun rights in an industry that has nothing to do with gun rights, veganism in a non-food industry, how much better a latte tastes with or without vanilla, or any other personal view you may hold. Even though you may be biased as far as all these subjects are concerned, your job delivery need not suffer.

Professional confirmation bias is the more serious kind of prejudice a person can hold. It creeps up on us even when we are not aware—when we are actively trying to avoid making warped decisions based on our confirmation bias. For example, when conducting research for a new product idea you may have just had (which is bound to happen among product managers eventually), confirmation bias creeps up on you even without you being aware. In the following manner, you ask your team to design a research study to find the viability of a product you honestly believe to be the next big thing, either in the company or in the whole industry.

Straight off the door, your team is biased. All the information they will gather from the public will be to confirm or rule out the viability of your idea. But (and this is where it gets even trickier) because they are biased, they will most likely present questions in such a way that the respondents give them whatever information they are looking for. They will definitely not do this intentionally because confirmation bias often exhibits in some of the most well-meaning areas like impartial studies. But the results from the study will be biased and probably lead to a loss-making decision.

To avoid this particular and very expensive confirmation bias, be sure to conduct studies in a truly neutral and impartial way. For example, instead of asking respondents whether a certain feature would be good for a product, ask them to rank the existing product features in terms of their importance, then ask for recommendations on improvement. That way, you will be asking the customers to point out what they would like in a possible product instead of shoving your idea in their face. Whatever product you make from a study of real preferences for customers is likely to be more successful than the one that you created of your own volition.

With that being said, it is important to point out that confirmation bias exists where objectivity does not. The surest way to remove any confirmation bias from a discussion and the interpretation of evidence is to take a step back and evaluate all the information neutrally. In a teamwork situation, the best way to avoid sliding into the slippery slopes of confirmation bias is to have a *devil's advocate* in your team. This role might not be very suitable for you as the manager because some employees will take your word as the gospel truth. Recruiting an outspoken person and encouraging them to speak out on every discussion—however contrarian their views might be—could save you a lot of trouble because you are more likely to spot holes and contradictions in an argument that way.

There is all the incentive for you to seek to remove any hint of confirmation bias from all your decision-making. Amazon is one company that has built its foundation on an objective analysis of market needs and then worked to present users with exactly what they need. According to Jeff Bezos, experimentation and measurement have been a part of the company's culture from its foundation. Instead of looking for evidence to support his views, Jeff uses scientific methods to measure the support for every idea raised within the company. Only if the data supports a decision does he authorize it.

Amazon was built on a foundation of giving the customer what they want. To Jeff Bezos, any sort of confirmation bias influencing his company's perception of what the customers want would be contrary to the very essence of the company. The success of Amazon and Jeff Bezos, currently the richest man on earth, was possible only because he went out of his way to remove confirmation bias from his decision-making process and give his customers exactly what they wanted.

The thing about eliminating all traces of confirmation bias is that it gives you a very distinct advantage. When you make objective decisions that you can count on to be true as many as ten years from now, you can apply yourself to its attainment even if you do not see the gains immediately. Therefore, not only does the elimination of confirmation bias improve your ability to get the correct facts, but it also empowers you to pursue goals with full confidence that you are on the right path.

Framing

Framing is the foundation of mental models through which we look at the world. In essence, framing constitutes the different pathways through which we think and the concepts we employ to communicate with each other. In thinking, framing determines the ways through which we interpret the data we receive and decode our own thoughts. In communication, framing denotes the different methodologies through which different actors send out information. Studies have shown that the power of framing is even strong enough to swing political elections. The way a candidate presents their ticket vis-à-vis their opponents could change the issues voters prioritize when making their choice of candidate, making an unlikely candidate win.

The same concept is used in marketing. Products are rarely described using their qualities. Mostly, the benefits they bring to you as the consumer will be hyped so that you see nothing but the advantages of buying. Even is a product is not the best in the market, the fact that they made you associate their brand with the benefits of whatever product you are buying could endear their product to you far above their competitors.

When communicating, framing is of utmost importance. With just a few changes to the wording, the meaning of a whole passage could be changed and made to sound very different.

You can say two different things with very similar words or use very different words to say one thing. For example, in the stock market, when a share plummets in price, the word "correction" makes it more palatable and avoids the more anxious term like "plummet" or "tumbling." More ominously, depending on what source you hear it from, *genocide* could be referred to using the tamer phrase "ethnic cleansing."

It is for this reason that you should train yourself to speak articulately at all times, leaving no chances of misrepresentation of whatever you say. As a mental model, framing is a model developed through evolution to help our brains to deal with adversity. When you refer to death as a "loss," it falls into the category of lesser adversities like losing your keys, losing money, and such. It is a method of unconsciously lessening the pain that every human being invariably uses. And when used in this way, framing can be downright comforting. However, at the office, where everything needs to be clear and transparent, it might lead to misunderstandings or misrepresentation of facts.

The first rule of framing is that we get the answers to the questions we ask. And depending on the position we are on an issue, we will frame our thoughts about it in a particular way regardless of how objective we try to be. In communication, framing can best be described as "reading between the lines." Even though it does not tell you the whole story, it tells you enough to know a person's real feelings about an issue.

In thinking, framing is more deliberate. One person chooses to think of a problem as an opportunity while another looks at it as a challenge. Whichever way a problem comes, you choose to frame your thinking about it negatively or positively. Either way, you will find some supporting evidence to prop up your thinking. And when managing people as a junior manager, understanding framing can be valuable to ensure that you pay attention to cues that hint at deception among your employees.

Selective Perception

In a debate, each side is always coming up with ways to strengthen their position and convince the other side that they have it right instead of listening and attempting to come to an agreement. Just like confirmation bias, selective perception causes people to pick out the points they agree within a set of information and completely ignore the rest of it. Any information that contradicts your particular view is usually dismissed without a second thought, while you dwell on that which is more aligned with your principles. In the world of politics, this is why hot-button issues remain divisive even after events where one side of the argument is clearly in the wrong. The people who believe in a certain side of an argument will usually go out of their way (even out of the argument altogether) to find supporting evidence to defend their position.

The same phenomenon takes place in the office, especially with deeply ingrained matters like organizational culture, business model, and workplace policies. The veteran employees will often resist all possible attempts to change these aspects (however dated) at all costs. The same goes for business ideas and project management. Once a person takes one side of the argument, the ego drives them to dig in their heels and defend their position at all costs. It is a highly confrontational issue that could destroy not only the team spirit but also the efficiency and the ability to make money.

Selective perception exists in two different states—perceptual vigilance and perceptual defense. In perceptual vigilance, people will identify information that is contrary to their beliefs in any format that the information exists. Such people are likely to see opposition to their views, even where there is none. On the opposite side, we have a defensive perception, which focuses on keeping opposing opinions out.

So if a study is to be conducted to find out if the market is receptive to a certain product that someone is really invested in, the person with selective perception will scour the document to prove that a market exists. On the other hand, a person with a defensive perception will block out any information that seems to invalidate their view. Even more tellingly, people are willing to lower or raise the bar on the observations they make out of a situation just to validate their opinions.

Selective perception is formed based on a person's previous experiences, their attitudes, conditioning, age, and emotional state. People in similar categories among these demographics tend to have the same or similar selective perceptions about issues. As the leader, it is your job to learn how selective perception works and work as hard as possible to eliminate it from your own reasoning. This is accomplished by stepping back from your own views when assessing every piece of information and objectively evaluating the truth (or lack thereof) behind them.

Only when you have overcome all selective perception within yourself can you go to the next step of ensuring that the information you get from your employees is not warped either. You can do this by listening keenly to them and asking pointed questions to verify the source of their ideas and opinions. Only by resolving all disagreements on opinion can you then establish a work environment that is conducive to productive work. And when coming to a consensus, settling a point of contradiction with the resolution that you "agree to disagree" should never be considered to be a solution.

Ideology

In the world of philosophy, ideology is used to refer to a set of beliefs that a person holds. These beliefs close your mind up to other views, especially those opposed to your way of thinking. Every other piece of information that comes into our brains after we have formed an opinion about something tends to be examined through our opinions by accepting similar views and rejecting contrarian ones. On the other hand, business ideology represents the basic principles of a business, including the mission statement, code of ethics, and philosophies. All the decisions and actions that a business makes are meant to further the business ideology.

As a leader, you need to understand the ideology of your company so that you can work toward furthering it at the workplace. But you can also take it a step further and create your own ideology as part of your personal brand. Creating and working according to your personal ideology within the company will allow you to stand out from your peers in a huge way. There are also other ways for you as a leader to deal with business ideologies at the workplace.

When hiring, you should always ensure that the new employee exemplifies the business ideologies you are supposed to advance as a leader. The suitability of an employee to a position is best decided through ideological examination. After they have passed the ideological test, you can be assured that they will fit in the workplace just fine. Employees whose professional values are aligned with those of their employer have been proven to perform better and further the objectives more than those who are distinctly different.

The second way for a leader to deal with ideologies at the workplace is to be an example to other employees. The actions of a leader will always be scrutinized more than their words, so if you speak a big game but your actions do not reflect it, you will have a discordant group of followers. However, reflecting the values that you advocate will unite your team and make a more effective workplace culture. When making everyday decisions, you should consult your professional ideology and business philosophy. Just be careful not to make these beliefs into blinders that will cause you to have selective perception and confirmation bias. The ability to interpret all information objectively cannot be overstated.

Finally, as a leader, you are expected to be the ultimate authority on ideologies at the workplace. You should correct errors resulting from actions that are not based on the business ideology whenever and wherever they occur. Ideological differences are not the kind of discrepancies that you should wait to address during performance meetings. The cost to the business culture will be too great if errors are not fixed immediately and with conviction.

As much as ideologies prejudice people to discordant views, nothing unites people as much as a commonly held ideology. As a business leader, you should create an ideology for the workplace and ensure that your team adheres to it. The harmony that will result from this simple action will surprise you with how much it ties your team together and allows your team to work as a front toward a common goal.

Stoicism for Business

Among the most successful businessmen of this age, a common personality trait called Stoicism is very popular. It is a philosophy founded by Marcus Aurelius, an old Roman businessman who lost his treasure at sea and inspired generations of conquerors and super-achievers by his handling of that misfortune. Stoicism is a philosophy founded on self-control and resilience—the two most difficult values to observe as a man yet the most important of all if you are to live a life of purpose.

Stoicism has been adopted by the best business minds in the world today, including the likes of Warren Buffet, Charlie Munger, Bill Gates, and Elon Musk, among others. In fact, the concept of Stoicism is what appears to link all billionaires together despite the path they took to arrive at their fortune. Whenever any successful businessman talks about the path they took to get to their most successful stage in life, they will always emphasize personal grit, self-control, and perseverance. This is explained by the fact that business is tough and demanding. It requires a great sacrifice from anyone who attempts to the greatest heights.

The central tenet of Stoicism is that we must accept our mortality to live accomplished lives. The reason why Charlie Munger and other billionaires advocate thinking along the lines of mortality and death is that they had to overcome one common failing among us "mere mortals" to succeed. It is the proclivity to waste time and let other people waste our time with unimportant issues when that time would be better spent pursuing our goals. People are usually more selfish with their material possessions than their time, which is the exact opposite of what Stoicism preaches. The one thing we have in scarcity, according to Stoic Seneca, is time. At an unknown time in the future, each one of us will encounter death. Because that time could come any second in the future, you ought to live every minute like it is your last.

Today, you will often hear people use the phrase "What would you do if you learned that you had cancer and you would die in one year [or a month]?" People often hold off thinking about the things they want to accomplish until they get that terminal diagnosis. Others simply waste away, accomplishing nothing of what they set out to do because they failed to pursue their dreams. It seems like only the most successful businessmen appreciate their mortality and make the appropriate arrangements to ensure that their time here on earth is as fruitful as possible.

After a near-death experience while vacationing in Brazil back in 2001, Elon Musk laughed the matter off with the words: "I guess I learned my lesson now—vacationing will kill you." They were words said in jest, but they give you a very clear impression of his ideas about work and death. One is inevitable, and the other is a choice. Work does not invalidate death, but a death suffered without accomplishing all you set out to do definitely invalidates life.

Steve Jobs is another Stoic billionaire. He made a very poignant speech shortly before he passed away in 2011. In a commencement speech at Stanford University, he postulated that our time on earth is limited and that each one of us has a purpose. Rather than spend all our time trapped in dogma or another person's life, we should follow our heart and instinct and stop at nothing to accomplish our life's purpose. Of course, the first thing to do on that journey is to find a purpose and commit 100% to its attainment.

If nothing else, anyone hoping to succeed in management and leadership should adopt Stoicism because every successful man and woman that ever lived have observed it. Think about it. Can you name a single hero who did not go through tribulations or one who did not exhibit a superhuman amount of self-control? I will wager you anything that you will not find a single person to fit that description. Even if they did not confess to being Stoics, they observed the principles of this age-old philosophy. Therefore, if you want to become successful, living according to the principles of Stoicism will already have taken you further than any amount of hard work ever could because Stoicism will first require that you discover your life's purpose. But for the purposes of this book, the following qualities are associated with Stoics in business.

First, you must be authentic. To become a Stoic, you must embrace each and every one of your quirks and view your unique features as an asset rather than a liability or something to grow out of. Even if you have a role model or a mentor, you must be true to your real identity. Failure to do this results in a second-rate personality and mediocrity.

Second, you must always be rational and approach issues in a logical manner. You cannot be a Stoic if the negative mental models discussed above bias your thinking. And after taking care of the biases and prejudices that cloud your thinking, you can then take charge of your life by exercising self-control all the time. Remember, you cannot control/manage anything or anyone if you do not first control yourself.

The third principle of Stoicism has something to do with discovering your purpose in life. It entails engaging in purposeful action at all times. With your purpose in life clearly embedded in your mind, you can engage in ten different activities that all tie together in contributing to the attainment of a life goal. As you start working as a junior manager, you must discover your purpose in that position, write it down, and work every day to achieve that goal.

Emotional Intelligence in Business

Emotions affect many of the decisions we make. Even the decisions we think were informed by unquestionable logic and facts are usually influenced in some way by emotions. They are all around us. They control us. In most instances, they run our lives. That is why marketers rarely ever attempt to appeal to our logic when selling us on something. No, they go straight to our emotions, and soon enough, they have turned us into the ultimate consumers. While our emotions are an important part of our identity, they are also rather easy to manipulate. That is why emotional intelligence is such an important quality to cultivate.

Most remarkably, emotional intelligence, as measured by most companies before hiring, can be very critical to the remuneration and promotion process. On a higher level, emotional intelligence calls for us to get a stronger grasp on our ability to manage our own emotions as well as those of others. I use the term "stronger grasp" here to indicate that you can improve your handle on the emotions you feel every single day. This can be done the same way you improve your emotional intelligence (yes, it can be done)—through the disciplined practice of emotional training exercises like meditation. People with high emotional intelligence are considered better leaders because they possess some skills that others do not have, as discussed below.

Self-Awareness

Emotional intelligence is essentially the ability to understand one's emotions and the stimulus behind them. It also entails the interpretation of other people's emotions, which allows us to relate to other people. Emotions control our lives in very subtle ways. Every unexpected mood swing and every personality trait comes to us from some emotion or other. Being able to reach down to these emotions when soul-searching to understand exactly how they affect our behavior is an indispensable tool. It means that you are always aware of motives for different behavior not just in yourself but in other people too. The first step in finding a solution to a problem is to understand the underlying causes of that problem.

Moreover, self-aware people understand their limitations and their strengths. This kind of emotional balance and self-understanding comes in handy when you experience strong emotions like anger. People with high emotional intelligence are usually able to control their reactions to emotional stimuli. This, in turn, ensures that your emotions never have to interfere with your job, making you a reliable leader and effective manager.

Self-Regulation

Self-regulation is all about a person's ability to regulate their own emotions and act appropriately. It allows you to practice self-control, which in turn increases your personal accountability score. Successful leaders know that the first person you should conquer is yourself because you cannot take on the world while you are incapable of triumphing over your own personal issues. A person with high levels of self-control will not give in to compulsive habits like drunkenness and other self-sabotaging behaviors.

As a measure of emotional intelligence, self-regulation also measures your understanding of your own values and your own personal code of ethics. The things that you hold dear (e.g., truth and justice, fairness to all, and the pursuit of happiness) all fall under self-regulation. They form the red line across which you would never cross. In essence, they are the values that make you who you are.

Accountability, as mentioned above, is another important metric in self-regulation. The ability to take responsibility for good things and bad things is an important measure of emotional intelligence. If you blame others for things that go wrong around you or if you give others credit for the things you accomplished yourself, your emotional intelligence is sorely lacking.

Motivation

How driven are you? Do you want to spend your whole life in the bullpen? Or do you want to move into a managerial position and have your own office? Do you want to be a junior manager your whole career? Or do you dream of heading the whole company one day? The last is a dream only the boldest dare to dream, but whatever your aspiration, studies have proven that people work consistently better when they have a definite goal. The quality of work is also much better among people with big goals because they need to climb a higher distance than the rest. The level of your motivation counts toward your overall emotional intelligence score.

To be more motivated, first, you have to be doing something you love. It is advisable to write down a few reasons why you love your job to serve as your "why" and "where from." You can then set some goals to pursue as your "where to." If you hold yourself accountable and pursue your set goals, there is no reason why you should not achieve those goals, however high you set them.

Empathy

Empathy is the ability to put yourself in someone else's situation and experience an event from their perspective. Empathy is the highest level of care you can show someone. Even if you cannot really feel their pain or struggles, you at least try to relate. As a leader, empathy is critical to leading your team. The empathetic leaders are able to grow themselves and their teams. They constructively criticize those who need criticism to reach their potential, listen to those who need a sympathetic ear, and generally hold the team together. Studies have shown that while empathy requires that you go the extra mile to connect with your employees, the effort is well worth it. Empathetic managers enjoy significantly higher amounts of loyalty from their employees.

To grow your empathetic skills, you have to be adept at reading body language. People communicate loads using their bodies, and anyone who cares to pay attention could learn a whole lot from simply looking at them. Being able to read people from their body language is an important skill that comes in handy, whether you are being empathetic with an employee or measuring up a prospective partner in a negotiation. But with your newfound responsibilities and power, you will have to ask the odd employee (or your assistant if you get one) to work late nights from time to time. You could do it the old-fashioned way where you simply inform them, with the attitude that they can either follow through or look for another job. You can also respond to their emotions about having to work late and reassure them that you understand. That way, you will get more out of them and establish a rapport.

Decision-Making 101

Whenever someone else makes a decision that you are expected to enforce, the impulsive reaction is to criticize it as a bad decision. As a worker bee, you will spend a lot of your time criticizing your superiors for the decision they make. Your limited perspective on the bigger picture makes you walk around with the impression that you can make these big decisions better.

This is a common fallacy among thinkers. We all overestimate our decision-making capabilities and criticize everyone else. It is a common feature of the ego to inflate the view of self by playing our own skills up and underestimating other people. It is a fact of life that people only appreciate when they encounter the same situations that motivated the decisions they criticized. At the workplace, you will only understand why your work was not prioritized when you are promoted and start to encounter the complexities of running a company. Only then can you start to understand exactly where the priorities of the senior management lay in the strategic outlay of the company and realize that you were totally unequipped to make the very decisions you criticized.

Historically, even the most well-meaning business leaders have made the mistake of criticizing the decisions of others and blowing up their own decision-making capabilities. When he was starting Walt Disney Studios, Walt Disney established the most conducive workplace for his animators. He paid better than other companies, encouraged a spirit of informal camaraderie in the studios, and did not even require his workers to clock in their work hours. He thought it was the decision that made his company stay ahead of the park. In his reasoning, the decision to incentivize his employees with great working terms and the best pay in the industry was a proven winning strategy.

The rest of the animation industry maintained a more business-wise compensation and organization strategy. They paid standard wages and demanded a fixed number of hours' worth of work from their employees. There was no allowance for an "informal" atmosphere at Metro Goldwin Meyer or Universal Studios (the competitors of Walt Disney Studios) even though they produced cartoons like *Tom and Jerry* and *Oswald the Lucky Rabbit* respectively. The point is, despite being respectable companies producing iconic animated contents, Walt Disney looked down on them for the decision to treat their animation departments like any other department. He felt that his own decision to incentivize his employees with friendly terms of work was better than the rest of the industry.

In 1940, his workers were recruited into the newly formed Screen Cartoonist's Guild labor organization. It represented the workers from his competitors as well as his company. In a dispute that escalated with every passing day, his animators would end up striking and setting up a picket line in front of his studios in 1941. When he finally managed to negotiate a get-back-to-work deal, his company had gone almost a whole month with no one at the studios, and his debt situation (which had been bad before the strike) was approaching crisis levels.

Even though he had made the decision to treat his employees in a more informal manner to make their lives easier, his company suffered for it. In the end, he had to lay off almost half the workforce just to manage the wage bill his employees had arm-twisted out of him. His great shock was the realization that after opening his bank accounts with more than generous salaries and increments, his employees were not likely to be more loyal. When he was done negotiating to end the strike and open the studio for business once more, he was so disgusted with the whole situation that he decided to take a vacation to South America for months.

Walt Disney was more formalized with the clocks, timesheets, and quotas that he had previously decided against and derided competing studios for enforcing. The decisions of his competitors to formalize the workplace were not looking so misinformed after all.

When you become a leader, you become a part of the corporate model of your company. The role you play from the moment you are awarded that promotion that entitles you to the title of manager is advancing the objectives and goals of the highest echelons of the company. As a common worker, you are responsible for implementing the action plans that have been deliberated on by your superiors as being the most suitable stratagem to achieve certain goals. When you become a leader, your thinking should shift from implementation to strategic thinking. You become a part of the company's central nervous system responsible for devising and implementing action plans. The most effective managers are those who familiarize themselves to the company ideology and action plan, then make plans to make it easier for it to come to being.

Chapter 3: The Thought Patterns of Successful Managers

Successful managers tend to think in a very similar way. If you study the thought patterns of the top 20 richest businessmen in the world, you will spot some very distinct similarities. Even though they come from different industries and follow distinct paths to their massive success, you can connect their thought patterns. The most successful men in the world have always been bold thinkers. If not in innovating new ways of doing things to make them more effective, they have created value by coming up with new systems. Some, like Einstein, took a leap of imagination, came up with scientific theories, and expanded humankind's understanding of the world we live in. Every aspiring leader needs to adopt this kind of bold thinking if they hope to achieve even a fraction of what the likes of Einstein, Steve Jobs, and Bill Gates, just to name a few, have achieved.

In this topic, we will focus on discovering the thought patterns that made the most successful managers successful. We will start with decision-making before moving to more sophisticated systems of thought, including the Bayesian concept and reverse thinking. We will illustrate how distinguished thinking leads to successful careers wherever one may decide to establish their career. To do this, we will rely heavily on the life stories of some of the most successful thought leaders in the world, including Ray Dalio, Elon Musk, and Albert Einstein.

Decision-Making 102

In your capacity as a manager, you will be required to answer hundreds of questions every day. You will also make numerous decisions with far-reaching impacts. Every decision you make as a manager will affect the employees you lead, the company you work for, and the customers you serve. You can no longer take decision-making lightly. At the same time, the sheer volume of decisions you will be asked to make calls for the ability to make great decisions in half the time. In "Decision-Making 101," we addressed the fallacious perceptions of decision-making that most people have in which they have a bloated idea of their ability to decide while disparaging other people's choices.

In this section, we will look at the exact strategies you can follow to improve your decision-making skills. What follows is a systematic master plan that will streamline your administrative functions and make you a better leader.

Systemizing

As much as you need to make them, the small decisions in life tend to have a very serious clattering effect on your brain. They drain your mental energies so that you cannot dedicate the entirety of your mind to the important things. From the analysis of the decision-making habits of great managers, you will realize that they eliminate these questions from the word go, freeing up their time to more important pursuits. The solution is to cut down the hundreds of small decisions you will be required to make every day to a few huge critical ones. In the study of systemizing, we will study the habits of the previous president of America Barrack Obama.

As the manager of the world's biggest economy, there was obviously a lot of demands on President Obama's time. The decisions he made would affect the whole world, so it was even more important that he made the right ones. By cutting down decisions like his wake-up time, morning routine, the clothes he would wear to the office (he only wore blue or gray), and the breakfast he ate, he was able to save on his mental energies on the hundreds of more important decisions he would make on a daily basis.

It may not seem like much, but a routine like this one can go a long way in improving your decision-making capabilities. When paired with the other strategies that we will discuss in this section, it will play a huge part in transforming you into the kind of manager you have always wanted to become.

Vision

If I could give you a strategy to improve your decision-making capabilities, I would use "vision." When you make decisions based on a clearly defined vision, you will cut down on a big chunk of discordant decisions that you will be asked to make. This is how it works:

As soon as you take up the managerial position, you sit down and draft a vision for yourself and the department. This vision should take into account the overall vision and mission statements of the company so that whatever vision you write will fit your job description. Be as detailed as possible about the different dreams and goals you hope to achieve. You can work within the time frames set by the company, or you can create your own. Be careful not to overestimate your abilities or underestimate the time needed to accomplish a particular objective. That is the worst rookie mistake you could ever make, and it might cause you untold problems.

Any time you are faced with a question or decision, you will have a very specific way of answering it. You will simply ask yourself, "Does the action that results from this decision align with my vision?" If it does not align, your decision is made for you; and if it does, you can then set about attempting to accomplish it.

Being Resolute

One of the worst things you can do as a leader is to walk back on your decision. It gives the impression that you are weak and unsure of yourself, which can, in turn, undermine your leadership. However, there is a difference between being resolute and being stubborn. Stubbornness is when you continue holding on to a belief even after it has been proven to be wrong. It endangers your team, vision, and career because you could be holding on to a wrong decision. Your superiors might not look very kindly at resoluteness if it ends up costing their company money. In fact, it is the definition of a *wise person* to be able to accept it when they make mistakes and work to correct them.

The way decision-making works is that if you make your decision right, you will not have to revise it for anything. Therefore, resoluteness is created in the backend of decisions. When you evaluate the data, take care of all loose ends, and consult with the experts to make a decision. You will have all the incentive to stick it out.

This is the difference between an unpopular decision and a wrong one. An unpopular decision will be validated in the end, so you should definitely stick it out despite initial opposition. Soon enough, you will be validated as a visionary. Some of the most successful businesses of today were once considered to be terrible ideas before they were proven to be visionary.

When Steve Jobs made the decision to start designing the Macintosh, he was determined to make it the best-selling personal computer in the market. The decision was so unpopular that he was fired from his own company. Today, Apple is the only company in the world to have reached a market capitalization of $1 trillion. The company has been able to reach these great heights by capitalizing on the Macintosh technology Steve Jobs had once been fired for pursuing. Talk about vilification!

In conclusion, the best way to make the hundreds of decisions that you, as the manager, usually have to make on a daily basis is not to do everything by yourself. When creating a vision, ensure that the employees understand the common goal and base their actions on it. You can then focus on strategic planning and supervision for greater success. This also means that your department works as a system rather than as an extension of you. When a system is in place and functioning well, you can usually take off without worrying that things will go wrong. It is when things start going awry as soon as you are out of the office that you should be concerned.

Mental Models for Systematized Decision-Making

When creating a systemized decision-making and thought process, we try to prioritize outcomes. The idea is to create a system that allows you to maximize outcome with minimal time and capital resources. Systemizing should follow the thinking process listed below:

In the first step of establishing a systemized decision-making organization, you reflect on the vision and mission of your company. This allows you to identify the work process that is involved in the accomplishment of various tasks. The outline of the work systems should be work centered; otherwise, you will just entangle yourself more in the process. Second, you come up with an objective statement, paying attention to the strengths, weaknesses, goals, and the strategies you think would make it possible to attain the goals. You can then make a general operating procedure made out of work procedures to accomplish the most common tasks around the workplace. The procedures should be sensible, practical, and simple for every employee to understand.

The third and final process in systemizing the decision-making procedure in the workplace is to ensure that you keep tweaking it. Constant updating will enable you to cut off redundant procedures, add new ones as needed, and keep everything perfectly up-to-date. When the system no longer serves its purpose of freeing you up from the hundreds of decisions you have to make daily, you must adjust. Studies have shown that highly successful people all put in place systems to help them save time in order to improve their personal performance. The Pareto principle applies to decision-making—meaning that 90% of the decisions we make apply to 10% of the most intense job activities we engage in at the workplace.

As for specific mental models, the best one to apply for decision-making is the Eisenhower matrix. Eisenhower was the supreme commander of the US forces in World War II and 34th president of the United States. He was a highly productive leader, achieving great things both in his military and political career. His life was organized using the four-part box matrix denoting activities that fell into different categories of urgency and importance.

The first box contains focus tasks. It contains the most urgent and most important tasks in your diary. These ones should be prioritized over all other tasks and be done as soon as possible. The importance of the tasks that fall here means that a leader ought to address them personally.

The second box is for your goals. The tasks that go here are very important but not urgent. You can set a future time to do them and carry on with the urgent for the meantime. Any good goals in this category move into the focus box as soon as they become urgent.

The third box of the Eisenhower matrix contains fit-in tasks. The tasks in this box are urgent but unimportant. You can get away with delegating them to your assistant or any other employee in your team.

Finally, we have the backburner box. It contains the tasks that are neither urgent nor important. They are mere distractions that you should eliminate so you can focus on tasks that are more important.

The problem with many managers is that they waste a lot of their energy and time on the third and fourth boxes instead of focusing on the first and second ones. As a result, their productivity suffers. The only decisions you should make are the ones in the important boxes. With proper insight and planning, you can also eliminate the urgency from your decision-making by focusing on the goals box. This is especially critical if you do not perform well under pressure.

The Common Mistakes of Beginning Leaders

The skillset that got you to the manager's office will not keep you there or take you to the next step in your career. For most managers, the first few months or years of their job is spent making mistakes and learning from them. However, if you know these mistakes going in, you can probably save yourself some trouble and propel your career to great heights right away. In this section, we shall look at some of the common mistakes that beginner leaders make that impede their progress as leaders. It is meant to be a guide for you to avoid repeating them.

1. *You try to prove to the whole office that you are the best.*

After a promotion, it is very common for the new manager to feel the need to validate themselves. This is especially common if you beat out some serious competition to clinch the office. As a result, most new managers will continue to perform their old technical job long into the managerial position. What they do not seem to understand is that management is a completely new ballgame. Your priority as a manager should be to support other technical workers and help them reach maximum potential. Continued performance of the old functions even when you are expected to do other things communicates to the senior managers that you are not very confident in your own abilities to manage. You waste so much time proving that you deserve the promotion that you bomb it.

2. *You go out of your way to show everybody that you are in control.*

The natural instinct for a newly promoted manager is to go around doing things that indicate to everyone that you are in charge. In this mistake, most new managers will veto good ideas because they did not come from them, stubbornly push their bad ideas on everyone, and generally make a nuisance of themselves. What they do not seem to understand is that everyone gets that they are the new boss. Not everyone agrees—in fact, most people will have a very passionate idea about who would have been a better candidate to promote in your place, but everyone is acutely aware that you are the new boss. When you go out of your way to show that you are in charge, you waste time and energy that could better be employed in creating a rapport with solid strategies and vision. In fact, the more you try to show your employees that you are in charge, the more resentment you will generate.

3. *You immediately embark on a mission to change everything overnight.*

Unless you are Jack Welch and you have complete control of your department, going about your new job as if your predecessor did everything wrong hurts your credibility. When you are just a small part of a system, you have to show some regard to the system. Anything else sends the message that you do not respect the efforts that went into setting it up, which is an indictment of every employee that worked on it before. If you want to bring some changes, a better strategy is to invite the team to suggest changes, combine them with your own ideas, and then gradually put them in place.

4. *You fail to establish a rapport with your team.*

When you go into a new job as the outsider manager, you will have to take the time to know your team so that you can work at earning their trust. When you are promoted in your current job, you will probably alienate other peers who felt they deserved the promotion just as much. In both instances, you will have to reach out to create a rapport. However gifted you might be, you cannot accomplish anything without a team to support you; the team is indispensable. A one-on-one sit-in with every member of your team is a great place to start. It allows you to measure everyone up to identify their strengths, weaknesses, and career aspirations. Knowing all this information comes in handy because these people will likely occupy key positions and come in handy in helping you achieve your master plan for the department.

5. You take everyone at their word.

Now that you are the manager, the common employee will start viewing you as the establishment. Even if you worked in the company before your promotion, your old friends would start acting differently around you. At least until your relationship adjusts back to its old level (if it ever does), expect to be "boss" and not "Ronnie" or "Rick." Being lied to is one thing that comes with the new territory of being boss. Therefore, you must listen with your eyes as well as your ears to avoid getting taken for a ride. Even if you are a straight shooter, chances are you were not 100% with your old boss either. There were some things that you kept from them, and you probably exaggerated the difficulty of getting a task done to get fairer terms too. In fact, you will probably have some fun as you watch people act in a way that you have always done, thinking that you are none the wiser. As long as it does not hurt anyone, you can let the small things slide, which is actually another mistake that new managers make.

6. You expect too much from your employees.

You have probably gotten to the position you are in now because you worked yourself to the bone, observing long hours and going out of your way for the job. The sooner you understand that not everyone has the same work ethic as you, the better it will be for you. Some people only work because they need to pay the bills; otherwise, they would not be seen within a mile of the office. Not everyone cares about impressing the boss or delivering the best work on every project. Some are perfectly content with simply finishing the project and not being fired. It falls on you to motivate them to care more about their work. You will get more out of your employees if you can find a way to get them to care about the work, not just the rewards.

7. *You micromanage your employees.*

Very few employees would have micromanagement among the list of the most endearing habits a manager could have. In most cases, employees feel that having someone even check their work is an insult. When you assign a task to an employee and then keep checking in on them, what you communicate is that you do not trust them enough to deliver. Good bosses leave their doors open to any employee who needs guidance on any part of the task, but they leave them to their own means for as much as possible. If you are the micromanaging kind of person, a better option is to establish checkpoints when handing out the assignment in the first place. This way, you can correct any mistakes that might appear early on instead of when the whole task has been completed.

8. *You treat all employees the same way.*

Fairness is a virtue worth having, but there is a difference between equality and equitability. Among the people you manage, you will have the highly motivated and dedicated, the highly talented but unmotivated, and the ones who only do enough to deserve their paycheck among many others. You cannot treat all these people the same way. The thing that makes one employee feel valued (e.g., asking how their night/weekend was) could make another feel like you are intruding on their privacy. For some employees, extra work means you believe in them and is an endorsement of their skills, but for others, it is a punishment. If you do not know the difference between these two types of employees, it will get very tough when you get the need to pass on some work to an employee. As far as fairness goes, this is the most important area of managing a group of employees. Getting this wrong could result in resentment that stretches far into the future.

9. *You do not lead by the coach's credo.*

The coach's credo is a mental model in which the leader takes the blame for the things that go wrong but attributes all success to the team. The coach's credo is the ultimate leadership mental model. It heaps all the responsibility on you when responsibility is especially hard to bear and demands heaps of grace to share the praise when the praise is sweetest. If you can live by the coach's credo, you will prove your credibility as a leader to the whole team beyond a shred of doubt.

Mental Models to Prevent Mistakes

The common mistakes that new managers make are avoidable simply by avoiding them, but the mistakes associated with decision-making are rather difficult to dodge. But in all due fairness, mistakes are unavoidable when you are trying to do something important. In fact, in a way, it is the mistakes that make you know that you are trying something worth trying. Many (if not all) of the most successful business managers have failed at one point in their career. It is the power to continue trying that sets them apart from everyone else.

The happy coincidence about mental models is that they can be used to multitask. For example, the mental models that you need to adopt to avoid the common mistakes of new managers listed above are far fewer than the mistakes they prevent. And when you apply mental models to any process of your job, the benefits stretch far beyond the tasks involved with that particular process. In this section, we will touch on the mental models of Bayesian thinking, lifelong learning, and reverse thinking as the ultimate mental models for new leaders who are intent on improving their decision-making capabilities as well as their job performance.

Bayesian Thinking

Every good decision-maker applies critical thinking to their decision-making process. It allows you to assess the issues at hand, scrutinize every option available, and choose the most suitable one. Bayesian thinking builds on this process by introducing the concept of probability to predict possible outcomes for every course of action. Formulated by Thomas Bayer, Bayesian thinking posits that no decision, strategy, or model is perfect in its current state. There is always room for improvement that comes from additional experimentation and improvement.

Bayesian thinking has been applied in military search-and-rescue operations and on the battlefield to come up with the best strategies to win a battle. Essentially, every event presents an opportunity to evaluate the effectiveness of the original strategy. Managers who use Bayesian mental models to make their decisions are not afraid to make changes when it proves to be flawed. In turn, the decision stops being a personal choice you made and takes on a life of its own. When a change is made, it is not an indictment on your decision-making capabilities. Instead, it is an improvement of the same. This is the core principle in Bayesian thinking: situations are always changing, and a decision made any time in the past will be inaccurate to some extent now and will require to be updated so that it reflects the reality.

Applying Bayesian thinking to your work as a new manager means that whenever you make a mistake, you can make a change without feeling like a total fraud. Studies have shown that the biggest impact on decision-making is the personal element whereby a person loses confidence in their ability to do something when a previous mistake is discovered. Doctors who are sued for malpractice are more likely to make a fatal mistake on the operating table because their confidence has been shaken. The same applies to managers. Normally, a previous decision that turns out to have been wrong makes you doubt yourself and either makes you make more bad decisions or stop making decisions altogether.

Bayesian principles applied in thinking makes you recognize the exact areas of your choice that did not work out. This is called fluidity, and it posits that any opinion or decision that is turned around by new information is better than the last. Of course, you have to be willing to acknowledge your mistakes and assimilate new evidence for it to work. There is nothing to be ashamed about in a bad decision when you are willing to pivot. In fact, a bad decision has led to better things down the road.

When he was starting out with SpaceX, Elon Musk decided that the best strategy to get into the space rocket business was to use old capsules from the Russian space program to make his own. He tried numerous times to purchase these old capsules but failed every time. Instead of giving up and writing it off as a bad idea, Musk instead came back home and decided that he would make his rockets himself. This decision again appeared to have been wrong when more than ten of the first rockets he launched failed. One of these failed rocket launches crashed with millions worth of equipment belonging to the National Aeronautics and Space Administration (NASA) international space center. All through these bad decisions, Elon went back to the drawing board and adjusted until he finally got it right.

Reverse Thinking

Reverse thinking is a creative method of brainstorming that you can use to bring some fun in your team. Usually, brainstorming calls for participants to wrack their brains for the best possible strategy to do something. The increased pressure often makes it even harder for people to think. With reverse thinking, you turn thinking around and start with the worst possible ideas to accomplish something. You will realize that most people come up with ideas that are more creative when thinking in the negative. You then work backward from there to formulate a strategy to accomplish an objective.

Reverse thinking is also great for coming up with a worst-case scenario to help you focus on the goals you set. When used in this way, reverse thinking taps into another mental model known as *loss aversion* to motivate us into action. Loss aversion states that the emotions associated with losing are usually twice as great as those associated with gain are. In a similar style, the prospect of losing something motivates us to work harder than the hope of achieving something.

As a manager, you can use reverse thinking and loss aversion to make decisions by comparing the cost of not doing anything. Usually, the decision with the biggest opportunity costs also has the highest rewards. When you do not know what path to take, what better way to move forward than to think of the path you do not want to take?

Even more encouragingly, reverse thinking has been listed by Charlie Munger as one of the mental models he uses to find investment and run Berkshire Hathaway in his book *Poor Charlie's Almanac*. The reason why Charlie Munger uses reverse thinking is that it plays into loss aversion, which in turn affects stock investing in a massive way. Many novice investors have fallen victim to the negative effects of loss aversion. Some have sold their stocks at a loss when a little patience could have gone a long way in increasing their profitability. Others sell their most profitable stocks for fear of making a loss even when market trends indicate higher prices are yet to come. The worst are investors who hold on to loss-making shares past the make-sense price levels because they don't want to suffer a loss and would rather wait for the stock price to rise before selling. In the end, they usually end up losing even more money.

The same conundrum exists in the decision-making processes of managers. With every decision you make, there is the possibility of adverse events. If you are to take the time to consider all options, you could end up frozen and unable to make a decision. However, as soon as you start reverse assessing your options, the options will become clearer and, ultimately, easier to take.

Lifelong Learning

The concept of lifelong learning is as simple as it sounds. It states that we learn something new from every new encounter. Whether you make a mistake or you do something right, you can use this to make yourself a better manager by recording every part of your engagements. You will learn what to do from the triumphs and what not to do from failures. By adopting the mental model of lifelong learning, you take the sting out of losing and enjoy your wins a little more as you learn from both. Lifelong learning also means that you should read widely and endeavor to expand your knowledge base with lessons from those who have succeeded where you intend to venture.

Story Time

To emphasize the lessons learned in this chapter, we shall look at the failure to success stories of Elon Musk, Albert Einstein, and Ray Dalio.

The Story of Elon Musk

Elon Musk is one of the most outstanding CEOs in the world. He is currently valued at over $20 billion, with two of his companies Tesla and SpaceX being some of the most popular companies in the world. But Elon Musk has come a long way to be the man he is today. When he was starting out, he was a shy young man who could not even summon the courage to follow up on a failed job application he had sent to Netscape when Internet companies were hiring everyone back in 1995.

He could have decided to take it in stride and go ahead to search for another job in a more relevant industry, but Elon Musk decided to learn a different lesson from his failure. He developed a mental model of looking at failure as a motivational tool and embraced it as part of the growth process. The change in mental models converted him from employee to entrepreneur and employer.

As soon as he had changed his mental model, the pathways to success opened up to him in a great way. Instead of seeking a job in the Internet industry, Musk instead collaborated with his brother to start his own Internet company that they called Zip2. Being a founding member, Elon Musk worked as CEO in Zip2 until the board of directors ousted him.

Throughout his career, Elon Musk has encountered numerous failures. He has overcome them all because he understood that failure is not the end of the road. Even with his most successful companies, SpaceX and Tesla, Elon Musk has encountered numerous failures. But his mental model has always been that failure is part of the innovation process. Once he accepted failure as part of his journey in 1995, Musk has achieved more success than most men his age. For his courage in changing his mental model from his very first failure, Elon Musk became the ultimate definition of trial by fire, of turning lemons into lemonade, and of persevering through failure.

In his countless appearances on interviews on SpaceX and Tesla, Musk has given the world a great look into his thinking. He has indicated that his genius lay not in what he thinks but in the way that he does his thinking. Thinking, Musk believes, has been influenced way too much by conventional principles and our inclination to draw parallels to previous experiences. He advocates a manner of thinking that is bound only by the first principles, which means original thinking that is unimpeded by the ideas of the world around you concerning what is right and what is wrong.

Rather than starting an idea by intuition, Musk starts by finding out the truth about a subject. This way, personal bias and shortcomings in knowledge are avoided, and we get the most factual model of a subject. When he was starting his space company and he needed to build rockets, Musk first identified the physics associated with space flight. He taught himself the whole subject of basic rocket science. He discovered that the materials for rockets made up less than 5% of the total cost of rockets. The technology took not more than 10%, yet rocket travel had been made so expensive that it was virtually unexplored. This is the kind of first principles thinking that we are talking about. See, most people look at the space exploration programs at face value. Only the richest governments run them because they need so much capital investment. Any accidents (which are common) can be catastrophic to the business. So why even bother considering it? No one has tried that anyway—until Elon Musk discovered that he could make a rocket at less than 20% the cost of conventional rockets.

From this point on, his idea stopped being bizarre and became a genius concept of exploiting an opportunity that has been right in front of the world the whole time. The government never had any intention of space shuttles. In fact, the whole space program had been started as a measure of wills and macho between the United States and the USSR. No more advancement had been made in the last two decades. By daring to observe the world using first principles, he identified a massive opportunity that everyone else missed.

The same is true for the battery parks that have kept the auto industry from moving into the electric space for almost a whole century. When he applies his first principles thinking mental model to battery parks, he discovered that he could take the price down from $600 per kilowatt-hour to about $80. This is a level that can be commercialized, which is what he did when he started Tesla. He has a very specific way of thinking that questions everything, accepts only basic verifiable truths as fact, and results in billion-dollar enterprises.

And in hindsight, even though it is not recorded anywhere, it is very telling that Elon Musk formed an Internet-based company immediately after being rejected at Netscape. After being rejected because he lacked the skill set the company demanded, he went to the basic principles of the matter. It was during a huge Internet bubble, so it was extremely easy to succeed with an Internet bubble. If he handled the management part of the company, it would not matter that he was not a trained programmer. When he finally sold the shares to Zip2, he made a neat $22 million.

The Story of Albert Einstein

Thought experiments are meant to challenge the thinker to consider a concept or hypothesis deep and hard. With thought experiments, you come up with conjectures, and without even meaning to, you modify paradigms for no other reason than give a sensible answer to an insensible question or riddle.

One of the most popular thought experiments is the impossible barber: If a barber in a small town cuts the hair of all the people who do not cut their own hair and does not cut the hair of those who cut hair themselves, who cuts his hair?

This thought experiment makes you think, but regardless of how much you think, there will always be a loophole because of the way the question is framed. No answer can be definite, and questions will always be arising.

The existence of the world is one such question. Scientists have been asking about the origins of the earth from time immemorial. Starting with a simple experiment on a beam of light for a children's book, Albert Einstein attempted to follow a beam of light. Instead, his experiment led him to form the theory of relativity and propel scientific inquiry into the origins of the world into a new age of empowerment.

The Story of Ray Dalio

The story of Ray Dalio is that of intense thinking on the subject of problem-solving. According to Ray, people have a tendency to tackle a problem at face value, which results in a vicious cycle of bad decisions in which one problem solved creates another one with even more dire consequences. This is called the first-order kind of thinking, whereby a person simply looks at the impact and not the consequences of their decision.

First-order decision-making is best exemplified by government-funded regime changes in other countries. The United States is responsible for creating some of the world's most dangerous terrorists when they fund separatist "moderate rebels" and arm them to aid them in removing a leader they don't want from power. After getting to power, these rebels turn around and establish an even worse condition for their people, prompting the cycle to be repeated all over again with ever more calamitous results.

From the school of thought of Ray Dalio, the only way to improve your decision-making abilities is to try to think of consequences to the nth order. Anyone can do first-order thinking, but only people with higher mental capabilities can take their thinking to the second, third, fourth, and beyond level. After taking your thinking to the next level, you can then follow through with the appropriate actions in full confidence that the consequences will be as you wish them to be. The levels of thinking are what people refer to when they talk about things like "two steps ahead." It means that you can predict what will happen when an event causes another to happen and use that to position yourself in the right position to profit. This is essentially what Ray Dalio has been doing all through his professional life. He has billions in personal wealth to show for it.

Chapter 4: Systemize for Productivity

The level of productivity at the workplace is determined in a huge way by the kind of management strategies used by the leaders. Decisions and thought processes are usually interlinked in a series of cause-and-effect connections. Therefore, the decisions you make on day one will still be relevant a year into your term as manager. As discussed in the previous chapter, decisions can be systemized to create a semi-autonomous working environment and free your mental faculties for the making of important decisions about strategy and direction. In this chapter, we will look at some of the principles that can be used to streamline the management process for any leader.

Systemizing Organization Processes

Half the things you will be doing in your job as manager will be organizational processes, otherwise referred to as soft bureaucracy. These tasks are critical to the survival of the organization because they establish chains of command, responsibility, and accountability. However, they also take up much of the time that you could otherwise use strategizing for new ways to do things and enforcing these strategies for the good of the company. Organization processes also tie you up at the place of work, making it so that you cannot be absent for more than a couple of days without a stack of documents pile up.

Successful managers like Elon Musk come up with such winning ideas and shine on a personal basis because they can usually take time off to think, strategize, and pursue apparently unworkable ideas. You can also do this by systemizing the organization processes that take up so much of a manager's time. With a system in place, you will finish all tasks in record time and leave yourself enough time to work on the vision you have created for the department.

Organizational restructuring is not that different from personal improvement. After all, organizations are made up of people with distinct values, worldviews, and mental models. When you decide to restructure the organization culture of a company, the first place you should look to is the personal beliefs of the employees who work there. In most cases, you will be surprised to find that the people working in a company have very similar characters.

Organizational restructuring is a big deal for any established company. It changes the way the company does business and, when implemented properly, is all but granted to act as a stimulus to better profitability. So when exactly is the right time to approach your bosses with a restructuring proposal? Below are the indicators you can look for in an organization to determine if it needs to be restructured.

1. ***The old skills and qualifications of most employees do not meet the operational requirements of the business.*** In a world that is constantly changing, skills are growing old fast. When you find that the business outsources functions for which people are employed to accomplish, then it would be a great idea to propose a restructuring.

2. ***Communication channels no longer work.*** Companies use performance appraisals to determine the effectiveness of the labor force in delivering the company goals. When the results of these appraisals are

warped or they do not reach the senior management in time, the company could end up getting stuck in the same underperforming situation year after year.

3. ***Technological innovations have produced a change in the production process in many businesses.*** Sometimes companies adopt game-changing technologies without changing the structure of the company to accommodate them. As a junior manager, it is your job to communicate with the managers about any changes you feel might be needed when a game-changing technology renders some jobs redundant or more staffers are needed to exploit new technology to the maximum.

4. ***The employee turnover rate is significantly high.*** When you see employees leaving a job, you should know that there are underlying issues that are not being addressed. When proposing a restructuring plan because of high turnover, try to find out why people decided to leave the company. In this case, restructuring should also involve a section on new ways to retain employees. After all, training new hires is one of the most expensive business processes.

The best mental model for organizational restructuring is the subtraction theory. Here, just like when it is applied to individuals, you endeavor to do away with all the negative qualities about the corporate culture in a group by introducing positive traits that you want to teach. And even though you will be tempted to keep ideas like these from your boss and instead try them out risk-free among the employees, the better idea is to leverage the people in positions of power. These are the decision-makers and policymakers, so convincing them about a point will result in better penetration of your ideas.

The policymakers are also in the best position to advice on the suitability of a model presented based on existing business policies.

Decisions Based on Numbers

There is a common saying that numbers never lie. Experts have designed numerous strategies of using data to make decisions, including probabilistic thinking and hypothetical projection. With hypothetical projection, you calculate the probability of an event happening and then formulate a list of possible scenarios that could result from a particular decision. The common feature among all data-based decision-making strategies is that they seek to eliminate the human factor. Instead of being in the driver's seat on the decision-making process, you are the conductor changing gears in a self-steering vehicle.

Studies have shown that executives are relying more and more on data to make big business decisions. Artificial intelligence and big data have created systems that make it easy for managers to delegate decision-making to data. While data should constitute a central part of your decision-making process, you should not rely on them to make decisions for you. The numbers are supposed to be an aid to the decision-making process, advising you on the most statistically sensible decision to make. However, the ultimate judgment should come from you. Because for all their accuracy and impartiality, numbers lack one very important ingredient that only a person can bring to the decision-making process—instinct.

Moreover, numbers are often deceptive. They do not always tell the whole story, and when they do, it is as good as the person reading them to put it together. Most managers will scan over data and look for the figures that jump out at them.

This is called the bird's-eye view, and its main failing is that it does not give the complete picture. The alternative is to conduct a deep dive into the data and come up with insights based on critical analysis of the numbers. Few people have the right tools to do this credibly, which means that the bird's-eye view is used more than the deep-dive method.

The Minimum Viable Product (MVP)

The minimum viable product is a common product testing strategy that allows the creator to release an incomplete product to the market and rely on feedback to make improvements. Companies like Airbnb, Dropbox, Snapchat, and Uber all started as MVPs before being developed into the desirable products millions (if not billions) enjoy today. A minimum viable product serves the purposes listed below:

1. It helps you go from idea to market launch in a very short time. Usually, a product takes years and huge amounts of capital to develop. If you wait until everything is fixed to get customer feedback, you are gambling more than just the money spent on research and development.

2. MVP reduces the cost of implementing a product design. Even though it is offered in a crude and incomplete manner, an MVP will still be priced and marketed like any other product. This enables you to collect practical data on the willingness of people to pay for the product but also serves as a revenue stream for the company.

3. With an MVP, a company is also able to measure the demand for their product. This is especially important when the company offers an innovative product for

which there is no precedent in the market. If the demand for the product proves to be sustainable during the testing process, the MVP will be developed into the complete product.

4. When you launch an MVP, you can send a team to correspond with the clients and hear straight from them what they would prefer to be added to the product after using it for a brief period. This is called sampling, and it is highly effective for gathering product data.

5. The main purpose of an MVP, however, is to prevent the loss of huge amounts of money for the company down the line. A new product is usually a very expensive endeavor, so taking chances is not something any wise manager would do. An MVP enables you to sleep easy during the final processes of creating a product because you finally know exactly how your customers will respond to the product when it launches.

Creating the perfect MVP is an art that few managers are able to master. It requires that you find the perfect balance between an overly burdened prototype and one with insufficient features. To be able to make a good MVP, you need to understand the needs fulfilled by the product such that you can narrow down to the bare minimum features that offer those needs with no frills.

The early or beta adopters will then give feedback on the features you have provided in the MVP, and you can add them into the product gradually. However, you must ensure that every feature you add increases the functionality of your product in solving the customers' problems. Finally, do not forget the golden rule of MVPs: feedback is everything. If your early adopters do not communicate with you about the good and bad of your product, then improvements will be hard to make.

System Thinking

This holistic analysis method caters to the ways through which parts of a system interrelate and how systems perform as constituent parts of a larger system. The system's philosophy posits that the universe is made up of systems within systems within systems, with every system in turn containing a series of smaller systems within it. This sort of thinking can be very conducive to the mental models that promote growth in the workplace. Systems thinking brings about some very insightful mental models, as discussed below:

Bottlenecks

Bottlenecks are described by the theory of constraints, which states that every system usually has a single constraint that holds it back more than any other restriction. In most cases, a constraint exists at the point in the system where there exist massive congestion and delay. But the most relevant thing about a bottleneck is that the whole system can only be as good as the worst constraint within it. They tend to slow everything down—meaning, that the system will not be exploited to its full capacity. To improve an inefficient system, you must identify the bottleneck in it and improve it.

Leveraging

When you understand a system, you can usually influence it in a big way with very little effort. This is called leveraging. It entails applying your energy toward influencing a system at the highest level of efficiency. In leveraging, you can create the greatest impact in a system by mastering a specific area to focus on rather than distributing your energies to a number of different sections.

The Feedback Loop

The concept of feedback loops borrows from the biological concept of homeostasis. In essence, it states that the output of a system either inhibits or amplifies it, but the opposite reaction happens to keep the system at equilibrium. For example, when a normally functioning body experiences temperature rises, the blood vessels dilate, and the sweat glands open up and help the body to release excess heat, returning the body to normal temperatures. When the body temperature drops, the blood vessels tighten, causing the body to shiver, generating heat and taking us back to normal body temperatures all over again. This type of feedback loop is called a balancing feedback loop. In the end, the system is left in equilibrium.

The second type of feedback loop is called a reinforcing feedback loop. It tends to bring about the deterioration of a system. On the negative, reinforcing feedback loops mean that when you don't fix an issue when it is still small enough, you will end up having to fix a much bigger problem. As a positive force, the reinforcing feedback loop makes viral marketing possible. Interesting and shareable content will spread faster through social media networks because increasingly more people share it.

Feedback loops also exist in our personal lives. Those behaviors that we find desirable are propped using balancing feedback loops. They consist of our bodies, relationships, values, the environment around us, and culture. When we fail to maintain these systems properly, they could turn into vicious reinforcing feedback loops. On the other hand, we can improve our feedback loops with heavy lift actions to create positive reinforcing feedback loops. Ambition is one such heavy-lift matter that can be injected into a person's life to make them more driven.

Pareto Principle (80/20 Rule)

Generally, the Pareto principle states that 80% of the effects come from 20% of the causes. Because the Pareto principle applies to every situation, it has come to be referred to as the rule of "Less is more" and the 80/20 rule, among other names. The Italian philosopher Federico Pareto, who observed that about 80% of the healthy pea pods in his garden came from just 20% of the pea plants, suggested the principle in the nineteenth century. He then went ahead and validated it by studying the land ownership system in Italy at the time. He noticed that about 20% of the citizens owned about 80% of the land. In the industry, 80% of goods in every market were made by 20% of the factories.

This concept remains as true today as it was more than one hundred years ago. You can vouch for this within your office: 80% of the sales made come from 20% of the salespeople, and 20% of your clientele generates 80% of the sales you make every year. Even from the wardrobe, we tend to gravitate toward the same 20% of our clothes 80% of the time. You use about 20% of the applications on your smartphone 80% of the time, and you probably spend 80% of your social time doing the same 20% of leisure activities. So just how exactly can you apply the Pareto principle in your position now for greater success?

You can decide to go with the flow of nature and identify the 20% of everything from your workplace. Find out 20% of your customers, 20% of the most important part of a project, and 20% of the most hardworking employees. You can then dedicate greater effort to understanding what makes the 20%

such great performers and try to convert the underperforming 80% into high achievers too. There is one very important reason why implementing the Pareto principle at the office is such a great idea. You target 20% of your efforts on a goal and reap 80% of all rewards, which effectively means that you spend less time and less energy on fewer priorities for the maximum possible amount of gains.

One of the most common fallacies concerning the Pareto principle is that the percentage points in the equation must add up to 100%. This is not at all true. For example, if you decide to narrow it down, you will not get 10% of sales from 90% of the customers. It just does not work that way. In fact, at some point, it stops making sense that you are focusing your efforts on 20% of your market for 80% of the sales. Converting the 80% of the customers into 20% material might just blow up your sales figure after you have finished exploiting the 80/20 to the maximum.

Another common fallacy that arises out of the Pareto principle is that the other 80% is not important just because it accounts for such a small share of the outputs. This is false. In fact, studies have shown that completely ignoring the other 80% can have serious effects on the productivity of a system. As much as you should focus your efforts on the 20% to get to the 80% of outcomes, the other 80% and 20% of rewards are important as well. Neglecting them oftentimes leads to mistakes being made that imperil even the other 80%.

KISS Principle (Keep It Simple, Stupid)

The US Navy developed the KISS principle in the 1960s. The concept states that a majority of the systems are most effective when they are designed with simplicity in mind. Some of the best leaders in history use the KISS principle to cut through the noise and move past the debates, doubts, and arguments for and against an idea to get at the crux of the matter and come up with simple solutions that nonetheless solve the problem spectacularly.

The former general of the US Army Colin Powell is one proponent of the KISS principle. He recommends it for leaders as the one strategy through which they can cut through multiple choices and confusion to make important decisions in a compelling and transparent manner. Keeping it simple is definitely a great management strategy. Not only can you be firmer and more consistent with the decisions you make, but you can also display reliable leadership and integrity to your employees.

In project management, KISS principles tie teams together in their pursuit of project objectives because everything is communicated in a simple and uncluttered manner. It is much easier to focus on the priorities when all the priorities have been communicated in the simplest language, expressing simple goals. More importantly, simplicity reduces important points to the bare bones and ensures that workers are not bogged down in petty issues.

Negative Mental Models

Even before you move into the corner office as the department boss, you will probably already have a very good idea about the kind of boss you want to become. Popular culture has popularized the image of the reclusive boss who spends all his time at the office, has his finger on everything that goes on in the office, and pops Xanax by the armful every once in a while. Unfortunately, this picture is more often quite accurate.

If you are not very careful, you will slide into this self-destructive pattern in no time. We have discussed the mental models that allow you to build your managerial career with concepts and principles borrowed from some of the most successful businessmen and leaders in the world. But now it is time to show you the pitfalls that lie on your path to greatness. Borrowing from one of the mental models discussed in the previous chapter, we will look at these pitfalls in the reverse perspective.

Jack-of-All-Trades

It is very tempting to do everything when everything that happens around you reflects one way or another on you. As a leader, the outcomes of all members of your team will reflect one way or another on you. The senior managers will evaluate your performance as the manager of your division based on the division's output. If one team player bungles up, the whole team suffers, but you more than anyone else do because it is your job to ensure that everyone does their job well.

Managers often adopt the role of a jack-of-all-trades at the office, supervising everyone's work all through the work process because they feel their responsibilities as the leader in a huge way. Jack-of-all-trades managers interfere in their team's work and impose their own views on everything. But trying to do everything yourself does not make you a better manager; neither will you magically be able to multitask supervising everyone's work just because you are now the manager. The mentality that you need to keep your finger on everyone's progress to be an effective manager leads to working late nights and having dysfunctional lifestyles of typical managers discussed above.

Even if you can comfortably keep track of every department in your division or the work of every member in your team, there is no way you can do this and still have the time to lead. Some of the world's most successful managers run their multibillion-dollar empires from the comfort of their holiday homes. Richard Branson is one of the most hands-off managers, yet he is currently worth over $4 billion. I am not saying that you should be *that* hands-off, but it does pay to focus on one thing and trust your team to take care of their part of the bargain.

A manager who moonlights as the head of marketing, research and development, and customer relations will simply bring down the total output of these teams. First off, you cannot be as dedicated to these functions as the people who work there full-time. The fact that you are doing the same thing with other teams, fulfilling other functions at the office, also means that your focus is split. Not to mention the fact that everyone will probably be tempted to defer to your opinions on everything, which could be disastrous. So to put this in perspective, the only reason you should become a jack-of-all-trades manager is if you want to bring about the failure of every division in your department because that will definitely be the case if you involve yourself in every function at the office.

Perfectionism

There is nothing wrong with having high standards and expecting everything to be perfect. However, every rational-thinking person knows that perfection is a moving target that you will never hit. Likewise, perfectionism is a mental model that sadly attempts to attain the unattainable. In fact, perfectionism is associated with anxiety, depression, and in the worst-case scenario, suicide.

Perfectionism is not something that you should be proud of exhibiting. It is much healthier to be high achieving. High achievers aim for the highest rewards. However, they recognize that things won't always go their way, and they are okay with the occasional sub-par performance, as long as they feel that they have made efforts to achieve the best results possible.

It is especially impossible to do everything perfectly right after getting that promotion. In the first year or so, most of what you will be doing is getting acclimated with your new role and responsibilities. Until you have adapted to life in charge, you can then put in place the strategies to improve the performance of your division. Perfection, however, is a strategy that is fraught with impossible situations. For one, perfectionism is a very subjective concept. You cannot measure perfection, so it will always be a moving target. And while you might think that a moving target is good because it will keep you on your feet, just think about the anxiety you will feel from all that.

So instead of trying to do everything perfectly, you should set SMART goals and work toward the attainment of them instead. I am talking about the clichéd "specific, measurable, achievable, realistic, and timely." When you set a SMART objective, it enables you and your team to work toward a very clear objective. For example, you could aim at improving the work output of the whole team by 30% in the next quarter. This is both very simple and ticks off all the boxes in the SMART acronym.

In their younger days, successful managers like Bill Gates set smart goals in their ascension to success. Elon Musk recently set a smart but bold decision to stop receiving a salary from Tesla until the company reaches $100-billion valuation in the next ten years. Smart goals are more motivating than the pursuit of perfection because they attach an objective goal that you can chase. While Musk tries to propel Tesla to $100-

billion valuation in the next ten years so that he can get paid, you should set your own goals too. You do not have to make them so bold, but you should definitely challenge yourself.

Snap Decision-Making

We have been talking about decision-making from chapter 1. So by this time, you are probably fed up with hearing how much management is all about the decisions you make. But this issue cannot be overstated. Your legacy as a leader will boil down to the kind of decisions you make every day. And having discussed the right ways to make decisions, let's talk about bad decision-making for a while. Specifically, let us talk about snap decisions. Just for clarity, we are talking about deliberate decisions here, not the systemized ones discussed in chapter 3.

Snap decisions are those that you make rather spontaneously without thinking too much about them because "it feels right" or "there's nothing to think about there." These decisions can be very catastrophic, especially because they are likely to have far-reaching consequences that you did not take the time to consider. While there are quite a number of books advising you to make unconscious decisions because they are purer and your gut is always right, nothing could be further from the truth. Studies have shown that snap decisions are more than twice as likely to result in adverse situations that the decision-maker did not foresee.

Of course, this is bound to happen. When you make a snap decision, you compress hours' or days' worth of thinking into a few minutes—meaning, you do not have the time to consider all the angles. More importantly, the snap decision-making strategy goes against the principles of second-order thinking proposed and exemplified by Ray Dalio's mental models. With the limited time you have to make a snap decision, you are susceptible to numerous fallacies, including the value of information fallacy. This fallacy means that when you are under pressure to make a decision, otherwise irrelevant pieces of information carry more weight than they would have if you were not in a rush.

The final trigger to making a decision in such a scenario could be very irresponsible. In fact, people are more likely to make a snap decision because they are afraid of missing out. For example, you are being sold a great investment opportunity that expires in the next hour. The potential profits are out of this world, and you only have to commit to paying in writing for the deal to be yours. Later, you find out that the deal is highly risky or someone was divesting from a terrible investment.

Every decision worth making is a decision worth thinking very carefully about. Any opportunity that requires you to make a decision without thinking carefully about it is an opportunity you can and probably should do without.

Superman Complex

The superman complex mental model is a mindset in which a person carries an overblown sense of their own responsibilities over other people's affairs. It comes with the belief that other people are incapable of taking care of themselves or, in the case of the office situation, incapable of performing a task. When you have a superman complex, you will always be trying to do things yourself, and you will never ask or accept anyone's help. The main problem with a superman complex is that it deceives you into thinking that you are capable of doing it alone.

Another mental model that goes hand in hand with the superman complex is the martyr complex. While the former makes you feel an overblown sense of responsibility, the martyr complex gives you a saintly feel because you do so much to help others (even when they don't ask for your help) and shield them from responsibility. These two mental models are actually associated with responsibility deficit disorders, but instead of shunning responsibilities, you take on more of them than you should.

A superman complex is tiresome. Working at things alone because you do not want to ask for help is immensely tiring. The saying "Two heads are better than one" is universally popular for a reason; everyone needs the help of someone else. And when you are the manager, you don't even have to ask for help; you are entitled to the help of everyone in your department.

Another reason why you might feel the need to take on responsibilities that you do not need to is that you want very much to be the hero when things turn out great. This is actually one of the features of individuals with a superman complex. To remedy this particular impulse, you should train yourself to practice the coach's credo and actually give the credit that belongs to you to somebody else. It feels mighty good, believe me. And when things go wrong, you can take responsibility and even things out! (Hopefully, that will not be necessary.)

With bigger projects, you can go as far as collaborating with other departments to tackle them together for better results. Asking for help does not mean that you are weak; it means that you are strong enough to admit that you cannot do everything and that you are bold enough to ask for the help you need to improve your output.

Productivity = Time Worked

There is this common belief in management circles that you have to work long hours to be productive. In the 2015 Frankfurt Motor Show, BMW CEO Harald Krueger collapsed on stage while giving his presentation due to exhaustion. Studies have shown that while workers may benefit from working long hours (promotions are based largely on your job performance in your current job rather than your abilities to take on the new job), working too much as a manager could adversely hurt your health. Your value to the company as a manager is less about the number of hours you put at work and more about the kind of results that you can produce, regardless of how long you work.

As a leader, you need to be in the best state of mind (well-rested) to perform your duties, which includes reading and interpreting body language. Lack of sufficient rest also affects moods, making you easier to bait into arguments and verbal conflicts. This, in turn, creates a toxic workplace and brings productivity down. In fact, studies have consistently shown that overworking is a common trait among managers who aspire for outstanding productivity. While this would normally be a good thing, the implications turn sour when you consider that to achieve their inordinately high productivity levels, these managers pressure their employees into overworking too. The problem with overworking is that it does not quite work out. The most overworked employees are not necessarily the most productive.

Poor Work-Life Balance

Balancing your personal life and the office can get problematic when you are in a position of leadership. With technology, you can access your work files from any remote location, which means that you do not have to be at the office to be working. You could be vacationing in a sandy white beach and still be at work. This means that you do not really unplug from work. Your home life suffers, and so does your job in the end.

It is important that you maintain a good balance between your work life and home life. More importantly, never take the job home. And as much as the subconscious style of decision-making does not work on its own, the time you spend outside the office when you have a big decision coming up is a time you give your subconscious to mull the decision over for you. So as much as you need to hit the ground running and succeed spectacularly in your new job, take the time to exercise, meditate, and take care of you.

There are many reasons why you should take care of yourself first. The greatest of this is that without proper care, you will not be healthy enough to continue at that job that you are killing yourself over. And the worst thing about overworking and all the negative mental models is that when you are busy overworking yourself, what you are actually doing is sabotaging your own success. Former Apple CEO Steve Jobs spent thirty minutes every day meditating. He led Apple into becoming the largest company in the world by market valuation—an achievement that belongs to him more than anyone else, even though it happened after his tenure.

Poor Sleeping Habits

While it is not really a mental model, poor sleeping habits can be very detrimental to your ability to lead. Not getting enough sleep sets off a vicious cycle where you perform badly at work, get stressed about your poor performance, sleep badly, and so on and so forth. If you look at the lifestyles of the world's most successful leaders like Oprah, you will notice that they take their sleep very seriously.

The right amount of sleep every day (at least six, preferably eight) refreshes your mind, gives your body enough time to rest, and leaves you feeling energized. While you can manage to get by on 100-hour work weeks and little sleep for a while, you can maintain your productivity in the long run by giving your body the time to rest each and every day.

Burnout

When you do not give your mind and body time to recover from too much work, they often take the time out of their own volition. This is commonly known as burnout. This is a WHO-recognized condition that causes detachment from work and poor job performance. Too much pressure at the workplace is one of the leading causes of burnout. Feelings of hopelessness when goals are not met exacerbate burnout.

It is especially common for you to suffer burnout when you are working on a long-term project because the relief your mind gets after achieving a set goal just stretches into the distant future. When you combine insecurities about the risks associated with big projects, the pressure makes your mind very open to burnout. When working on a big long-term project, it is better to subdivide it into individual tasks and take the time out to celebrate the completion of every task.

Chapter 5: Negotiation—How to Make It a Win-Win

Negotiation is essentially a discussion conducted with the aim of reaching an agreement between two parties. In more technical terms, negotiation is what happens when both parties are mutually interested in reaching the agreement. For example, when one party is willing to sell and the other is looking to buy, that is a negotiation. With mutual interest established, all that remains is to reach an agreement on the terms of the agreement.

Negotiating is an art and science that only few business managers ever master. The ones who master negotiation thrive because they can always acquire what they need to pursue their goals while those who are incompetent negotiators will struggle to make headway in achieving their goals.

At one point in your managerial career, you will be asked to step up to the negotiation table and make a deal for the company. Negotiations are part of the running of a company. You will have to negotiate when you need to buy some proprietary software to streamline the business operations, when you hire a new employee, when you have to collaborate with business partners for any purpose, and in numerous other instances. It is very important, therefore, to understand and grasp the mental models of outstanding negotiators. In this chapter, we shall cover everything there is to know about negotiations.

Characteristics

Quid Pro Quo

Quid pro quo is a Latin term that means "something in exchange for something." The thing that you need from a negotiation is what guides your whole negotiation strategy, including the concessions you are willing to give. Just keeping in mind that the discussion is taking place because your negotiation partner needs something from you can help you keep everything in perspective. Quid pro quo is meant to reflect the values of fairness, but it can be used as a power tool just as easily.

When going into a negotiation, good negotiators assess the value of their concession against the rewards (what the other party is willing to give in return). The value both of you place on the things you are willing to give away to get what the other party has will determine the power dynamics of the negotiation. If your opponent senses that you are more desperate to reach a deal, they are likely to up their ante and take advantage. In the same vein, if either of the two parties is in negotiations with an interested third party, the probability of losing out if they go with the alternative deal shifts the power dynamics in their favor.

Same Interest

As much as your opponent will measure you up to determine your level of investment in the deal, the interests you share with them is one of the molding blocks of negotiations. Both of the parties in the negotiation table is usually looking to benefit by acquiring something the other party is willing to give. Your mutual and complementary interest with the other party connects you together. Whenever the interests of the parties involved mismatch, negotiations tend to go sideways. In fact, most negotiations fail because the two parties do not see eye to eye on their respective interests. If you are hunting for a willing partner to negotiate some sort of deal with, always look for one with whom your interests are aligned. Otherwise, you will be selling your deal to a disinterested party, which is much harder to do.

Compromise

Compromise is an important part of a negotiation. Even though you share the same or similar interests, most often than not, a deal will not be struck until one of the two parties or both are willing to give up or take less than they were hoping to get.

Reluctance

Especially in a persuasion, one party is usually an unwilling participant in the negotiation process. The reluctant party position is one of prestige because it falls on the other one to bring you to the table with a sweetened deal. A reluctant participant holds all the cards until the crafty negotiator arouses their interest with a dangled carrot and makes them want to negotiate.

Trade-Off

Every person in a negotiation gives something up. This is what makes it a negotiation; an exchange of some sort must take place. The trade-off is a characteristic of a successful negotiation. When a negotiation falls apart for whatever reasons, no trade-off takes place.

Mutual Benefit

The mutual benefit aspect of a negotiation is very important. The only reason why people enter into negotiations is that they want something the other gives, and they are willing to pay for it. The antithesis of mutual benefit in negotiation is the hostile takeover where an interested party foregoes pursuing a merger or acquisition and takes ownership of another business by buying out their shares and leveraging them to get what they want, usually a stake in a successful business.

Anchoring and Adjustment

When two parties start a negotiation, they both set parameters. If the parameters match, the negotiation could just be a handshake, and then the parties sign an agreement. Where they do not match, negotiators are anchored by the lowest or highest price past which they are not willing to go. Adjustments are then made to move closer to a mutually acceptable agreement.

Bargaining Zone

To illustrate this characteristic, let us look at a negotiation to buy a house. The seller quotes $500,000, and the buyer makes a counter-offer for $400,000. The gap between what the buyer is willing to pay and what the seller is willing to sell for is called the bargaining zone.

Negotiation Skills

As with anything else that you will do as a manager, it is always better to build your negotiation skills. And apart from building the confidence that allows you to charge into the boardroom and boldly ask for what you need, the following are some of the skills that are critical for effective negotiation.

Set Some Negotiation Goals

You know exactly what you are looking for in that deal; there is no doubt in your mind about that. But is it enough to know what you want? The answer is no. You have to be very clear about the goal and the concessions you are willing to give to get the thing you want. In setting the goals for the negotiation, you should consider the best-case scenario of the discussion, the bottom line, and the plan B. This way, you will have all your bases covered.

If you walk into that negotiation room and receive an offer that is within your range, you can take it right away, subject to a few considerations. Body language is one thing that you can read to determine if the person you are negotiating with is a straight shooter of the kind of person who enjoys a drawn-out haggling. If you accept the first offer of a haggler, they might take it as an offense and rescind. Haggling with a straight shooter when they have given you a fair deal is also a bad idea.

The bottom line is the lowest price you are willing to accept for something you are selling or the highest one that you can pay for something. This price point should be set based on data analysis and should never be violated.

Your plan B is what is referred to as the "best alternative to a negotiated agreement" (BATNA). Without a plan B, you could be forced to take a bad deal simply because you have no fallback plan.

One should have a *core negotiation strategy*. A negotiation strategy is like the viewfinder in a sniper rifle. You can try to shoot without it, but it is highly unlikely that you will hit anything. In a negotiation, you find the one thing about the matter at hand that the other person really cares about and use that as a bargaining chip. The core negotiation strategy allows you to get all over your opponents business and find their one weakness that you can focus on to get your way.

Elon Musk has managed billions of dollars' worth of tax concessions from the US government. He did this by selling government officials on the idea that his electric vehicles will not just spur innovation in the automobile industry but that they will also help combat carbon emissions and advance the war on global warming. The truth is that he would have made those vehicles even without the tax concessions. However, because he went in with a winning negotiation strategy, he managed to earn himself an enviable tax break.

Be in Touch with Your Negotiation Signature

Every one of us has our own distinct style of negotiating—from the people who give nothing to those who give everything, from negotiators who enjoy haggling to those whose first offer is the only offer, from people who go through the process of bargaining but are unable to close to those who can "close" anyone. It is all about understanding what you want and what the other person wants and finding the best way for both of you to come out of the discussion happy or at least satisfied with what they came out of the negotiation with.

Whatever your style of negotiation is, you will need to be completely aware so that you can measure yourself against your opponent. If you have no experience with negotiating and you are feeling nervous just before a big negotiation, you can practice with an employee or friend. As much as it is not the same environment, it will give you a bit of exposure so that you do not go in completely detached from your negotiation style.

Find Out the Reason the Other Side Wants a Deal

Negotiations are all about power, and there is no greater power than the power of knowledge. By looking carefully at what you bring to the table, you can try to work out exactly what your opponent wants from you. When negotiating with a professional, you may find that money is not the only motivation. Exposure is also part of the reason why a professional might be interested in scoring you as a client, or they could be using you to get to other clients associated with your company. Finding out information like this gives you an edge that you can use to haggle for better prices.

Play the Reluctant Party

In negotiations, just like in life, reluctance is a powerful tool. When you express reluctance about striking a deal, you force the other party to persuade you to come to the negotiation table. Persuasion gives you greater power over the opponent, which means that you can get concessions from them that you wouldn't receive in an even playground.

The first rule of negotiation is "Never show your weak spots." Eagerness is one of the worst vulnerabilities in a negotiation. It brings with it a measure of desperation, which can be exploited for a bigger share of the bargaining zone. So even when you need something, try as much as possible to come up with backup options so that you don't come to the bargaining zone with the least bit of eagerness.

In the real negotiation, your body language should communicate nonchalance and reluctance. This means that you should be relaxed, sitting back from the table, with no tension in your body whatsoever. This way, you will be communicating reluctance to the other side. If they are good, they might actually call you out on it. If not, you could make a deal at a fraction of the market price.

Mental Models of a Negotiation

The following are the mental models that the most successful managers use to get what they want.

Haggling Model

Everyone goes into a negotiation with a competitive mindset. The aim of negotiating is usually to try to get a bigger share of the bargaining zone. Negotiations are usually very competitive, and haggling is the ring where negotiators square off against each other. In haggling, you can exploit a position of power to force the opponent to accept your terms, or you can exploit their interest in whatever you are selling for the same purpose. Whoever enjoys the power and the interest in the negotiation (or manages to convince the other that they hold these cards) always come out on top.

Cost-Benefit Analysis

You will be forced to make several decisions in the course of the negotiation about whether or not you want to take whatever deal has been negotiated at that point. Every time an offer is made, you must decide whether you will accept or reject it. The decision about taking an offer relies on the negotiation goals you set at the start of the negotiation process. Unless the deal on the table reaches the bare minimum, you should definitely not take it. However, if it is higher than your bare minimum but you still think you can milk your opponent for a few more concessions, you can make the decision to hold out, even if they insist that it is their best offer.

Partnership Negotiation Models

Negotiations are not always about seeking to advance your encroachment on the bargaining zone. Sometimes, the best deal is one where both parties meet halfway, enjoying greater benefits from a friendly alliance. Everyone in this model gives some and takes some. Some of the world's largest mergers have been made along the partnership model.

For example, in 2018 AT&T merged with Warner Bros to create Warner Media, allowing each company to consolidate their standing in their respective industries. From that partnership, the streaming service HBO Max was created to compete with Netflix, Amazon Prime, and other such services in the industry. From that deal, Warner Bros was able to capitalize on AT&T's large user base to compete in an industry that has been disrupted by new players Netflix and Amazon. AT&T's cable services also reaped the rewards of an extensive library like Warner Bros'.

Problem-Solving Models

Business operations are fraught with conflict. When the conflict reaches certain levels of escalation, the bottom line of both companies suffers. Sometimes people are forced to seek conciliation by negotiating with their business rivals, establishing clear-cut boundaries to de-escalate an otherwise disruptive conflict. Problem-solving negotiation models are ideal when both parties are hurting from a conflict. Even if you are the one instigating the talks, you will still be coming from a position of relative power because the other party also has vested interests in a cessation of differences.

When this is not possible, you can seek to strengthen your position in the conflict by negotiating with a different player. Even if you cede some ground to make the new deal possible, you will be in a better position to compete, probably even turn the tables on the original conflict to your favor.

In 2009, the Walt Disney Company acquired Marvel Entertainment in a deal valued at over $4 billion. The deal was negotiated at a time when both companies were facing massive competition in their respective fields. Marvel Studios was especially in need of reprieve from their main competitors DC Comics that had been gaining ground since Time Warner acquired them two decades previously. Having gone through a bankruptcy in the past decade, Marvel was in need of reprieve. Their problems were all solved when they folded under the protective custody of the Walt Disney Company. By capitalizing on the expansive distribution channels of Walt Disney affiliates like Buena Vista, the Marvel comic line has since had a resurgence that took them to the top of the box office just a decade later.

Common Mistakes of Beginning Negotiators

When starting out as a novice negotiator, business managers often make huge mistakes that cost them greatly. Losing a negotiation could end up costing your employer millions of possible revenue, and they will possibly not be very grateful. In fact, you are most likely to be reviewed or fired after dropping the ball on a negotiation you were entrusted with by your bosses. So to make sure that you don't make those mistakes that could put your career in jeopardy, below is a list of common mistakes to avoid when you are handling a negotiation.

Not Preparing Enough

You can never be too prepared, but you can definitely be underprepared to handle a negotiation. As noted above, negotiation is all about power and taking advantage of openings to encroach on the bargaining zone. To do this, you must perform all the necessary due-diligence studies to ensure that nothing surprises you during the negotiation phase.

Rigorous preparations also have another advantage. It makes you feel more confident going into the negotiation, which counts for more than just appearances in a negotiation. Sometimes even a partnership negotiation could turn predatory if the other party senses that you are ill-prepared to handle the talks. An undisclosed liability suit, a defective product that has been hurting the company's bottom line, contracts with competitors and partners restricting the business from engaging in certain activities—all these are worthwhile when you are walking into the negotiation room. Even if you expect mutual goodwill from the other party, preparing is 100% your prerogative.

Combativeness

Nothing hurts a negotiation worse than a warlike negotiator. In fact, the evidence points to the contrary. Agreeable negotiators sometimes make more headway in the negotiation table than the aggressors. Nelson Mandela is recognized by Harvard Business School as the world's best negotiator for his handling of the peace talks that abolished apartheid in South Africa. His negotiation style is described as amiable but firm. Without escalating the situation, he could push a point in a patient, practical, and strategic manner that left both parties satisfied that the best deal has been reached. In his negotiation for the lifting of apartheid, he made concessions that allowed the Afrikaans in South Africa to retain their holdings in the country—a contentions point that nevertheless allowed the country's economy to continue thriving.

Combativeness makes it harder to reach an agreement because it establishes a hostile atmosphere. People are less likely to concede a point they would concede in normal situations when they feel threatened. Furthermore, combativeness sacrifices rapport and common interest. It hardens the anchor points, making it that much harder to reach a deal.

Blindness to Options

In a liberal economy like the United States, your options start far before you walk into the room to negotiate. Whatever the gains you are looking for with one party, you can get the same from any variety of other options. You can create options by doing a BATNA study beforehand. And just because you have committed to negotiating does not mean that your only option is to make a deal. Sometimes, it is better to walk out of the room and away from the possible deal, especially if reaching a deal would mean breaching your bottom line. For the inexperienced, negotiations are taken to their bitter end, even if it means destroying any hope for a deal. Of course, you won't know this when you continue slugging it out with the other side past the sensible walk-away point.

From the moment you walk into the negotiation, you can calculate the possibility of reaching a deal by reading your opponents for the telltale signs that any experienced negotiator can read from a mile off. Does the negotiating team look open and willing to reach a deal; the facial cues and body language can tell you that. Are they eager, or do they look indifferent? Depending on what their bodies are saying, you can capitalize or adjust your strategy accordingly. And talking about walking out, did you know that sometimes walking out from the first negotiation saves the deal? Walking out means that you know exactly what you want, which often prompts the other side to revisit their options and come back with a better deal.

Underestimating the Opponent

Just because you come from a major corporation and you are facing off against a startup does not mean that the negotiation will be a walkover. Keep in mind that all successful businessmen of today started out as tiny startups. Jeff Bezos and Steve Jobs all started their multi-billion companies in garages, but they build them up through patience and resilience into the mighty conglomerates they are today.

The worst thing about underestimating the opponent is that you are more likely to make other mistakes like being underprepared and thinking that the other team does not have any option but to bow down to you. This could, in turn, lead to retaliatory bad faith, like the subcontractor who takes their skills to your competitor because you showed that you do not appreciate them. Remember, no matter how good of an opportunity your deal presents, emotions come into play more than any other factor in the making of decisions.

Caving in Quickly

Unless the person you are negotiating with send all the signals that they don't care to haggle, you should never deny the other party the chance to do it. Making a deal after haggling makes everyone feel like they walked away with a better deal, which is good for their peace of mind afterward. Let us say that you are negotiating with a real estate agency about leasing some space for a satellite office. You go in there and take the first deal they offer you and send the message that money is not an issue. They will possibly be left feeling like they did not ask for enough, and a few months later, they might be tempted to hike your rent payable. On the other hand, if you haggled hard and threatened to go to their competitor a few times, they will sign the documents with immense relief. After that, instead of sending you rent-hike letters, they will be sending you a Christmas card and going out of their way to ensure that the space is well maintained—what they should be doing anyway!

As preposterous as this concept sounds, it has been endorsed by some of the best scholars on business negotiations. If a product is negotiable, you should always start by offering less money. Even if you end up paying the asking price, the seller will feel that they deserve it more because they worked harder to clinch the deal.

Gloating

You have outdone yourself in the negotiation, and you have gotten a deal so sweet you feel like breaking into song on dance right there. Don't. Just do not. Gloating has the exact opposite effect to giving the other party a run for their money, only more intense. When we discussed the mental models of loss aversion, we established that people feel worse about the things they lose than the things they gain. When you gloat, you simply make your opponent feel bad about losing out to you. They will be sure to extract their pound of flesh should the opportunity ever arise.

Any wins on the negotiation table should be taken with grace and dignity. If your emotional intelligence is good enough, you will even give the other party a pat on the back for a battle well fought. Even though that will not assuage their feelings of loss, it will surely endear you to them. That rapport could come in handy sometime in the future.

The Psychological Insights of Negotiation

In his text *Influence: The Psychology of Persuasion,* Robert Cialdini discussed the results of his life-long study of the psychological insights of negotiations. His study resulted in a list of six principles of negotiation termed "weapons of influence." Anyone who is privy to these insights holds in their hands the power to influence the actions of others, whether it be in the negotiation table, at the office, or in the retail business. In this section, we will discuss these six principles in detail.

Reciprocation

Human beings are very transactional in nature. We all feel the irrepressible need to pay a good deed with another good deed. The principle of reciprocation transcends cultures, age groups, and social and economic classes. Reciprocation is deeply ingrained within us from years of evolution, so the impulse to give back when you receive something is virtually impossible to avoid. In fact, the temptation is to give back something whose value exceeds the value of the gift you received.

While negotiating, it is much easier to come to an agreement when one party makes the first gesture of conceding ground. Depending on how well balanced the other party is, they will either match the concession with another one of equal or greater value. This transaction is not just expected; it is often demanded. You will observe that when you are haggling, both parties tend to keep a close eye on the concession given by the other party. If you are buying something worth $100,000 and you quote a price of $80,000, the final price will either be $90,000 or within this range.

Commitment and Consistency

Caldini discusses the correlation between commitment and consistency. After paying the opportunity cost on a decision, we become almost irrevocably committed. Even if you were not sure about buying that house or hiring that questionable Fayetteville State University, you would feel more confident about your decision as soon as you have made the initial decision to do it. Satisfaction levels with decisions increase after the fact because consistency takes over.

After making the initial decision, your brain forces you to be consistent in your commitment to it as well as in making other decisions. A decision, even one that was flawed at the time, will often be followed by other decisions of similar nature simply because our brains are wired to behave in a consistent manner. So once you give some ground at the negotiation table, you are more likely to concede a few more points because your brain forces you to act in a consistent manner.

Social Proof

The most accurate way to describe social proof theory is that when in doubt, do what everyone else is doing. Caldini found that people were more likely to do something when other people were doing even when they were fundamentally against such behavior. He gives a great example of canned laughter in television sitcoms. Viewers and the artists behind the productions were unanimous in their repulsion to canned laughter, yet studies show that viewers laughed more and for longer when they were watching television programs with canned laughter.

Social proof is driven entirely by the deeply ingrained desire for us to fit in. When someone does something, we are forced to do the same even though we would never have done the same thing first. During negotiations where an impasse has stretched for a long time, the person who attempts to break it almost always wins because they take the position of leader, assuring the other party that it is okay to give ground.

Liking

Caldini's study found evidence that people are more willing to concede to someone they like than a total stranger. He also found that people tend to like people with some qualities more than others. Physically attractive people are thought of as being more honest, intelligent, kind, and talented, even when there is no evidence to support these assumptions. We also connect better with people who share our looks, values, or lifestyle. This has a calming and disarming effect, forcing us to look at the other person as a friend rather than whatever appropriate tag we ought to assign to them.

Outside the negotiation room, it is for the above reasons that salespeople are usually attractive, with generic clothes to avoid offending any sensibilities. A good salesperson will talk football with you as easily as they would talk 3-point shots with another person if they think it will endear them to you. Good negotiators know how to appeal to the interests of their opponents.

Authenticity

The philosophy of authenticity is based on authority. We are more likely to do things without considering the outcomes when we do not anticipate shouldering the responsibility of the consequences. In the study, when employees were reminded that they were not responsible for the mistakes they make under the instruction of their employer, they were more careless with their decision-making. This applies directly to negotiating. When you are just representing a third party, you should be careful not to make the mistake of careless decisions just because your employer would ultimately be responsible for it.

Scarcity

Finally, we have the theory of scarcity. Caldini found that people were willing to go out of their way to invest in shady deals just because they were harried in their decision with the warning that the opportunity would not be available for much longer. The fear of missing out (FOMO) comes into play here as well. Given a choice between getting something we don't really need or want now and the risk of never getting it (even if we want it in the future), most of us will choose the former.

In negotiations, you can normally get a person to agree to a deal just by taking it off the table. As soon as you do this, if previous observations are anything to go by, the other party will want it more and probably settle for less favorable terms than they could have gotten otherwise.

Persuasion

Even though persuasion is part of negotiation, there are times when the two are quite different. When one party is more invested, the negotiation occurs as more of a persuasion, whereby the interested tries to persuade the other into doing something they are not actively trying to do. For example, when you go to the board of directors with a proposal to fund a new product, you persuade them to see things your way.

The process of persuasion is relatively straightforward. Since you approach them, the tables are tilted in the other party's favor. They hold all the cards and may name whatever price they want, and you may have no option but to acquiesce to their demands. In the example given above, it is entirely up to you to convince the board that your idea is worth investing in. The decision to go along with your idea is entirely up to them (to a certain point). Even though the odds are stacked against you, it is still possible to get your way with an unwilling party.

The first thing you need to do is find something they really want. If you understand company policy and the long-term goals the senior management has set forth, the obvious way to win them to your side is to show how your proposal would help the company achieve these goals. You can then use framing to make the alternative (not going along with your deal) sound like a bigger opportunity cost. In another example, let us say you have identified a great opportunity to cross-market with another business in a complementary industry. You have to sell the deal to them by highlighting the benefits they stand to gain from it. It then becomes their prerogative (in part) to collaborate with you. Everyone has their price. As long as you can identify it, you can persuade anyone to do what you need them to do.

Conclusion

Mental models are systems of thought that affect the way we interact with the world around us. By using mental models, you can improve the way you manage time, apply your energies better for more efficiency in all areas of your life, and achieve success. This is possible because mental models, as used by the most successful businessmen in the world, constitute a higher order of thinking that challenges norms and encourages individuality.

Some of the most common mental models include success by subtraction, outlier algorithm, and the protégé effect. Success by subtraction posits that when we remove negative influences from around us, we are better able to achieve personal success in any area of life. The outlier algorithm sets apart and rewards unique thinkers by giving them the ability to spot opportunities that other people miss out on. Finally, the protégé effect postulates that people who endeavor to mentor others are more likely to succeed in life themselves. It implies that as we try to help others climb to greater heights, we are forced to climb even higher to continue guiding them.

However, before you can go about adopting new mental models, you must first search yourself to make sure that you are not the victim of decision-making bias. Even the most capable thinkers have been known to err in making decisions under the influence of confirmation bias, picking out specific information to digest. It is very critical for managers and leaders to understand how these biases affect their decisions because mistakes and poor decisions can have very serious implications.

Emotional intelligence is a very important building block for success. It prompts us to get a more profound sense of self through self-awareness, which in turn makes us more receptive to other people's emotions. With a better understanding of personal values, emotional intelligence builds our accountability and prompts us into a higher level of self-control. With accountability comes the push we give to ourselves to work even harder toward our goals. Thus, emotional intelligence builds on our passions and, having allowed us to get in touch with our deepest desires, fuels our motivation to pursue them. The most important element of emotional intelligence is empathy. It prompts us to relate to the emotions of other people, especially those we are responsible for leading.

Along with emotional intelligence, the most successful businessmen in the world also exhibit high levels of Stoic behavior. It is part of the mental model used by Elon Musk, Charlie Munger, and other highly successful businessmen. Stoicism allows leaders to persevere in the face of massive challenges. They also appreciate life, you can say, a little more than the rest of us because they have accepted their mortality. Stoicism calls for authenticity, rationality, critical thinking, and living a purpose-driven life.

Next, we discussed decision-making. The career of a manager comprises of a lot of decision-making exercises, with these decisions having a significantly greater weight because it affects the employees, the employer, and the customers. A systematized decision-making process has the effect of making life easier for any manager who practices it. Eliminating decision-making in small matters (e.g., what to wear and what to eat) has been found to free up our mental reserves to focus on decisions that are more important.

New managers make more mistakes in the early days of their

managerial careers than at any other time. Some of the most serious mistakes include flexing their muscles to prove to everyone that they are in control. This alienates team members and makes your job of leaders infinitely more difficult. Micromanaging is another serious and common mistake of new managers. Not only does it annoy the team members, but it also indicates an unwillingness to trust your team to deliver.

Systemizing is a strategy that has been used by business and political leaders to simplify their decision-making processes. In this, the concept of subtracting comes in very handy. It entails creating a well-defined vision for your department and ensuring that your every decision is made in service to that vision. To follow through, you should use the Eisenhower to classify your tasks into a matrix based on urgency and importance. You then focus on doing the urgent and important things and, if you must, delegate the rest.

When designing your systems, you should keep in mind that, by the Pareto principle, 80% of rewards come from 20% of the efforts. You should select the areas you want to focus on very carefully but not neglect the other 20% of rewards that come from 80% of the work. Another concept of creating systems is the KISS principle. It dictates that every system you create should be easy to use for any person and that your vision should be easily communicated and implemented. Some of the obstacles you will have to observe to create an efficient system include bottlenecks, feedback, and leverage. You should endeavor to remove bottlenecks, leverage on your advantages, and use feedback loops to motivate your team and yourself.

Another very popular mental model for systematized thinking is the Bayesian concept. In this concept, you use probabilistic thinking to predict the probability of a desired or undesired event from happening. It bears a close resemblance to the second-order thinking mental model that has been used by Ray Dalio to amass a fortune of over $18 billion. In second-order thinking, we are supposed to think beyond the immediate outcomes of the decisions we make. Failure to do this leads to a chain of events of ever-increasing calamitous impact.

Negotiations are central to a career in management. However little your experience in negotiation might be, at one point, you will have to step up and negotiate a deal for the department or the company. Negotiation requires a specific set of skills. Reciprocation is one such skill, and it can be both a friend and foe. When going against seasoned negotiators, you might get baited into an argument with concessions, conceding far beyond your bottom line. Another strategy used by negotiators is social proof, driving discussions into an impasse and then offering an icebreaker that unwitting victims are likely to fall for.

Being a reluctant party in the negotiation gives you a position of power, forcing the other party to persuade you to take the deal you wanted all along with better terms. The most commonly used strategy to close a negotiation when you hold power is to take the deal away, shocking the other party into a scarcity-induced acquiescence to your terms.

Negotiations in which you discuss a deal with an unwilling party are more like persuasion than anything else. At one point or another in your career, you will have to persuade someone to do something they are not necessarily eager to do. The secret to persuasion is to find the other party's price, then pay it.

Emotional Intelligence in Business

EQ: The Essential Ingredient to Survive and Thrive as a Modern Workplace Leader

Introduction

> *"It is very important to understand that emotional intelligence is not the opposite of intelligence. It is not the triumph of heart over head. It is the unique intersection of both."* – David Caruso

Imagine that you are a team manager working for a large multinational company. Due to economic crashes having taken place over the world, the company is now in a complete tailspin and looking to downsize. It is something that you have found out recently. You have been called into a meeting by the upper management and told that there are specific issues that you need to address in your own team, including dedication and productivity.

Shocked and caught unaware, you walk back to your own corner office and call your entire team in.

"I have really bad news. I was informed by the higher-ups that our team performance is absolutely abysmal. We need to straighten up; if we don't pour our number by the end of this business quarter, we will have to lose members. Since none of us want that, I have decided to make a few major changes so that we can meet the deadline and targets. The first order is that all sanctioned vacations for this quarter are officially canceled. You will all have to be here at work in your most productive behavior and meet the weekly goals no matter how hard it is or how long it takes."

How does that little speech make you feel? Do you feel motivated? Are you pumped to work harder than ever and make sure that you and your colleagues stay safe? Do you feel like there is something wrong with the way that you just spoke? Can you identify the problems with what you said?

We understand that it's hard when you can't, but on the bright side, that isn't a problem you need to live with anymore, because we're going to walk you through every basic and advanced skill associated with emotional intelligence.

First off, thank you for downloading this book, *Emotional Intelligence in Business - The Essential Ingredient to Survive and Thrive as a Modern Workplace Leader,* where we will carefully walk you through not just how emotional intelligence works but also what the common models are and how they apply to the workforce in today's world.

You see, the thing about emotional intelligence is that it is more than just basic logic. While human beings tend to use emotional reasoning when incidents relate to themselves or their own well-being, they oddly do not have that same instinct when they work with others. The initial gut reaction is to be logical, which is not always enough. That is why understanding and honing your emotional intelligence is such an important part of industry growth right now.

Imagine that you are dealing with an extremely pampered child who does not know how to cook. He will be living alone in the next few months on a shoestring budget, and so restaurant meals are way too pricey to be considered. What is your knee-jerk reaction to that? Some may be quick to say, "Learn to cook!"

It's the same with emotional intelligence. It may be a skill that you do not possess, but the industry standard demands for it. Thus, you have to acquire it.

Emotional Intelligence in Business - The Essential Ingredient to Survive and Thrive as a Modern Workplace Leader is more than a theoretical book on emotional intelligence theory. It is a comprehensive study on how your emotional quotient (EQ) can not only help enhance your quality of life but also promote and cultivate personal and professional growth.

Let's go back to that example about the team manager earlier. Now, we will get to the content of his message later, but we should focus on how the information in question has been delivered.

The team manager's delivery of the message was clearly not optimum. The members attended the meeting and came out with bad news. It gave them no time to process this bad news; the manager immediately conveyed the information in such a way that basically made the entire situation worse.

It seems obvious, but what is causing this?

The problem is, not everyone can put their finger on why this specific briefing sounds off, and perhaps neither can you (well, not yet, at least). However, if you keep on reading, you will soon find that the reason is that the team manager has failed to deliver in accordance with the basic emotional intelligence models that we are about discuss below. What makes it worse is that the three factors that he happens to completely overlook include self-awareness, self-management, and empathy. Because they are so fundamental to the application of emotional intelligence, the entire speech itself is void of any form of EQ. By failing to insert EQ into his leadership, it has made the team manager's ability to lead questionable.

Why YOU Need This Book!

"As more and more artificial intelligence is entering into the world, more and more emotional intelligence must enter into

leadership." – Amit Ray

Ever heard of the saying "Knowledge is power"?

Well, there is no better way of describing what damage emotional ignorance can cause, particularly in terms of your own health and worth as a business leader.

Today, some of the most successful leaders in the world have gotten to where they are because they have made an active choice to use emotional intelligence in their day-to-day lives and interactions with their company, as well as the teams and employees under it.

First off, Ursula Burns, former CEO of Xerox, is specifically known for her assertiveness and ability to use mission-based goals to create motivation in her employees. Burns rescued the company from near bankruptcy and was also the first female to take over for another female as a CEO of a Fortune 500 company.

Jeff Bezos, the multi-billionaire CEO of Amazon, utilizes self-deprecating humor to make employees feel more at ease. Aside from being extremely fair, his values also managed to translate over to his team managers and employees positively.

Indra Nooyi, PepsiCo's first female CEO of Indian origin, practices empathetic employee motivation schemes as well. In addition to making a point to stay approachable, Nooyi makes sure that she appreciates and acknowledges all the hard work that her subordinates are doing. An example of which would be her personally written messages that were sent to the parents of 29 senior Pepsi executives to let them know that they raised great kids.

Another amazing leader worth mentioning is Oprah Winfrey, the dynamic talk show host and self-made millionaire. She is one of the most well-known African-American females in the world, if not *the* most. Winfrey advocates active listening and is so engaged with not just her viewers but also the people that she brings out as guests. Her ability to get them to open up has eventually gotten its own term, which is Oprahfication.

On another note, did you know that people with a higher EQ make almost $300,000 more than individuals who rely solely on IQ every year even in 2019 on an average? If you think that it does not apply to your job field, you might want to know that emotional intelligence increases add almost $1500 to the salary of professionals across any job field per point.

So, do you think that any of these leaders would have approached the problem we chalked out earlier any differently? Odds are, they would!

Let's talk about the team manager in the first example again. His main mistake was that he lacked self-control. Also known as an amygdala hijack, the team leader received bad news and could not process it. As such, he basically threw it all back at the staff without even bothering to think about how this information would impact the employees that he was in charge of. His leadership value at that point was zero.

The first thing that the team manager should have done was to identify and process the information. What did the bosses mean, what changes would they need, how could they fix this, what were the most prominent problems, and how could they address them? Five minutes of evaluating the information would have told her that it's not necessarily as bad as it seemed. Even if it was, creating panic was not the way to deal with it.

Fortunately, as we have said before, you will not be in this position. At least, not once you finish this book. *Emotional*

Intelligence in Business - The Essential Ingredient to Survive and Thrive as a Modern Workplace Leader does not focus on emotional theory but on a comprehensive lifestyle. Starting with forming a clear understanding of basic human emotions and how they can form combined emotions, the book then goes into their impact on businesses and how the emotion-versus-logic showdown tends to pan out. Once we have managed to construct a basic understanding of what emotions are, we will take over and explain what the three master EQ models are and how they act as the blueprint for all successful leaders. We will even talk you through how to identify and address personal emotions, as well as teach you the control paradigm, which is a crucial component of EQ application.

The book also goes on to explain the importance of self-motivation and breaks down ways to motivate yourself and the people around you. Since motivation is such a critical part of optimism and positivity, it is also an extremely vital component of positive emotional influences in business settings. Once we are done establishing its value and applying self-introspection techniques, the book will work on ´extrospection´, which deals with the ability to recognize emotional cues in other people and address them. It helps leaders understand how many of the emotional triggers can also be controlled.

Nevertheless, it does not end there. *Emotional Intelligence in Business - The Essential Ingredient to Survive and Thrive as a Modern Workplace Leader* is a complete workbook that provides you with a concrete 30-day plan to help you cultivate your emotional intelligence, bit by bit, and then learn how to best implement all that you have just learned over the span of 4 weeks. Amazing, isn't it?

That's exactly what it's meant to be. In a world of alternant fax when people were supposed to unify us, we are actively working to use our fears and weaknesses to control, well, us. It is essential that every leader in businesses and everywhere else starts to demonstrate awareness of the human factor in the future. After all, entrepreneurs need strong leadership to drive organizational success.

And it was with this thought in mind that Peter Salovey and John Mayer ended up coining the term "emotional intelligence" in the early 90s, defining it in their own terms as "a form of social intelligence that involves the ability to monitor one's own and others' feelings and emotions, to discriminate among them, and to use this information to guide one's thinking and action." But this wasn't necessarily the beginning or ending since Edward Thorndike had already brought up the issue of "social intelligence" in the 1930s. Years later, Daniel Goleman studied emotional literacy at the Fetzer Institute and went on to publish *Emotional Intelligence*, one of the biggest books on the topic. Goleman's work particularly focuses on the emotional architecture of the brain and talks about the way in which feelings often bridge the gaps between logic and rationality. We tend to pick up where he left off and show you how to implement emotional intelligence for leadership purposes.

Remember the words of Ray Kurzweil: "Emotional intelligence is what humans are good at, and that's not a sideshow. That's the cutting edge of human intelligence."

It means that, as of this very moment, our emotions are no longer a dirty secret to be hidden away and looked at and mulled over. How we feel emotionally matters just as much as how we feel physically. That is why we need to be consciously educated to understand emotional balances just as we are educated to understand basic academic knowledge.

Once we have finally managed to grab ahold of our own mind and feelings, we will know exactly how to make it in the world.

The revolution of emotional empowerment is here. So, are you ready for the journey of a lifetime or will you be a mere spectator?

Chapter 1: Human Emotions

"In my 35 years in business, I have always trusted my emotions. I have always believed that, by touching emotion, you get the best people to work with you, the best clients to inspire you, and the most devoted customers." – Kevin Roberts

Emotions are a basic human feature. Just like the nose on your face or your hands and limbs, they are intricate and inevitable parts of your existence. And since feelings are a basic component of being human, they are also vital in almost all human interactions, including the ones pertaining to business or professional spheres.

The problem is, unlike our arms or legs, which we tend to use and flex regularly, most human beings do not exactly know how their emotions work. They just kind of do. This lack of fundamental knowledge makes us similar to one of those bad restaurateurs in Gordon Ramsey's show. They are entirely dependent on the whims of the cook and have no real clue on how to run a kitchen. It makes us incompetent. As any good business leader knows, there is nothing worse than incompetence when it comes to holding a leadership role, particularly in the workplace.

Nonetheless, don't worry; we've got you covered. We will give you a crash course in human emotions and start with the basics. For instance, what are the most common human emotions? What do they build into? Where do they stem from? How do your body and mind react to it?

But hold on! Did you think that was it? We are all about leadership here. So, what's the most important task a leader has to undertake? Answer: Making decisions.

Here's the best thing though, we've gone ahead and covered that too! Once you have managed to get a basic understanding of how emotions work, we will show you what functions emotions have when it comes to leadership roles, particularly during the decision-making process.

Basic Human Emotions

> *"If you are tuned out of your own emotions, you will be poor at reading them in other people."* – Daniel Coleman

Every basic emotion has three major parts. The first one is a subjective component. It refers to how you are subjectively experiencing the feeling in question. The second part is the physiological component, which details how your body reacts to every emotion. Finally, there is the expressive component, which refers to how you behave in response to the emotion in question.

Each individual feeling has a different trajectory, and there are hundreds of emotions that can make you react and act in a different way. Whereas anger can cause you to lash out at a co-worker or employee, anxiety can cause you to make wrong decisions or panic. That is not something you want to do as a leader.

At their core, however, every human reaction stems from eight basic emotions. They are like primary colors building into all those other shades. Everything starts with these feelings.

Anticipation

From the get-go, you have anticipation. It is generally a

positively geared emotion that entails looking forward to a specific action or thing. Anticipation is everywhere. You can see it, for instance, when you are in the grocery line to buy yourself chocolate milk. You anticipate owning and drinking that bottle of chocolate milk. At the same time, when you sit in an exam hall, worried about the questions, you tend to look forward to the questions that you will face. This, in turn, means that the emotion can be both positive or negative, although it does tend to tilt towards the former, especially when the individual is healthy and neutral.

What do we need to know about anticipation as a leader?

Well, for one, anticipation, if used right, can lay out a road map of exactly how you need to behave in order to get people to react the way you want them to. Remember, anticipation is not about reaction; it is a precursor to a reaction. It is similar to a crystal ball that shows you a bunch of possible actions that lead to specific reactions, and all you need to do is pick the reaction you want and act accordingly.

Fear

Fear is a negatively charged emotion that is often considered as one of the most powerful emotional forces there is. Not only does it behave in a more controlling and overwhelming manner, but the emotion is also inherently reactive. It is different from anticipation in which the emotion is easier to guide and control.

What do we need to know about fear as a leader?

You need to keep in mind that fear is more than just an emotion. It is almost like a disease that impacts the present and leads you to change how you react in the future. Because this emotion induces panic, it also takes away your ability to think clearly. Meaning, once you feel fear, it is hard to get away from it. It does not simply exist; it breeds hatred, envy or both. Thus, any good leader must know how to be fearless in the face of everything.

Disgust

Another common negatively charged emotion that we encounter more often than we realize is disgust. Referring to a tendency to reject or feel revulsion towards something that one considers distasteful or offensive, disgust tends to influence your morals and all those prejudices that you may have not known you have. It starts from racial prejudices to sexual preferences, which seem to arise inexplicably even though there is no scientific reasoning to assume that one is better than the other.

As a matter of fact, these moral judgments that we regularly make tend to be among the main causes behind our snap moral judgments. Back in prehistoric times, these generally stemmed from lack of knowledge and kept people from eating poisonous berries and food, making disgust an essential safety tool. However, it became redundant in modern times, considering the emotion not only reflects on food and safety anymore but also on thoughts, morals, and beliefs.

Joy

Coming back to positive emotions, joy is commonly used to refer to how human beings feel when there are positive things happening around them and they sense an impending gain, be it monetary or otherwise.

Joy itself is a very buoyant emotion. It is usually triggered by success or some sort of happy event, such as the birth of a child. It is the equivalent of a golden star from our limbic system, telling us that we are doing all the right things. Joy can also be a form of encouragement so that we continue to do everything.

Sadness

Joy is often directly contrasted with the emotion called sadness, which is the most known negative feeling. While the former stems from a sensation of gain, the latter is closely related to the concept of loss, be it material (when you lose your favorite necklace), emotional (a bad breakup or a the loss of a loved one), social (loss of fame or social accolades), or even professional (a demotion or a pay cut). The resulting feeling that tends to overpower the mind is a deep sorrow that connects with the need to seek refuge and comfort, as well as protection of the mind and soul from the loss in question.

Generally, sadness acts as a base or supplementary emotion for many other common feelings that we deal with, particularly disappointment, pity, and anger.

Anger

Another extremely strong negative emotion is anger. Although it is considered as a secondary feeling, recent studies have shown that the feeling of anger is more dominant than we realize.[1] The emotion tends to arise from a sense of urgency, generally directed at some form of action or injustice that the

---

[1] Petrides, K. (n.d.). Trait emotional intelligence [PDF File]. Retrieved from https://www.thomasinternational.net/getmedia/6bf0569a-8da3-4646-bfc0-ce7e2aed07d5/Trait-EI-Presentation-General-(2016).pdf

individual in question believes requires rectification. Anger indicates that the immediate reaction to a situation is the need for some change and can manifest in many ways, starting from irritation to indignation or even, in extreme cases, rage, or fury.

A typical misconception regarding anger is that violent outbursts, which are simply known as 'venting,' are good for the individual and a healthy way to rid oneself of rage or anger. In reality, venting is like putting a bandage on the emotional condition; it does nothing to solve the problem. The best way to approach anger is with logic. Figure out what causes it and why, how this emotion can be dealt with, etc.

Surprise

This brings us to the feeling of surprise, which is a sense of amazement or wonder that develops or arises from a sudden or unexpected occurrence. Surprise can be both negatively and positively charged. The former can come from the expectation of something that we have projected to take place but still has not, while the latter can stem from a positive circumstance that we have not even anticipated happening.

Interestingly, 'surprise' is one of the most important emotions as well, regardless of whether it is positive or negative. The reason is that surprise brings in dopamine and acts as a shot of stimulus to the human mind. Aside from giving our brains an energy boost, it also helps us focus.

Trust

The final primary emotion we deal with another positive emotion, which is known as trust. It refers to your ability to rely on another person or the confidence to depend on someone else or an institution outside of oneself with any sort of positive expectation.

Here's the thing, though: we know that trust is a feeling, but is it really an emotion, too?

Well, as it turns out, yes! Trust is not just an emotion; it is also an emotional feeder that acts as a base for other emotions, such as interest or rage. Most secondary emotions stem from the existence of trust itself.

Understanding Advance Combination Emotions (ACE)

> *"The most successful business leaders are often experts in emotions."* – Chip Conley

Complex emotions are like compounds built from the original primary emotions in which circumstances and external factors add themselves into the mix to form an instinctive drive. It can be both biological or induced from one of the basic emotions such as fear or joy and act as variations or supplementary emotions, which help in the production of a specific emotion and in the overt behavior displayed due to the emotions in question.

When it comes to being a business leader, the ability to understand, employ, and even exploit or identify these emotions is critical. Hence, while there are over 33 complex emotions out there, we will only be covering 8 of them, which happen to play the strongest role in business communications.

Love

Love may seem like one of the most basic emotions, but it is genuinely a combination of joy and trust. Both of them are essential for modern-day leaders as they make the transition from transactional to transformational leadership smoother than ever.

A key example of businesses flourishing from consumer love and care is Apple, one of the tech giants in the world. When Apple receives a complaint, the store managers handle it through lengthy phone calls, which are not just time-consuming but also extremely expensive. Regardless, Apple chose to continue the practice and later reported that it generated over $1,000 in sales for every hour the spent on the phone. The company actively cultivated trust and joyful experiences, thus making love a natural byproduct of their actions.

Optimism

Optimism is another positively charged emotion that is based on joy and anticipation. Combining the two together formulates a positively minded form of anticipation, which can be anything starting from a good experience to a happy event.

There are a lot of businesses that use positive anticipation to promote the company's sales. Tom's Shoes, for instance, donates a pair of shoes to a child in need for every pair purchased from their stores. The anticipation of a positive event occurring or stemming from their action is a great way to boost sales, and Tom's is evidence of this with over $250 million in profits in 2013 (Krell, 2017).

Aggressiveness

Negatively combined emotions also manifest as ACE and have the exact opposite effect. Aggressiveness, for instance, can be directly contrasted with optimism as it results from a combination of anticipation and anger. There was even a report in which the downsides of aggressive sales techniques have been highlighted with specific reference being drawn between aggressive sales and consumer maltreatment.

Contempt

Contempt is another negative emotion, which stems from anger and disgust and is an extremely visceral reaction. Due to its inherent nature, it has a tendency to result in subsequent behavior that may be harsh or unethical in nature. Think about it, individuals who are faced with disgust are more open to indulging in self-interest and self-interest-based actions than others. This is part of the reason why cleanliness needs to be emphasized in business contexts. The cleaner an environment is, the healthier the mindsets of the employees tend to be, which is something that leaders like you need to watch out for desperately.

Disapproval

Most business leaders know to be wary of is disapproval, which comes with sadness and surprise. When consumers or employees are shocked by the company's actions, this feeling is not exactly positive. That emotion has appeared when BP Oil, for instance, announced a £14-million payout for their CEO. In recent days, another major company that has elected the same emotional reaction is Uber, whose sexual harassment allegations have caused a major drop in consumers and its lack of transparency on the matter only increased the disapproval that the company faced.

Awe

Surprise, however, doesn't always combine with sadness; it can also combine with fear. And when it does, the resulting emotion is the shockingly positive emotion of awe. In businesses and HR contexts, being able to create awe is an essential part of being a good leader. This is because a good leader needs to be able to be unpredictable and worthy. If your employees or consumers see you as a predictable human being, you lose control of your company image automatically. The idea is that you should be untouchable, someone who is looked up to but cannot be measured up to at the same time.

This is why so many companies have surprise events for their customers. The more a consumer attaches the element of positive surprise with a company, the more they feel like being a part of it. The same goes for employees; the more a boss can positively surprise their employees by giving out bonuses or praises, the more connected and attached the employees will feel and more inspired to continue to work toward a new goal.

Remorse

Another common feeling that a lot of business leaders have to contend with is remorse or, as it is more commonly known in business circles, buyer's remorse. It stems from two primary emotions, disgust and sadness, and lead to a feeling of contrition, which is best communicated to the masses. Previously, organizations or companies functioned as demi-gods and reasoned that they were so high-and-mighty because they were untouchable and used to be one of the only choices.

However, in recent years, if there is one thing that a buyer does not lack, it's options. As such, the manner in which those companies have operated also need immediate change.

Apology culture is and has always been a major part of businesses, particularly in the United States and, more precisely, in the healthcare sector. The CEO of Cerner, an IT company that specializes in this industry, for instance, was caught in a scandal over a derogatory email sent out to his management team. When the email became public and Cerner's stocks took a nosedive, the CEO himself not only acknowledged the issue but also offered a public apology. It does not only minimize costs but also helps companies understand modern company culture, as well as the mistakes they are making in terms of it.

Submission

Submission, which happens to be the last emotion that is dealt with in this segment, stems from the combination of fear and trust. Like the others above, it is a critical emotion for any business leader to master. Because submission indicates a level of compliance in addition to the trust that is being put into a person or institution, the ability to cultivate submissive behavior matters for any successful merger or acquisition. It is also essential to improve the leaders' own personal standing. Employees are more willing to listen to leaders who can elicit submissive behavior and are more likely to stay true to the aims and objectives chalked out by their superiors.

All these, however, are merely examples of some of the main feelings that a company's employees and consumers deal with on a daily basis. It emphasizes as well that the ability to control these specific emotions plays a major role in determining the strength of an individual leader. What they do not explain, unfortunately, is the origin of the feelings and why we have them.

Why Do We Have Emotions?

> *"Our emotions amplify what's going on at the moment and our cognition transforms the emotion to provided further information."* – Dr. Mary Lamia

As odd as it may sound, there is no basic difference between emotional and physical reaction. Imagine that you are in an abusive relationship; every single time your partner sees you on the phone, you end up in the ER, in need of stitches. The next time your mobile rings in front of your partner, you may undoubtedly cringe or flinch at once. This isn't you deciding on any actual action, though; this is your body reacting to preserve yourself from harm. Emulsions act in an exact way, so emotions are the result of your body and mind judging a specific situation to be either safe or unsafe, good or bad, happy or sad before reacting in a manner that it finds to be appropriate.

The easiest way to understand it is to mentally put yourself in a situation where you feel a very strong emotion, e.g., disgust. Imagine that, as you walk down the street, you are suddenly assaulted by an extremely unhygienic person in smelly clothes who then proceeds to vomit all over your new shoes. Now, while your brain is processing the loss of your brand-new kicks, the financial loss is deemed to be less important in the face of the immediate repulsion that you feel due to the vomit being in such close contact with your body. While your mind processes this uneasy and queasy feeling, it also makes a mental note to automatically feel disgusted the next time you see someone, who does not look clean at all, moving towards you.

This is, however, a basic emotion. Moral emotions are also a large part of the human experience. They accompany psychological and physiological changes after a period of self-reflection. This is why moral emotions are so distinct, even though they happen to have basic characteristics as primary emotions. They are more than simple involuntary reactions to stimulus and are rather the result of careful consideration and passive and active judgments passed in regard to specific situations.

Why Are Emotions Important in Business?

"The most important thing in communication is to hear what isn't being said." – Peter Drucker

While there are nine types of intelligence, including spatial and linguistic intelligence, one thing that seems to be building an increasingly larger role in the business is emotional intelligence. Now, what you need to understand is that every individual has to find a way to figure out and identify their own capacities. That being said, a business leader similarly needs to discover how to effectively apply their intelligence in a manner that will allow them to recognize opportunities, solve present problems, and effectively collaborate with other teams and people. This ability to integrate is a crucial steppingstone to becoming a strong business leader.

To be more specific, managerial positions have found that emotional intelligence is a critical part of relationship building and the development of dynamic leadership.[2] That is exactly

---

[2] Goleman, D. (2015). Self-regulation: A star leader's secret weapon. Basic emotions, complex emotions, Machiavellian emotions. Royal Institute of

why you will find that more managers and organizations nowadays have stepped away from the hierarchical or authoritative form of running a business. On the contrary, you will find that most start-ups and up-and-coming organizations have opted to introduce a flattering form of managerial policy. Simply put, it will be a lot more like democracy than dictatorship in the office.

Currently, the core business leadership models are undergoing a massive shift from being transactional in nature, to relationship oriented. That is to say, previously managers were used to having simple transaction-based encounters with staff and consumers. These were based on simple give and take mechanisms, where the managers were giving the money and instructions, and the employees taking the money and acting in accordance.

However, business models have now changed in such a manner that business leaders (and yes, even a manager is a business leader), now find themselves in need of composing and implementing an empowering shared message, that will both boost staff morale, and help develop a more organic managerial system through genuine workplace relationships.

Emotions vs. Logic

> *"If you cannot control your emotions, you cannot control your money." – Warren Buffett*

All of this finally brings us to what modern-day business scholars consider as one of the biggest obstacles to an appropriate, effective, and fully functioning decision-making process: the application of logic beyond passion and emotion. For years, managerial techniques have advocated the absolute removal of emotion and passion from all forms of business management. The idea is that in order for it to be effective, all business and corporate strategy needed to be a purely analytical and logical process. Unfortunately, people tend to forget that businesses revolve around people, both in terms of those running it and making it flourish. In short, the presumption that a *rational* human being would always behave *rationally* is perhaps the most *irrational* assumption ever.

The Role of "Emotion vs. Logic" in Decision Making

> *"Emotions have no place in business unless you do business with them." – Friedrich Durrenmatt*

So, how big is this role of emotion in terms of businesses and corporate strategies? Well, according to some experts like Daniel Goleman (2015), emotional intelligence contributes to over 80% of business success. This is exactly why you'll find that when you enter a job field that there are a lot of managers who are not necessarily very educationally advanced but who are in charge of plenty of highly intelligent people.

Even though logic plays a strong role in human actions and reactions, it is not the sole component. A rational human beinFg is still prone to emotional outbursts, while the ability to distinguish between logical and emotional appeals is entirely subjective. When an appeal is in tune with what the listener wants to believe, it is considered logical. On the other hand, when it is not, it is labeled emotional.

How can we avoid logical missteps and focus on building a

more balanced response then?

Well, one way is to be on the lookout for logical fallacies as they present themselves.

1. Faulty Cause

Faulty causation works on the basis of assumptions. The logical following here is that due to incident X, incident Y has taken place. The only problem is these two circumstances often have nothing in common. For instance, Alice wore a red cape; therefore, she must also be Little Red Riding Hood.

2. Sweeping Generalization

Sweeping generalizations are another major logical roadblock. The problem is that it promotes the idea that if one specific thing is true, then everything similar to it must also be true. Say, the common theory about Asians being good at math is a sweeping generalization - and a racist one at that. Thinking that someone must be good with numbers due to their race takes away the individual's identity and makes leaders short-sighted. This is a mistake that you definitely want to avoid.

3. Illogical Parallels

Another logical fallacy is the thought that if two things are similar in one way, they must be similar in all others. For instance, if you are a team leader who was forced to fire a 16-year-old because he was not punctual, and you refuse to hire any other 16-year-old because you think everyone in his age might be tardy, then that's wrong.

4. Faulty Signs

Another mistake is to allow specific individual associations build into a broad assumption – so for instance if you saw a person wearing a black suit and a white shirt and decided that they must be a lawyer, you are kind of stretching it. Making similar conclusive assumptions is a major no-no.

5. Double Dead Ends

A double dead end is when you are framing a point in such a manner that there is no way to disprove it. For instance, if someone was to claim that you disagree with them about everything, they would point out that you just did it again after expressing your disagreement.

6. Authoritative Appeals

An authoritative appeal occurs when an individual uses famous or authoritative sources to establish and justify a decision. For instance, look at how endorsements work. If Nike is good enough for Colin Kaepernick, Nike must also be good enough for the new quarterback of the high school football team.

7. "What if" Arguments

Then, there is the "what if" argument. An easy way to trip up logic is to offer an alternative, however unlikely it is, as a plausible substitute. For instance, the Game of Thrones finale might have been bad, but what if Missandei had got the crown and she became Queen, wouldn't that have been worse?

These seven roadblocks may seem to be unremarkable, but they ultimately destroy the bowl of emotion in logic. That is especially true if you are using emotion-driven logic to establish a claim simply because that is a claim that you wish to have come to fruition. You are using the worst of both worlds as a leader. Your job is to find balance, feed a greater cause, and not drive logic and emotion to meet your personal cause.

Chapter 2: 3 EQ Models Every Business Leader Needs to Know

"Effective Leaders are alike in one crucial way: they all have a high degree of emotional intelligence." – Daniel Goleman

As we open the door to the notion of emotional intelligence, we find that, as a leader, we are forced not only to deal with a diverse group of people daily but also continuously confront the same questions. How do we make the right decision? How do we motivate our team? How do we do things better?

The core of everything, however, is the same: a willingness to changes and adapt to suit the needs of the workforce and the company. We will soon learn that if we can properly balance and redirect the way we lead.

Once you begin to understand the importance of emotion and emotional intelligence, you will automatically realize that you are in need of a solid theoretical base from which you can work forward – this theoretical base is henceforth provided in the form of the three most important models of emotional intelligence produced by modern research.

These three models once properly understood and instilled can and will act as the gravitational center of all your leadership decisions, and will act as an anchor and a tool to help you simplify and tackle any upcoming and current problem. It is, in other words, your light at the end of the tunnel, not just a beacon of hope, but also a guide to lead you forward.

Now, are you ready to brush up on your theory?

Emotional Intelligence Ability

"Perhaps the most irrational assumption we can make is assuming that people should behave rationally and unemotionally." – Dean Tvosjold

The ability model is an EQ model developed by Yale's Peter Salovey and University of New Hampshire's John Mayer. It is based on four individually standing yet interconnected emotion-related abilities. when combined, they can basically measure the level of emotional intelligence that an individual has. These four abilities have been identified and are discussed in detail below.

Emotional Perception

The first and most basic ability is perception. In order to accurately master and apply emotions and emotional intelligence, one must first be able to not only understand the verbal emotional cues provided but also accurately identify the non-verbal cues that workers and peers use in their regular interactions. Non-verbal cues include body language, facial expression, tone, vocabulary, and even contextual behavior or omission of an act. To become a good leader, you need to pick up these cues and identify them masterfully.

Sample Scenario

Jon Snow is a great leader. When he's told about how his people are feeling and what goes on around him, he can make the right decision and always put them first. He is also a righteous ruler who never places his own personal wants or desires above the needs and rights of the people he is in charge of.

The only problem with Jon Snow is that he "knows nothing." Meaning to say, as a leader, he lacks the ability to perceive or identify the thoughts and needs of the individuals he serves. He is also unable to understand the motives or intentions of the people he surrounds himself with unless he is specifically told in some overt way about, say, the burning down a city. As such, Jon's ability to lead is entirely dependent on the information he receives.

Question: Can you still say that Jon is a great leader?

Answer: No. In order to be one, Jon should be able to identify and then assess the threats and possibilities that surround him. While he is capable of making the right decision, he can only do that when he is spoon-fed with information, which, in reality, is not something that is always going to happen. Due to his inability to accurately perceive the thoughts and emotional triggers of the people he is supposed to lead, therefore, Jon Snow is effectively blinded by ill-meaning folks and rendered unable to become an effective leader.

Use of Emotion

The second most important ability according to the ability model is the capacity to control and use one's own emotions, as well as the emotions of other people, to your advantage. It is an undisputed fact that feelings play a major role in the decision-making process. We have already highlighted how emotions can even influence logical decisions and lead to emotion-based ideas and logical fallacies. However, what we haven't really touched upon is the truth that, despite all this, every decision not taken by a robot or AI is still influenced by some degree of emotion. As such, it is critical for a leader to know how to mold and manipulate their feelings to achieve their desired ends. This is particularly vital when a leader is dealing with an issue that needs to be resolved at once.

Sample Scenario

Let's say you are in the middle of negotiating a merger between Microsoft (a company that you lead) and Apple. Apple is represented by a man named Ross Geller, who is the head of its corporate negotiations team. Unfortunately, he is also currently dealing with mental distress because he happens to be going through a bad breakup with Rachel Green, his girlfriend. This woman works for your company as the chief of corporate strategy, and so she has to represent Microsoft in the current dealings. Inexplicably, the merger keeps on facing irrational obstacles that are usually generated by Mr. Geller every time he comes across a point being put forward by Ms. Green.

Because you are unable to understand how to use emotions, you don't understand why Mr. Geller can't seem to come to a rational compromise.

Question: Are you being a good leader?

Answer: No. Although the idea of Mr. Geller representing Apple and Ms. Green being in attendance for Microsoft seems good at first, and while removing either of them from the negotiations can be unfair because they are both entitled to be in the meeting for their respective companies due to the posts that they hold, you, as a leader, seem to be missing the point entirely. Your job is not only to cater to logic but also usher in an effective and positive progression. Because of the emotional baggage that both parties hold on to, it is irrational to expect them to behave reasonably. Therefore, you should know better than to expect them to be able to come to an amicable settlement.

Instead, if you send other members on your team who are equally or adequately equipped to go to the meeting, you will be using your EQ to navigate the current situation in a manner the is beneficial to you and your company. This is the mark of good leadership. Alternatively, if you want to stall the deal because you are also in talks with Yahoo! for a similar merger, you may continue to have Mr. Geller and Ms. Green as the representatives of their respective companies. Doing so can buy you some time and allow you to see how the second option pans out.

Understanding Emotions

Another important part of EQ is the ability to properly comprehend the depth and implications of emotion. Now, unlike what most people seem to think, identifying an emotion is not always enough. Furthermore, it is hard to navigate through it without understanding its root and effects first. For instance, if you were dealing with an individual who happened to be angry, your first question as a leader should be "Why?" By unmasking the reasoning that the individual is using, whether or not you agree with it, you are also giving yourself insight into the possible future actions that he or she may take. When it comes to anger, after all, a possible future action can be seeking revenge, attacking, or retreating fearfully. As a leader, you need to have that insight into all of your employees and other people you interact with. Remember, knowledge is power, and EQ is emotional knowledge at its peak.

Question: How can understanding emotions differ from emotional navigation? How does it change the way you approach the workforce?

Answer: Imagine yourself as Dany Targarean, the CEO of Unsullied, Inc. As such, you have been put in charge of a failing company called Westeroes, which just declared bankruptcy last week. Now, you have decided to employ Ms. Cersai Lannister, former CEO of Westeroes, as the CFO of your company, even though she holds a major grudge against you for taking over and blames you and Unsullied Inc. for the financial ruin of Westeroes. As a CEO, have you made the best possible decision by putting Ms. Lannister in charge of its financial future?

No! Of course not. While it is entirely likely that you were attempting a gesture of good faith or that Ms. Lannister was Sheldon Cooper's counterpart in the world of financing, the fact remains that Ms. Lannister bears a grudge towards you and your company for some reason, logical or not. Hence, she is unlikely to want the best for the business and may genuinely wish to see its financial downfall. If you cannot spot an emotionally vulnerable employee, it entails that you are a liability to your own company as well.

Managing Emotions

This brings us to the final emotional competency measured by the ability model: the management of emotions. Managing emotions deals with three main factors - is the person in question being able to adequately take into account the emotions that they are perceiving? If they are, then are they comprehensively using those emotions to control the root cause and reactive elements in question.

Mixed Model Intelligence

> *"When your intuition is highly developed, you don't have to work to turn it on. It stays on; it flows. It becomes part of the way your heart and senses relate to every experience and*

circumstance." – Robert Cooper

The good news is, unlike IQ, which is mostly built in and fixated after our teen years, our EQ is learned and can be learned at any age. In fact, there are five specific components of emotional intelligence that help buoy your ability to function with better emotional stability, which is covered in the David Goleman model of EQ, a.k.a. the Mixed Model.

Self-Awareness

The development of self-awareness as a business leader is critical. As a business leader, after all, you need to be aware of your own moods and emotions so that you can also follow and anticipate how they will impact others. It is also important because self-awareness allows you to understand what motivates you as an individual. The more in tune you are with your personal strengths, weaknesses, interests, and disinterests, the better you will be able to control and influence your own actions.

Self-awareness allows a person to have a strong sense of self-worth as well. This is super important as it lets you identify your own strengths and teaches you how to accept criticism, which is a critical part of human development. Such a need intensifies when you become a business leader because the more you develop self-awareness, the more your organization can grow under your leadership.

Sample Scenario

As a leader, it is important that you understand what impact you have on the people you are leading. Imagine for a minute that Lord Voldemort decides to have a board meeting with all of his Death Eaters to gain their opinions on how he should treat Harry Potter, who happens to be their current prisoner. Given the reputation that Voldemort has forged, it is unlikely for his followers to tell him what they genuinely think he should do. Due to his fearsome nature, it is more possible for him to receive lip service.

Now, imagine that you are the CEO of MAC, and you have developed a tendency to lash out at the bearers of bad news, often by firing or demoting them. You have recently assembled a board meeting to ask your senior executives how a lipstick that you have personally been seeking to produce may fare on the global market. How likely is it for your senior managers to speak up?

A good leader understands not just what other people are prone to do but how they behave and impact others as well.

Self-Control

Self-control is another extremely important competency. Unlike self-awareness that focuses on the understanding of the self, self-control concentrates on the ability to conform and redirect actions or reactions. This way, the things that we do are not impulsive. Self-control works to actively increase the process of rational thinking under pressure and is meant to encourage and boost productive actions.

Sample Scenario

Let's go back to the Lord Voldemort scenario that we have just dealt with. Like Lord Voldemort, you have been made aware that your tendency to lash out and use Avada Kedavra on all of your opinionated Death Eaters has somewhat turned you into a tyrant. You now have two options: acknowledge and disregard this information or act on it. The thing is, emotionally stable and intelligent individuals would choose to do the latter. As such, the Mixed Model seeks to measure one's ability to impose self-control to see how emotionally intelligent a person is.

Now, let's take a look at the MAC scenario again. Lack of self-control means that even though you are aware that your actions as a CEO cause you to lose valid opposition or something as simple as a second opinion, which, in turn, makes your company garner unnecessary and preventable losses. Neither of these things add up to you being a smart or great leader. In contrast, if you taught yourself how to be more accepting of changes, you would be able to not just adjust your product but also come off as more approachable and less of a tyrant. In the end, you can't just always be right, because no one ever is. As a leader, your job is to be right for the company, even at the cost of your own pride or emotions, and that is where self-control comes in.

Motivation

It is extremely important to keep in mind that one's ability and will to work do not merely depend on the logical factors that generally govern work-life balance, such as monetary gain or professional advancement. There are many times in which a person's desire to work comes from something more basic like their passion or determination to do well and succeed in life. And these factors, when combined together, are what we often call as motivation. The thing is, it is more than just drive. It is the force that allows someone to easily overcome the obstacles that they will undoubtedly face as they continue to pursue their goals. That is exactly why any good leader needs to have a strong grasp of what motivates their employees and how to increase those motivational levels best.

Why?

While being aware of how you impact your employees is great, so is being able to control your own emotions. Nevertheless, what's genuinely important is having the ability to handle your employee's emotions, which is basically what motivation does.

Sample Scenario

Once upon a time, Walt Disney didn't have enough money to make movies. So, he went to his brother, but then he got turned down. Walt went to a man named Mike Vance and asked him to get more money out of Disneyland. Mr. Vance did it by putting together a team of seven people, who recommended that they should open the park on Mondays and Tuesdays, which were holidays at the time while providing a corporate discount. The idea was a massive hit. As a thank you, Walt Disney personally sent over Mickey Mouse to each of the seven members with an envelope containing 100 shares of Disney stock, $25,000, and a handwritten note that said, "It's fantastic. You're fantastic. Do it again." Now, what do you think happened the next time Walt called them in?

They came in, of course! That is exactly how motivation works. It not only gets the job done but also makes sure it keeps on getting done, which is what every great leader should aspire to!

Empathy

Empathy is also very important, particularly for business leaders. It allows a good leader to feel what other people - more importantly, what their co-workers or employees - feel. Even in cases wherein a leader is unable to completely understand others' emotions, the mere establishment of the intent to reach out, understand, and work through these problems is a core skill for any mentor. Especially for people in diverse work cultures, that is such an integral part of today's business world.

Sample Scenario

We've talked about this before, but it is worth repeating that we are no longer dealing with one-dimensional transactional sales anymore. Company sales depend on the experience the consumer is gaining and not on the simple product that is being purchased these days. As such, it is crucial for companies to learn how to sell their image, which - surprise, surprise - is so much easier to do when the business comes off as nice. Think of Walgreen's for a minute. The company, thanks to its then-VP Randy Lewis, began a disability inclusion program, which showed significant business gains after a year. Turns out, when a company comes off as empathetic, the consumers tend to like it a little bit more. Who knew?!

Social Skill

Finally, we find ourselves dealing with social skill. Despite being able to empathize, understand, and even control our own emotions, it is impossible to be a good business leader if one cannot demonstrate strong and consistent ability to deal with conflict situations and manage mutually beneficial relationships. This skill to be whoever their consumer and employees need them to be is always common in every great leader.

A person manages to do that by obtaining and maintaining a high degree of emotional intelligence, of course!

Sample Scenario

Imagine that you are the CEO of a Fortune 500 company but are unfortunately extremely awkward. Not only do you have a hard time keeping up with your peers; you also have a tendency to offend and cause problems among your allies. You will basically end up being the Donald Trump of the business world. Aside from ruining the company's image, you will also come off as incompetent and destructive. None of your EQ is worth anything if you cannot attend to the situations you are faced with in a manner that is appropriate. Remember, in order to rule the roost, you need to be a rooster first!

Emotional Intelligence Trait Model

"Before you can lead others, before you can help others, you have to discover yourself." – Joe Jaworski

The final model that we'll be dealing with here is the Emotional Intelligence Trait Model, which has been defined by its developer Konstantin Vasily Petrides, as "a constellation of emotional self-perceptions located at the lower levels of personality." This specific model does not merely test one's perception of their own emotions, but it does so in a manner that allows self-assessment to help build the EQ framework. It has often been criticized for its vulnerability to result in manipulation. For instance, if a person decides to answer dishonestly, their EQ would theoretically be scored incorrectly; however, the model itself has been known to reject such implications. A basic Trait Model EQ test imposed on an adult would consist of the measure of 15 major points.

Adaptability

Adaptability is an individual's emotional intelligence trait that is considered to indicate his or her flexibility. It refers to how rigid they are in their own thought pattern, as well as how capable they are of adapting to newfound situations or conditions. Adaptability is a key component of emotional intelligence, considering the only way to bolster teamwork is by putting together a cohesive team and showing a willingness to change their ways, which is something that any good leader should be on the lookout for.

Assertiveness

Next up is assertiveness. It is a sociability trait that determines the individual's ability to stand up for the rights that they have inherited or gained, as well as communicate their feelings or opinions in a frank and forthright way. The higher the assertiveness of an individual is, the more emotionally intelligent they are considered to be. After all, the trait is indicative of clarity and consistency of mind.

Emotional Expression

Emotional expression is a similarly important trait. Unlike assertiveness, however, emotional expression is an emotionality trait that determines how capable a person is at communicating their thoughts and feelings to other people. The higher a person scores on their emotional expression, the more in tune they are with their emotionality and personal views. This serves as an indicator of high emotional intelligence.

Emotional Management

Another sociability trait is emotional management. This is thought to measure how well an individual can use their other sociability skills, such as assertiveness, to control and influence other people, especially their thoughts and feelings. The more adept a person is at managing or controlling others' emotions, the higher their emotional intelligence score is, considering the entire objective of emotional intelligence is to be able to exert some sort of control over other people through emotional manipulation.

Emotional Perception

Unlike emotional management, though, emotional perception centers more around the emotionality factor and is used to check how comprehensive one's understanding is of their own feelings, as well as the others'. It is another extremely important factor since most actions are undertaken due to the individuals' understanding of the emotional state of the other person or even themselves.

Emotional Regulation

Emotional regulation, on the other hand, falls under the category of self-control and is a trait that assesses how capable the individual is when it comes to not only influencing but completely controlling and regulating how people feel regularly. The better a person is at handling their own emotions, the better and more balanced their decisions will be, and the more likely it is for these decisions to be good. As such, emotional regulation is another key factor measured.

Impulsiveness

Another self-control variety that trait models measure is the scale of impulsiveness that is displayed by individuals. Unlike the other sectors in this book, the lower the impulsiveness levels a person shows, the higher their emotional intelligence is deemed to be. The reason is that being impulsive is the exact opposite of acting with emotional intelligence. In truth, it has a tendency to destabilize any decision because it is usually a not-well-thought-out reaction.

Relationships

Another emotionality-based trait is relationships. A critical part of measuring emotional intelligence is weighing a subject's ability to not only perceive or act on but also fully function in an emotionally balanced manner to maintain personal relationships that are meaningful and fulfilling. Think of Sheldon Cooper's ability to keep friendships and relationships as opposed to a normal person - that is what you're trying to avoid. Sheldon from the first season of Big Bang Theory is not very high on the EQ scale, and maintaining personal relationships is challenging for him. His other friends like Penny may not have a high IQ level, but they are quite capable in terms of EQ maintenance.

Self-Esteem

How a person views himself or herself is also an important part of emotional intelligence. You should keep in mind, however, that the trait test is not a simple case of high means good or low equates bad in terms of its scoring. On the contrary, each score is contextually based. As it involves self-assessment, it is based more on the perceptions that someone has of himself or herself instead of the actual measure of competencies or skills that the individuals hold. Nevertheless, positive well-being is determined by higher levels of self-esteem, among other factors.

Self-Motivation

Self-motivation is one of the auxiliary facets of the test that is used to assess how driven an individual perceives themselves to be and how likely they are to either succeed or persist in their attempts to achieve a goal despite the situation at hand. In other words, it seeks to measure how much drive an individual has when it comes to how they approach issues daily.

Self-Awareness

Interestingly, self-awareness, which is a sociability factor, differs from self-esteem and self-motivation, in the sense that it does not measure any positive view that one may have or think they have about themselves. Instead, it seems single-mindedly focused on identifying how accomplished a person is in terms of how they perceive their own social skills and subsequent networking abilities. It matters to keep in mind that awareness does not depend on how good one is about their skills but how well they can realize whatever abilities they have.

Stress Management

Emotional or stress management is another sociability factor and the last of the three used to measure trait EQ. An individual's perception of their ability to withstand and work under stress, as well as their perceived ability to regulate or control the stress levels imposed on them are both identified through stress management.

Trait Empathy

Another emotionality trait measured is empathy. Here, the individual's perception of how far they can commiserate and objectively see the world from the eyes of another person is identified and accounted for.

Trait Happiness

The happiness trait, on the other hand, deals with how a person perceives their ability to be happy, how happy they think they are, and how satisfied they are with their own lives. Hence, the well-being of an individual is judged in part by the happiness trait.

Trait Optimism

The last trait is measured by trait optimism, which, as a rule, checks how likely an individual is to confidently look at the positives - or on the "bright side," as people put it.

With EQ tests measuring different parts and many other factors, it is clear that emotional intelligence plays a critical role in terms of predicting job performance. As such, it has a very specific impact on contextual happenstances. It practically means that there is a positive correlation between the two. Emotional intelligence can be used to approach organizational behavior as a tool, which will not only help explain problems in the workforce but actively and effectively navigate through its waters as well.

Chapter 3: Introspection

"To thrive, all businesses must focus on the art of self-disruption. Rather than wait for the competition to steal your business, every founder and employee needs to be willing to cannibalize their existing revenue streams in order to create new ones. All disruption starts with introspection." – Jay Samit

Introspection is a vital element when it comes to the expansion and comprehension of every individual business' inherent building blocks. The easiest way to understand introspection specifically in terms of business leadership is by thinking about it as an opportunity to understand the inner workings of one's own mind.

Intelligent business leadership, of course, views introspection not as a byproduct but as a fully functioning tool, which is used to weed out inconsistencies and hostility in the business environment. The reason is that introspection, when properly conducted, does not merely work on building a clear understanding of one's company or leadership. More importantly, it uses the opportunity to focus on a leader and businesses ability to regulate or control one's impulses and motivate themselves. All these three factors matter for the expansion of a business and the true establishment of a well-rounded business leader.

Self-Awareness and Introspection

"We cannot change what we are not aware of, and once we are aware, we cannot help but change." – Sheryl Sandberg

This need to properly introspect business leaders and their

motives brings us to the ageless concept of self-awareness. The idea is simple: use the truth, a clear unvarnished version of it, to recognize, accept, and embrace the changes required for you to become a business leader. It's like being a president who doesn't always go off saying that he has the best words. Rather, he makes a point to listen to the concerns that people raise, as well as works to address them instead of suppressing them. Running a successful business is no different from running a country, after all. It's not always about gaining more traction or adding more land; it's also about how you rule and make sure that you know the best possible ways to do things. Remember that a strong foundation is nothing but that. When you are watering the soil it is standing on, the minute you stop, the very thing you are standing on goes from solid ground to shifting sand. Then, your traction, footing, and ability to remain upright - much less your ability to move forward - are all automatically compromised.

Self-Esteem vs. Values and Priorities

> *"It's not hard to make decisions when you know what your values are."* – Roy Disney

Two of the hardest things to do as a business leader are finding time for the things that the company values and prioritizing and balancing that with the self-esteem quotient of the people you seek to lead. This is particularly prominent in terms of schedule-based management systems in which the production of a specific outcome is practically the most important thing on the agenda.

Or is it?

Individuals with low self-esteem will say 'yes' and stick to the safe bet. They do as they are told, but if you are not questioning and implementing specific judgments, why are you even bothering with hiring people? Just stick to AI. The fact of the matter is that your strategic goals are what you need to look out for as a business leader. You need to ensure that your employees feel empowered enough to find better ways to keep on putting these values and priorities ahead of company culture and past trends. Think about Goldman Sachs and E*Trade for a second. Both of these companies work with financial services. Now, considering Goldman Sachs is so much bigger and more famous than E*Trade, the latter has sought to emulate the former's model to a T. How successful would they be? *Not very.* Do you know why?

If you tried to measure your success on the same scale, you'd still feel like a failure, and so would your employees.

The reason is that they are not the same company. Goldman Sachs works with high-end customers and needs to focus on one individual sale, whereas E*Trade is more grassroots and gets its push from the mass influx. While Goldman Sachs can rely on client relationships, E*Trade has to set their eyes on being competitive, as well as more technically advanced options.

You need to teach your employees and future leaders how to see things in context, especially when you are trying to introspect. After all, you can't judge the skill of a fish by how high it flies.

Furthermore, the self-esteem of the employees you are working with is critical. The better they feel about themselves, the more invested they will be in their jobs. By teaching them how to replace their negative behaviors or perceptions with positive actions, you give an idea on how to identify the company's priorities and needs over their insecurities. That is essential for building a better tomorrow for your business.

Self-Confidence vs. Curiosity

"The four Cs of making dreams come true. Curiosity, courage, consistency, confidence." – Walt Disney

Self-confidence is the next major wing of self-awareness. It also has a big part of what allows you to change and grow, as well as shepherd such growth as a business leader. In fact, curiosity is perhaps one of the most important elements of effective self-awareness. It gives you cause to question what lies beyond the limits of your knowledge. As such, it constantly lets you accept and seek out more.

The only potential roadblock here is self-confidence, which is considered as an important part of leadership. Now, here's the thing: does confidence still matter when it comes to the realm of business leadership? *Yes!* Every successful business leader needs to always seem like they know exactly what they are doing. You will not be able to move forward or lead if your words or decisions do not sound absolutely certain. A business leader is a rock in everyone's eyes. They know; they don't guess. They lead; they don't flounder.

While all that is true, the only true way to foster growth is to keep reaching into the abyss and pulling yourself forward. Believe it or not, even business leaders don't know what to expect.

They aren't supposed to.

They are supposed to be curious and constantly seek information. A good CEO isn't necessarily the best financial graduate that has walked out of Harvard or MIT. It's the kid who knows he or she is not the best but is willing to ask the right questions and push the company and employees in the direction of prospective change while confidently maintaining the economic status quo. Curiosity is something that can be built into businesses. It was done by 3M whose concept of Post-It Note was developed by Dr. Spence Silver during the company's allocated curiosity window.

Assertiveness vs. Feedback and Circumstances

> *"Your most unhappy customers are your greatest source of learning." – Bill Gates*

Another important part of self-awareness, particularly when you are a business leader, is the whole notion of being assertive or forthright in one's own opinions. Assertive matters, but it is also equally - if not more - essential for every leader to know how to temper this characteristic with the feedback that they receive and in light of the circumstances they are in. These two factors are the basis of accountability, which is perhaps one of the - if not *the* most - crucial parts of leadership.

When a business leader is assertive when they are unaware, unwilling, and unable to admit their mistakes or the reality of the situation. The same thing occurred with the former CEO of Turing Pharmaceuticals, Martin Shkreli, who famously increased the prices of Daraprim (a drug used to treat toxoplasmosis, a disease that targets the immune system of cancer patients and HIV positive individuals) from $13.50 to $750 per pill. This markup of $736.5 was not the only thing that costed the company, however. Shkreli's unapologetic tweets and statements that subsequently followed did that as well, including his statements at the Forbes Healthcare Summit where he stated, "I probably would have raised the price [of Daraprim] higher ... I think healthcare prices are inelastic. I could have raised... [the price] higher and made more profits ... this is a capitalist society; capitalist rules, and my investors expect me to maximize profits, not to minimize them or go half, or go 70%, but to go to 100% ... [like we] are all taught in MBA class." He further tarnished not just his own image but the image of pharmaceutical companies everywhere.

Identification of Personal Emotions

> *"Just because you are a CEO, don't think you have landed. You must continually increase your learning, the way you think, and the way you approach organization. I've never forgotten that." – Indra Nooyi*

As a business leader, the most important reason that any individual needs to either cater to or learn to reign in is our emotions. There is a theory that our thoughts control our actions. In truth, actions are never controlled by thoughts unless they are specifically allowed to. That is exactly where mindfulness comes in.

Mindfulness is like the express version of self-awareness. Whereas awareness centers around your ability to act on autopilot - that is, to do something without even thinking about it, without resistance or judgment - the whole purpose of mindfulness is to use these same tools to identify and label your thoughts. Instead of avoiding them, you challenge yourself to understand and accept how you are thinking and why you are thinking in that specific manner by objectifying your ideas.

All of this is important because, to truly understand ourselves and our personal motives, we need to stop being overconfident. That is impossible to do without identifying the emotions surrounding us. Once we manage to do so, however, we are afforded key insight into our own values and thoughts, which allows us to bridge the disconnect that we've had between our functioning self and our theoretical self. This, in turn, allows us to become not just more productive but more successful as well.

Self-Regulation and the Control Paradigm

> *"It's okay to have your eggs in one basket as long as you control what happens to that basket." – Elon Musk*

The thing that most people tend to forget about emotions is that they are, for the most part, biological impulses. While the impulses themselves may be hard or even impossible to control, the actual emotion itself is not. Having said that, we will concede that, in the heat of the moment, it is easy to forget that our conscious choice to manage or ignore emotional reactions will determine how you function as a business leader or even a regular person.

Self-regulation is about more than just making room for emotional intelligence. It is liberation from the shackles of impulse-based behavior and the responsible undertaking of reflection and control in the face of current climates and uncertainties. They are all tempered by integrity, which gives individuals the choice to say 'no' to those impulsive tendencies.

The thing is, regardless of how it is perceived, self-regulation is a crucial part of business development. In truth, it is one of the most underrated skills that the business leader needs to have.

Why is this even more important now more than ever? Well, for one, businesses today require extremely higher productivity rates in order to stay competitive in the market. The only way that business leaders will be able to sustain high productivity while maintaining safe and fair environments for their workers is if they make a point of creating environments where high-profile, effective, and competent workers want to come and work for their companies. Frankly, this is something that they cannot do if they have a reputation in the industry for blowing their top all the time or creating drama.

Furthermore, self-regulation builds its way into the concept of trickle-down economy. The more the leaders apply this technique, the more the employees will follow suit. Remember, as a leader, your actions will be emulated, so make sure that your workers can pick up characteristics that will take your company forward.

Basics of Self-Control

"Rockefeller and his associates did not build the Standard Oil Co. in the boardrooms of Wall Street banks. They fought their way to control by rebate and drawback, bribe and blackmail, espionage and price cutting, by the ruthless efficiency of the organization." – Ida Tarbell

As a business leader, one of the major problems that we tend to face is the manner in which our emotions and logical brain seem to clash or face off. It is only natural for leaders to battle with their emotional reactions and be expected to provide rational decisions at some point. Despite that, this is where emotional self-control comes into play. Destructive emotions and impulses are a regular part of our day-to-day lives, even if we don't always recognize them as such. Something as simple as not wanting to wake up early in the morning - although you know that you have to be early at work - is a prime example of how destructive emotions can be to your behavior. It can also control the actions that are taking place - and will continue to take place - as the leader of your workforce and company.

So, how do we get a grip on our emotions and start to decide on what we're going to do, logically and not impulsively speaking?

Well, why don't we start with Dr. M. Seligmans' ABCDE model of worry management? The reason why you should use such a tool, in case you have not already guessed it yet, is that worry is the exact polar opposite of control. Meaning, if you can manage your worries, you will automatically be putting yourself in a position of control!

A - Adversity

The first thing that you need to do in order to establish self-control is to describe your adversity. Who is the problem? What is the problem? When did this problem arise? Moreover, where is this problem taking place?

By making sure that you are using specific terms to accurately describe the adversity in question, you automatically ensure that you are establishing objective statements. That will help you to form a rational decision in the near future.

Sample Scenario

Imagine that a product that you have launched has failed in the market. This failure is adversity. It's not about you feeling unwell or sad. It's not about the fact that your distributors were an hour late to the launch last week either. The problem is the product itself and its failure to attract consumers. Once you know and accept this, you can start working on the problem directly.

B - Belief

Considering you have identified the adversity, your next job is to recall what you say to yourself when facing such a dilemma. This is extremely important because much of what you speak of later translates into actual beliefs. For instance, if you are dealing with a tough problem, you may tell yourself, "I can't do this" or "I just can't cope with the pressure." You will honestly be unable to cope with the pressure because you have taught yourself to believe that you are incapable.

C - Consequences

This is where the concept of consequences starts to form. Once you have identified your adversity and then recorded the belief pattern that you have either verbally or mentally established, you may take note of the subsequent consequences of your ideas. For example, when you told yourself that you could not cope with the pressure of work or do a certain thing, how did you feel? Did it empower you, as if it was something you could do? Or, did you feel even more helpless, like your ability to overcome obstacles had been completely taken away?

This idea is not that uncommon. Keep in mind that the feelings and emotions that you deal with stem from the beliefs that you instill in yourself.

D - Disputation

Now, let's move on to the action items. Go back to your beliefs and ask yourself objectively, "What is wrong or inaccurate with the belief that I put forward?" Identify it, then dispute it. For instance, when you said that you could not cope with the pressure, you could challenge this event by recognizing the multiple instances in which you managed to deal well with pressure.

E - Energization

That's how you bring yourself to energy and organization. Energization is where you identify how to apply your energy in an organized form so that you can build towards a better future. Instead of saying "I can't do this," try telling yourself that you need to work harder and make sure that you will.

Importance of Identifying and Quelling Impulsive Behavior

"Timing, perseverance, and 10 years of trying will eventually make you look like an overnight success." – Biz Stone

The biggest problem with impulsive behavior is that it can be downright destructive when it comes to the success of any business. As a business leader, it is essential to not only have the ability to organize and coherently plan but also be able to lead by example and ensure that your behavior is both rational and deliberate.

Let's put this into context, shall we?

Imagine that you are the CEO of a multinational company. Among your current goals is to improve productivity during work hours, and you believe that the best way to do this is by avoiding unprofessional working environments. One morning, you walk past the office kitchen and notice a gathering of five or six employees who are chatting as they make their own coffee.

You instinctively decide that workplace conversations such as these are responsible for the lower productivity of the company. Therefore, you issue an e-mail to all of the individuals you have seen, stating that employees are no longer allowed to visit the kitchen for a coffee break. If they want to have coffee, they merely have to push a button, and a server will bring them coffee. The only problem here is that you have not consulted the chief operating officer or head of human resources. Also, you don't exactly have a coffee server at the moment.

Almost immediately, your organization is in a state of absolute chaos. It can effectively extend to smoking breaks; if it does not, then smokers have an unfair advantage over non-smokers. So, you suddenly find yourself bombarded by thousands of questions from hundreds of employees. This problem may have been avoided by holding a small meeting with the COO and head of HR department first.

What's worse is that your impulsive behavior has led your employees to label you as an irrational and erratic leader - a name that is obviously not for PR.

Emotion Management: Leveraging and Controlling Positive and Negative Emotions

> *"Happy employees lead to happy customers, which lead to more profits." – Vaughn Aust*

The thing is, emotional management is difficult to do, especially when it comes to stressful situations at work. Unfortunately, it is also much more common. But this doesn't mean that you need to allow yourself to be controlled by negative feelings. So, why don't you start by trying to identify the calm and negative emotions that can be found in the workplace first?

Remember that being aware of your emotional state is the first step to controlling your emotional state, just like we have laid out in the mixed model for emotional intelligence.

Now, coming back to the negative emotions that we are faced with, one of emotional this stress in the workplace arises from frustration or irritation. This is generally stemming from the form of helplessness.

Say, you have a boss who is deliberately sexist or racist. If you want to get out of this situation, you first need to stop and evaluate if such labels are truly applicable for your superior. Then, ask yourself if that is why you are feeling this way. Is there a better more tactful way to deal with this issue?

Take your time to think things through. After doing so, you will find that you feel calmer and more in control. Now, you can move on and look for a positive way to deal with the situation. One suggestion is to recall the similar incidents that you or your peers have been in and see and learn from how those situations have been tackled.

Nevertheless, this is not merely about frustration and irritation. Every other negative emotion that you may experience in the workplace, such as worry or anger, nervousness or aggravation, dislike or disappointment, and unhappiness or dissatisfaction, can be resolved in the exact same manner. It's all about understanding what negative emotions you have and finding a rational and effective way to deal with them.

It is important to keep in mind that introspection is a major part of running any business. As a leader, the ability to examine your own motives and feelings matters not only because it will give you a clear vision of what you see yourself doing in the future but also because it will allow you to lead the people who follow you with much more clarity.

Self-Motivation

> *"Leaders become great not because of their power but because of their ability to empower others."* – John Maxwell

In a world of over seven million people where no two people are the same, diversity is the lifeblood of businesses, as well as all the possibilities that lay before you. But what are these things? Furthermore, how do you teach someone that the #1 thing you need is the motivation? Frankly speaking, employees are a dime a dozen; great leaders, however, are not. The only question is: How does a leader become great?

For one, a great leader must be self-motivated. They must know who they are, what their needs are, and how they intend to fulfill their needs. Most importantly, they should have a strong, unbreakable drive to achieve their goals while simultaneously ensuring that their personal objectives are in tune with the needs and goals of the organization that they lead.

How do you ensure that you have maximized your self-motivation as a leader? Well, why don't we start with nine easy tricks to get you going?

Use Words to Boost Your Motivation

> *"Wanting something is not enough. You must hunger for it. Your motivation must be absolutely compelling in order to overcome the obstacles that will invariably come your way."*
> – Les Brown

Talking to someone about the things that you want to do is an excellent way to motivate yourself. Not only does talking help communicate your ideas to your team; it also helps you! By simply hearing your own ideas spelled out aloud, after all, you can see what other people see, hear what they hear, as well as identify where you have gone wrong or where you need to refocus your attention.

Be Optimistic

> *"Entrepreneurial business favors the open mind. It favors people whose optimism drives them to prepare for many possible futures, pretty much purely for the joy of doing so." – Richard Branson*

Another great way to make sure that you are holding onto your personal motivation is by looking at everything through rose-colored glasses. In other words, be optimistic. Remember that obstacles come and go; the one thing that remains constant throughout is your approach to dealing with these obstacles. Are obstacles going to scare you, or will they be seen as another challenge that you can soon overcome? The choice is yours.

Find Out What Interests You

> *"Life can be much broader once you discover one simple fact, and that is everything around you that you call 'life' was made up by people that were no smarter than you. And you can change it, you can influence it... That's maybe the most important thing. It's to shake off this erroneous notion that life is there and you're just gonna live in it versus embrace it, change it, improve it, make your mark upon it."*
>
> *– Steve Jobs*

It's hard to stay self-motivated if you are neither interested nor absolutely in love with what you are doing. If you can't find something to love about the task that you have been given, try to look at the bigger picture and mentally envision how you do minor tasks as a building block for the ultimate big picture.

Acknowledge Your Achievements

"Never give up. Today is hard, tomorrow is worse, the day after tomorrow will be sunshine." – Jack Ma

Another important step is to make sure that you acknowledge the achievements that you have. It is challenging to stay motivated when you constantly feel like a failure or as if you are not achieving or amounting to anything. Instead, try making sure that you take time out to acknowledge things that you have achieved something, then point yourself towards the things that you hope to attain in the future.

Monitor and Record Your Success

"There is a difference between losing and failing. Losing reflects the score; failing reflects our attitude." – Simon Sinek

Speaking of self-acknowledgment, try keeping a record of how successful you are. Having your failures and successes written down in black-and-white will not only allow you to physically see how far you've come. Instead, it will also act as a map and indicate how much farther you need to go in order to achieve the success that you wish to have.

Boost Your Energy Levels

"Leadership isn't a title. It's a behavior. Live it." – Robin Sharma

Motivation, however, is hard to hold onto unless you have the right energy levels. Besides, maintaining the right energy levels means maintaining a healthy lifestyle. Eat right, sleep right, and make sure you exercise. Your body is your temple. While businesses may seem to want your brain more than they do your body, it's not really possible to have a brain that is fully functioning if the body it's attached to is failing.

Motivate Everyone You Can

> *"We can't help everyone, but everyone can help someone." – Ronald Reagan*

Another technique to boost your own motivation is by sharing your own ideas and thoughts to boost motivation among the people you surround yourself with. Healthy, motivated peers can automatically recharge you and keep you motivated and on track.

Be Open to Learning

> *"An organization's ability to learn and translate that learning into action rapidly is the ultimate competitive advantage." – Jack Welch*

Always, always, always be open to learning. There is no such thing as "enough knowledge." More importantly, as cliché as it may sound, knowledge is power. Always keep your mind open and take on each obstacle as a challenge that you not only need to overcome but learn from as well.

Break It Down

> *"The journey of a thousand miles must begin with a single step." – Lau Tzu*

As a pro tip, when it comes to self-motivation, you should always use stepping stones to make your way to your bigger goals. Having such things can seem daunting, but what's even scarier is not even wanting to take it on because your motivation levels will be low. Instead, breaking your major project into smaller, more approachable pieces not only ensures that you are more confident. It also ascertains that your project gets done on time. A win-win situation, indeed!

Chapter 4: ´Extrospection´

"Beyond doing the right thing for their workers, companies have another reason to lean into workforce development initiatives: their own competitiveness. As demand for skills for the intelligent era heat up, so too will a war for talent." – Sarah Franklin

Although emotional intelligence models have already taught us the importance of clear emotional perception, the specific use of emotions and the thorough understanding of emotions still seems to escape us. This is why trait EQ models focus heavily on the characteristics of various emotions, as well as the impact that they have on themselves and other people. At the moment, we have already figured out how to understand ourselves and manage our own emotions. As leaders, we cannot merely perceive what our customers and employees think about and how they feel. We also need to find a way to share the experiences they endure since that is the only way to genuinely figure out what motivates them and what holds them back.

We will go through this process in the same way we have approached the EQ models. It will start with understanding and recognizing the emotions. Then, we will make our way down to the complex side of managing and controlling them.

Recognizing Emotion in Others

"Businesses often forget about the culture, and ultimately, they suffer for it because you can't deliver good service from unhappy employees." – Tony Hsieh

Imagine being able to read people's minds. How much easier

would it be when you walked into a board meeting - or any business conference for that matter - and practically knew exactly what your opponent was thinking about, how they felt that way and why, as well as how there emotional state was without playing word games or throwing shade at each other. Imagine knowing how receptive someone will be to an idea after having an idea of what to say, when to say it, and basically be Jean Grey in a suit.

Well, buckle up because we are about to teach you exactly how to do that!

Facial Expressions

Remember all those primary emotions we talked about back in Chapter 1? Well, it turns out that you can literally express almost all of them simply by using your face! As a beginner on the topic, why don't we start you off with the seven common micro expressions first?

1. Surprised Micro Expression

Usually, a surprise is identified by raised eyebrows that are generally curved in nature, horizontal forehead wrinkles, the whites of the eye showing both above and below the pupil, and on occasion with a dropped jaw teeth generally parted, and a tightly stretched brow.

2. Fearful Micro Expression

When depicting fear, human beings have a tendency to raise eyebrows once again. However, such brows are drawn together usually in a flat line instead of a curve. Their eyes are also enlarged, but the lower whites of the eyes are generally not visible and the mouth is typically drawn back in a taut expression instead of simply leaving it open.

3. Disgusted Micro Expression

Disgust is generally depicted with prominently raised eyelids and a curled lower lip. The nose wrinkles, as well as the corners of the eyes. You will also notice that individuals depicting disgust also tend to have raised cheeks, which combine together to show an overall sense of revulsion.

4. Angry Micro Expression

When it comes to anger, the facial expressions are very similar to those of disgust, the lower lip is tensed but usually not curled as it is with disgust, the eyes are hard and protruding, while there are lines between the brows again, although these are anger lines, which are vertical and not horizontal, like the worry lines we have noticed earlier. The lower jaw is also prone to be jutting out, and the nostrils have a tendency to be flaring, depending on the individual's level of rage and breathing capabilities.

5. Happy Micro Expression

The micro expressions that denote happiness are almost the exact opposite. The teeth are generally exposed, the lips are upturned, and a wrinkle forming from the nose to the outer edge of the lip. The cheeks are also raised; depending on the age of the individual, you may notice wrinkles near the corner of the eyes as well. This last factor distinguishes genuine laughter from fake laughter. As such, it can be extremely important when dealing with client satisfaction.

6. Sorrowful Micro Expression

Sorrow is also quite easy to spot. The eyebrows are a definite factor, the inner corners of the eyebrows are pulled toward the center and then upward, the lips are drawn downward, and the jaw comes up with the lower lip protruding outward. Because of the complexity of the factors involved, this also happens to be the hardest micro expression to fake.

7. Hateful Micro Expression

Then, we have hatefulness. Also projected as contempt, it is depicted with relaxed eyes and brow and a lower lip smirk to one side of the face.

While it is relatively easy to express emotions when your entire face is projecting the same thing, micro expressions also allow you to pick up the tiny non-verbal cues that perhaps haven't even registered to the individuals themselves regarding how they feel.

Bodily Expressions

Facial micro expressions are not the only way to recognize what a person is thinking or feeling, though. One of the more prominent forms of non-verbal expression is the use of bodily cues, such as crossing arms, which indicates defensiveness, or crossing legs, which shows being closed off. Similarly, standing with one's hands positioned on their hips is an almost universal sign for aggressiveness or alternatives for strength and control. Holding one's hands behind their back is indicative of boredom or anger, while fidgeting or repetitive motions can be used to identify impatience, frustration, and even boredom.

All in all, being able to identify micro-reactions, both in facial expression and bodily cues, allows individuals to not only communicate more clearly but also allows interpret and understand the non-verbal signals being put out so that they can adapt their verbal communication to be more effective and impactful.

Sympathy and Empathy: The Great Divide

"In a very real sense, we have two minds: one that thinks and one that feels." – Daniel Goleman

One of the biggest problems when it comes to leading employees is that, at some point, there seems to be this insurmountable wall between leaders and followers. Think about it; in the last three places you worked at, how connected did you feel with your boss? Alternatively, if you have been working in a management position for a while, how have you felt about the team you lead? Have you noticed a noticeable distance that you can't seem to figure out no matter how hard you try?

Do you know why it's like that?

Believe it or not, it is because of one simple oversight that many of us don't even realize we are making: using sympathy and empathy as interchangeable terms. Since it sounds like such a bland topic, why don't we start by directly covering the trademark differences between the two pillars of emotional intelligence and then dissecting the corporate behavior patterns wherein they are adopted?

Sympathy in Leadership

We'll start with sympathy because, for the most part, people tend to be a lot better acquainted with it. The origin of the term means "together with feeling." Meaning, 'sympathy' inherently implies a sense of proximity with another being, and a feeling of connection is implied *but* generally not felt.

Now, what does that entail?

Well, simply put, sympathy refers to a sense of acknowledgment, or a commiserative nod, so to speak, in which you admit and agree that a person is indeed going through a difficult time. Generally, sympathy arises as a human reaction to a situation and acts as a bandage of sorts. The problem is that when it comes to business atmospheres, particularly when you are dealing with management or leadership, sympathy is not a mere reaction. It's more of an excuse that you are employing with one goal in mind: to be approved of or liked. And as Twitter's Ben Horowitz says,"'Managing by trying to be liked is the path to ruin."

Imagine if you are at work, and of the three employees under your control, two keep coming back with various excuses about why their work isn't on time. You've been in charge of this team for almost a month now, and you've been feeling like this for quite a while. However, every time you go to point this out, they talk about how they have not gotten to work on the project they want to work on, and you feel compelled to agree with them about how unfair it is. Subsequently, they end up not telling them how their work ethic has been problematic.

Sympathy is getting the better of you, isn't it?

This, dear reader, is exactly why sympathy is so looked down on.

Because the main objective of sympathy is to display your concern for another person, it becomes more of a show-and-tell scenario than about actual feelings and real condolences. This is not just a superficial "Oh, you don't' really care" problem. It's a tangible problem in the workplace because when your employees start feeling like they are not being heard or cared about, their productivity also has a tendency to drop.

For sure, this is not really what you're gunning for as a leader. So, what is the solution?

Allow us to introduce empathy.

Empathy in Leadership

Empathy doesn't work like sympathy. It's not about trying to find out how you come off as the nice guy. It's about *being* the nice guy.

Whereas sympathy is about pretending that you care about someone who is going through a rough time, empathy is about regularly stepping into their shoes and visualizing their own pain as if it's yours. As a leader, it is crucial to not only understand that your employees are hurting or dealing some difficulty but feel exactly how they feel so that you know first-hand what changes need to be made to ensure your employees aren't suffering. Think about it, if your employees are unhappy and secretly trying to figure out how they can quit instead of looking forward to coming to work, what does that say about the company you are running? Furthermore, always remember a happy employee is a productive one.

The best thing about empathy, though, is that it has a tendency to be reflective. Because it does not have a motive in and of itself like sympathy, whose foremost objective is to appear amicable, empathy tends to be reflected back to the empathizer, which can create a positive cycle of organizational behavior. When a leader is empathetically leading his team, the latter automatically feels well cared for and acknowledged and works harder, as if the simple act of kindness has manifested as a group motivator. It also helps keep leaders grounded. The more you are in tune with the needs and wants of the employees you are dealing with, the more you ensure employee loyalty, which is critical to good corporate governance.

How to Master Social Skills

> *"If your emotional abilities aren't in hand, if you don't have self-awareness, if you are not able to manage your distressing emotions, if you can't have empathy and have effective relationships, then no matter how smart you are, you are not going to get very far."* – Daniel Goleman

Regardless if you are employing sympathy or empathy, one thing that you have to keep in mind is that leaders, as a rule, must have exceptional social skills. Brilliant scientists are a dime a dozen, for instance. Unfortunately, being brilliant at what you do, be it science, engineering or whatever you choose, does not matter unless you know how to translate what you have to offer into something that the public want and need.

How do you do that? Well, by being a master salesman.

Contrary to popular opinion, being a salesman does not mean you need to be able to sell ice cream to an Eskimo. A huge part of making sales depends simply on your exterior appearance. For instance, are you coming off as a likable person? Do you seem trustworthy? Are you humorous? Are you a good listener?

This begs the question: How do you get to be that person?

Social skills is the answer to it.

Here are some of the top social skills you can work on

mastering.

Fake It Till You Make It

Being a social skills master isn't something that just happens overnight. In fact, one of the best ways to improve your social skills is by pretending that you are good at it. Pretending like you're a social person gives you an added confidence boost, so you don't struggle with the whole "but I'm not good at it" spiel. Instead, you can focus on what's important, which is the communication of ideas. Arunachalam Murugunatham, who is known to be a revolutionary in the female hygiene industry from India, is known for speaking in broken English, as is Alibaba's Jack Ma. Both promote this concept of communication above perfection, and their records speak for themselves!

Start Small

If you struggle with your social skills, a boardroom isn't probably the best place to practice getting better. Instead, try small one-on-one conversations with your employees and work on building up your empathy levels while you're at it. Not only does it work as a stepping stone; it is also a major confidence booster.

Be inquisitive

Pretense and building blocks aside, there are actual techniques you are going to need to master, and being inquisitive is one of them. Ask questions, for one. The most questions you ask, the more interested you seem, and the longer you can keep a conversation going without having to invest too much of yourself. It takes off a lot of the pressure if you are learning how to do better with your social interactions.

Learn to Listen

You can't ask questions just so you don't have to talk, though. Listening is a crucial part of communication; when done well, it is always an active element that many of us mistakenly tend to think. Active listening allows you to gain better insight; in turn, it allows you to be a better and more informed leader.

Be Generous With Your Compliments

When you are talking, however, a great way to break the ice is to use compliments. We are not talking about empty flattery; instead, be genuine and kind. Even if what you need to talk about is something that the team has done wrong, always start the conversation with the things that they have done right and you want to appreciate. This ensures that your employees are no longer in a defensive mental state once you've been able to bring them down off that ledge, then start explaining the problems that you face due to a specific action that they or their team generated. Once you manage to communicate your issues, discuss the possible solutions and remind them of all the good work that they have been doing. Furthermore, make a point to reinforce how you believe that they are capable of so much more.

Study Up

Another helpful trick is to read up on your employees and social skills. The more you know about how to interact, the easier interactions will be for you. The more you know about them, the easier you will understand what kind of conversations and approaches they are more amenable to.

Work on Your Non-Verbal Cues

Non-verbal actions account for a lot to monitor what messages you convey through your face and body. Sometimes we may come off as aggressive, whereas we feel defensive and can't seem to understand why the other party is suddenly so offended. Well, now you know; it can be anything, from crossed arms to a smirk to an unintentional yawn. Whatever the action was, the result was that it led to a negative reaction, and that's what an emotionally intelligent leader needs to avoid.

How Should You Respond to Other People's Reactions?

> "Before you become a leader, success is all about growing yourself. *When you become a leader, success is all about growing others.*" – Jack Welch

As a leader, you will soon find that a large portion of your time is spent trying to understand the needs, actions, and reactions that your employees or team depict. The problem a lot of leaders tend to face is that they don't know how to react or respond best to these external actions or reactions coming at them from all corners. The thing is, they are not based on actions or decisions that you have taken. On the contrary, external factors play an extremely large role in workplace reactions, and you will never be used to distinguish between how much of that reaction is genuine and how much of it is stemming from an outside factor until and unless you teach yourself to stop and listen.

So, let's make this easy, shall we?

Instead of always assuming that there is a backstory, you can try using a leadership response technique. Dr. Rathe of the University of Florida developed a technique called Background-Affects-Trouble-Handling-Empathy (BATHE), which he began to use to communicate with patients and found it extremely helpful.

According to BATHE, the first thing you need to do when you are dealing with employees is to initiate conversation about the **background** of the issue. Ask yourself, "What is going on?" "When did it start?" "How did it happen?" "Who was involved?"

Once you've assessed the incident, ask about how the situation impacts or *affects* the company or team. When the topic arises, you will soon find that the employees will start to discuss the **troubles** they face. As they make a point to ensure you are listening actively to their problems, you'll find this helps you understand their pulse a little better. In turn, it helps to tell you how to **handle** the crisis best. Usually, showing parallel examples and offering fresh solutions bring back positive emotions, which you can then reinforce with **empathy** and understanding.

The BATHE technique not only provides a structure; it also gives leaders time to think and process. Instead of being forced to automatically react to situations, they now have the flexibility to rely on a specific structure to give them the same information that they will get through a complex conversation. The best thing is, this doesn't take away from the leader's ability to take knowledge or information; it just gives them a little more room to breathe.

How to Leverage Positive Emotions in Other People

"A leader can be very destructive or very inspiring. It comes down to their level of emotional intelligence." – John Mackey

Quick question: On a scale of one to 10, how happy do you feel when you go to work - a five, maybe a six, if we're lucky?

Now, ask yourself, "How long do you spend at work?" Most of your waking hours, right?

Do you feel that regret building in your chest? Imagine, if you could fix that, if you could do something that made going to work in the morning to look forward to. How much more productive do you think you would be? According to corporate studies, a lot!

Why don't we teach you a few tricks of the trade?

Express Gratitude

One easy way to increase the positive emotions in your employees and team is to by creating a culture of positive recognition. Think about it; just saying something like "thank you" can make the recipient feel recognized and valued. By learning to count your blessings, particularly in a business atmosphere, you are fostering positivity in every individual team member. Because positivity is a reflective emotion like empathy, it tends to reflect back and add value to the team as a whole.

Ideally, a great technique to inject gratitude into daily business dealings is by starting meetings with positive feedback session. Meaning, talk about the good and reinforce it before you even touch upon the problems that need to be addressed.

Build Connections

Another important way in which leaders can build positivity into their teams and companies is by encouraging the employees to build connections among their own teams. Happiness research has shown that positive moods are practically contagious, which means that even if you are personally not in a good mood, simply being in contact with someone who is can help with your mood and those around you.[3]

You need to encourage staff to celebrate little successes or personal achievements; small companies and family-owned companies tend to do this by employing "employee of the month" or "manager of the week" strategies, which can entice employees to do better. It also gives the staff a sense of community; that, in turn encourages, workplace friendships, which is very beneficial to productivity and company growth.

Embrace Strength and Values

Another pro tip is to use goals and opportunities to attract employees to work on their strengths. Goals give employees a sense of purpose, particularly since the big picture isn't always easy to imagine. By allowing employees to do what they are good at and giving them more opportunities to shine, we are effectively strengthening organizational goals and facing developmental challenges with the best possible candidates for the job. Doing something well in itself is a good feeling; as

---

[3] Waters, L. (2015). Why happiness is contagious. Retrieved from https://www.weforum.org/agenda/2015/10/why-happiness-is-contagious/

such, it makes it easier to make people feel good about themselves as well.

How to Deal With Negative Emotions in Other People

"You can conquer almost any fear if you will only make up your mind to do so. For remember, fear doesn't exist anywhere expect in the mind." – Dale Carnegie

Unfortunately, leaders don't always get to deal with positive emotions. In truth, a big part of being a leader means dealing with the problems and crises that your company and team are going through. As you experience these negative incidents, it's easy to get sucked into a vortex of negativity, which is something that you can't afford as a leader.

The trick here is to center yourself and your employees. Before you let the problem swallow you whole, ask yourself, "What is its source?" "What is its result?" "How can you or your employee fix it?"

Action plans play a big role here; use your expertise to mentally guide your employees through possible solutions. As you do, teach them to process information productively instead of panicking. This allows you to use negative situations to your benefit, which later helps diminish the sense of panic your employees or team feel when faced with difficult situations. Always remember that, as the leader, you need to lead them forward no matter how difficult the situation is. Meaning, *you* don't get to panic or feel overwhelmed. There is nothing you can't handle.

Chapter 5: 30-Day Emotional Intelligence Booster Program

"Research shows convincingly that EQ is more important than IQ in almost every role and many times more important in leadership roles. This finding is accentuated as we more from the control philosophy of the industrial age to an empowering release philosophy of the knowledge worker age." – Stephen Covey

Understanding the role of emotional intelligence is one thing, but being able to apply it is completely different. When we started this book, we walked you through what basic human emotions were, how they impacted our logic faculties, and what roles they played in decision making. This is perhaps a leader's most crucial job. But we didn't just talk about them; we also showed you how these emotions fell into specific categories based on emotional intelligence models. It allows you to then develop a sense of self-awareness as you worked on the internal emotions you deal with, and then the reactive element or the external emotions you deal with.

Sounds pretty comprehensive, right?

Well, it is, but it's mostly theory, and theory and practice are two totally different dimensions. Think of this as a diet plan. Knowing what healthy foods are and what kind of junk food you should be avoiding, and then eating healthy and avoiding junk food, are diverse. In order for you to properly master emotional intelligence, you will need to pull yourself together and apply everything we have taught you to your workforce and surroundings daily until it becomes second nature.

Don't be too scared, though; we are not going to make you walk in blind. We have formulated a complete 30-day emotional intelligence booster so that you can practice with training wheels before you have to go at it alone.

Week 1: Learning to Recognize Emotions

> *"No doubt, emotional intelligence is more rare than book smarts, but my experience says it is actually more important in the making of a leader."* – Jack Welch

For the first week of EQ training, we will focus on emotional recognition. As we go back and revise what we already know about emotion recognition and use the EQ models discussed previously, we will use each individual day as an opportunity to concentrate on a new element of emotional recognition. By the end of the week, you can recognize all of the major elements of emotional intelligence to improve as a future business leader.

Day 1: Emotional Recognition

The basis of emotional intelligence is the ability to identify, understand, and even predict human emotions as they occur real-time. The process is literally such a crucial part of business leadership, considering there are actual companies that work solely with recognition technology.

Earlier in Chapter 1, we have talked in depth about eight basic emotions and how each of them manifests not only as individual emotions but also as supplementary or complementary feelings based on the context. These emotions that you need to be able to identify are anticipation, fear, disgust, joy, sadness, anger, surprise, and trust.

Golden Hours

Early in the morning, before you start your day, is when you are most likely in the best position to deal with emotional recognition. Any time between 7 A.M. and 10 A.M. gives you the opportunity to practice taking your own emotional temperature. You are also similar to a blank sheet at that period; external influences do not usually take hold until mid-day. Thus, you are now in a position to identify some of the core feelings you are dealing with.

Mid-Day Reboot

During the middle of the day, roughly 11 A.M. to 1 P.M. is when most of the basic emotions we feel tend to take on a life of their own. If you have been feeling tired, you get cranky; if you have been feeling mad, you lash out. This is because your body has now moved on from the relaxed state it was in earlier and is dealing with physical needs like hunger, which make you more susceptible to emotional outburst. The emotions that you see now are usually exaggerated versions of the emotions you feel – keep that in mind.

Wrap and Reflection

You have your wrap-up and reflection time from around 2 P.M. to 5 P.M. One of the major mistakes that people make is that they assume that one should not be working on recognizing or reflecting on their emotional state till they are home, tucked in their beds and about to go to sleep.

The problem with this is that you are usually too tired to properly reflect by then. Secondly, you have also most likely forgotten how you feel exactly at a certain hour. Instead, take time out from your workday to focus on your emotional state and then mentally reflect on it while you still have the energy to do so. In the end, you can use a journaling technique; this can be handwritten or typed, whichever is more convenient.

Sample Scenario

If you start your morning fresh and happy, then you start to feel stressed out or overburdened by mid-day, it is obvious that you are feeling a combination of negative emotions in the workplace. Your job is to find your trigger so that you can work on the problem at hand.

Day 2: Finding Your Trigger

Today, we will walk back through what we have done yesterday and take it a bit further by locating the trigger behind our emotional reactions. By identifying what causes us to act the way we do, we are equipping ourselves with the ability to not only control that trigger but also change it. The mixed EQ model deals with issues stemming from control and awareness directly and make them central to how emotional intelligence is measured.

Golden Hours

Since you are basically like a black slate in the morning, it's a lot easier for you to shift through your feelings any time from 7 A.M. to 10 A.M. Start by monitoring how you feel and make a conscious note of how those emotions are changing throughout the day. By following the flow of your emotions, you're also giving yourself the opportunity to zero in on the exact reason why your mood is shifting.

Mid-Day Reboot

Any time from 11 A.M. to 1 P.M. is when your emotional state is easiest to perceive. How you feel about what you've been doing tends to come out, and you are also much more likely to know why. Make mental or, if necessary, actual short notes on the emotional changes that you have had due to specific factors.

Wrap and Reflection

Later on, during the later quarter of the day from around 2 P.M. to 5 P.M., make an active choice to evaluate how you feel and how certain actions have changed or enhanced that feeling, as well as how it has changed it.

Sample Scenario

Recently, you've been going into work, but even as you do, you've been feeling dull and lethargic, not excited or upbeat like you used to. This tells you that the emotions you feel are not solely trigger based and have been around long enough to embed themselves into your regular daily life. Then, as the day goes on, certain factors start intensifying this feeling, e.g., missing lunch plans with friends due to work or being asked to complete Team A's assignment because they have somehow been set behind. By the evening, you feel like you can't escape work, no matter how hard you work to power through keeps on piling up even if it isn't your own. As you start journaling these factors, it becomes clear that the emotions you are dealing with point to one thing: you are burnt out, and that is where the negativity is coming from.

Day 3: How Did You React?

The next thing that you need to actively take into account is,

"How did you react?" Being able to identify how you have reacted and which part of your behavior serves as a reaction to external stressors increases your emotional intelligence. Your behavior tells what you are what, but your reactions tell you more, specifically if your life is generally working in a positive manner. It also helps to identify exactly what portion of your life does not function. When do you feel most positive? What makes you the happiest? Conversely, when do you feel most negative and upset?

Golden Hours

Since 7 A.M. and 10 A.M. are your golden hours, this is the best time for you to journal your emotional journey in the previous days. Reaction journaling is different from everyday journals. In the heat of the moment, it's easy to say and do things we don't necessarily feel, but you won't be able to see your actions for what they are until the next morning. For just this one area, therefore, morning reflective journaling is extremely helpful.

This gives you the rest of the afternoon to process how you feel and react to the day-to-day events that you face. Once the emotions have processed fully, you can use the later quarter of the day from 2 P.M. to 5 P.M. to identify your triggers and reactions. Sometimes, even if you have the same reaction, you may be dealing with different triggers, and that helps you figure out how much of your reaction is valid.

Sample Scenario

Imagine that you have a bad boss who tends to yell at you a lot. You, in turn, have been yelling at the team under your supervision to control your own stress levels. You'll notice that you tend to be acting out more on the days when your boss is worse. The journal also allows you to recognize your behavior for what it really is. Odds are, you weren't yelling at Mark because he made the same mistake that Jon made last month, which you allowed slide. You were yelling at him because you just got yelled at as well, and that made you feel powerless. Hence, you were asserting your feelings.

Day 4: How Balanced Was Your Reaction?

Once you have begun to identify the various emotions and reactions, as well as zero in on the trigger points that have led to specific reactions, the main thing you need to start to consider is how balanced or rational your reaction has been.

Every action has an equal and opposite reaction. However, what is the reaction that you showed that that's not equal? Imagine that you got berated for failing to submit a report on time, and you decided that you didn't want your six-figure job anymore. Thus, you quit without any further thought. Does that seem like a rational balanced reaction? *Probably not.* Still, let's go by the book on this one.

Golden Hours

Always remember that 7 A.M. up to 10 A.M. are your golden hours. This is when and where your emotions are most balanced. If you want to compare the rest of your day against a standard, this is the best time to use. In contrast, the next three hours is when most of your reactions start to develop, which means that that's also when the problems come to light. If you feel that the emotions you deal with are extremely powerful enough to justify your reaction, then you're in the clear. However, with a calm head, evaluate the morning journal of your reactive actions from the previous day, not all of your actions made sense, and not all of them were justified. Make a point to use this period to reflect on what parts of your reaction were out of line and mentally visualize a more beneficial reaction to the situation.

Sample Scenario

When you go through an explosive situation that causes you to react disproportionately, the best thing to do is to actively work to normalize what's happening. A great way to do this is by listing and reflecting on the closest similar action that you had to undertake in the recent past. Imagine that you are a doctor, and the resident on call whom you have been training overslept during rotation. Instead of kicking him off your team entirely, start by trying to find a way to rectify his behavior. Say, you can force him to make up for the shift that he has missed, as well as apologize to his peers who have had to cover for him. The more balanced your reactions are, the more beneficial your subsequent actions will be to you and your team.

Day 5: What Are the Positives That can Help This Situation?

But where exactly does one get positive, balanced reactions? Can you just buy them at a super shop? Unfortunately, not yet. Positive reactions that will help balance out the situation are always subjective. There are certain positive actions that you can take to improve the quality of your interactions, even if they may sound a little hippie to you at first.

Golden Hours

For starters, try using your time from 7 A.M. to 10 A.M. to put yourself in a super zen mode. If you can begin with a positive mindset instead of the neutral mindset, you can positively impact the rest of your day. In fact, just starting your day with a positive outset isn't all that can help you. Your mind is an organ just like the rest of your body; making sure that you are taking care of your physical health by eating properly and on time builds up your emotional resilience.

Be smart. Be strong. Be in control.

Sample Scenario

Let's say that your team has been causing your emotional outbursts for the past two months. You recognize that your emotions are not always balanced. So, what do you do? Well, you should seek professional assistance and lower your personal workload. Often, reactions tend to stem from being overworked and tired, and a professional can help you recognize that.

Day 6: What Are the Negatives that can worsen the Situation?

On day 6, we will work on actively assessing the negatives that tend to worsen the scenario as a whole. Since negative emotions start to kick in by mid-day, we'll be skipping over the golden hour so that we can focus solely on the wrap-up and reaction time.

Sample Scenario

For instance, you are dealing with a difficult teammate. That person not only has a tendency to not finish the work on time; they also tend to hamper your work. Yelling and screaming or lashing out is hardly going to be of any help. Instead, try to work through your emotions in an appropriate way, talk to the individual personally, explain what the problem is, and ask them to look into it.

Day 7: How Can You Best Bridge the Knowledge-Doing Gap?

Your final action item of the week doesn't deal with journaling at all. Today, your job is to evaluate, go through the last six days, think of the things you've learned, and focus on how they have impacted your daily life. Look back at the suggested steps and make a mental note of how many things you have been able to implement.

Remember that knowledge isn't power unless it is put to use; as you start to work your way through each individual day, focus on the theme and contrast what you have learned that day about your behavior with your actions of the following day. There is no point in knowing your triggers unless you can manage them, so make sure that before you move on to the next seven-day stretch, you have already mastered the emotional response techniques we have taught you here. If necessary, go through the seven-day exercise again. Repeat it until you are ready.

Week 2: Learning to Use Emotions

"When you're on a team where individual team members lack self-control and emotional intelligence, the outcome will often be an unfavorable or destructive one." – Ty Howard

We've talked before about how the entire business market is shifting from being transactional to experience-based. That is why any good team now requires its individual members to be emotionally intelligent and knowledgeable in their own respective fields. Daniel Goleman, one of the pioneers of emotional intelligence in business, has gone on to speak about how emotion-centric businesses and leaders have become. In fact, he even uses a combination of the ability model and Eisenhower's Matrix to formulate better and more self-awareness management techniques. Goleman himself believes that in order for a leader to be inspirational and worth following, they must first devise a plan to influence and develop others. When properly executed, this type of emotional awareness can help in conflict management, teamwork building, and increased productivity during collaborative exercises.

Day 1: The Golden Circle

As a leader, when you start making decisions, each one needs to be recorded in logic and rational thinking. The only problem with it is that they are not very effective when you are trying to get your business up and off the ground. Think about it like you are a regular Starbucks drinker and your average cup of Joe costs you about $2 to $5 everyday. Now, any logical person will perhaps save themselves about $100 a month by investing in a coffee machine or alternatively start buying coffee at local cafes where the costs are only a fraction of that price. Still, that's not something you're doing. Have you ever wondered why?

Simon Sinek developed a business model that addresses this specific decision-making part of your brain. He calls it as "the golden circle." In Sinek's circle, the first element you find yourself dealing with is the product and the purpose. The brain identifies what you want with what is being offered and will initially register if the good fulfills the purpose. Then, the brain seeks to identify the 'how' of the matter. For instance, how does this product propose an impact? Also, why is this person or organization selling to me?

Now, imagine converting this into leadership. When your

employee is being difficult, you can start out by identifying exactly what they are doing and what the purpose of their action is. Say, if they are acting out, are they doing it for attention or because they feel genuinely frustrated? How are they acting out? What methods are they using? Why are they using these methods? You need to be able to answer these questions if you are going to use a person's emotions in a proactive manner. Once you've figure that out, gear their emotional outburst in the direction you want them to go. If they want attention, teach your team that more evolved accomplishments equate to better screen time and more opportunities. Automatically, they will shift their energy from complaining to working extra hard. You just have to know what matters to them and work with it.

Day 2: Benefits Over Features

As you start working with the concept of emotional manipulation, you will soon find that you constantly have to reshape how your team and employees think. As tiring as it may seem, this is a necessary task, though. Your appeals to logic are pointless unless you are dealing with a robot because we've just showed you the human brain and it doesn't think in a consistently logical manner.

Any good leader knows that in order to build a strong and proactive team, you need to make your team feel like the aims and objectives on their job posting are more than just words. Make them feel as if they matter, like their job accounts for something. Always remember, though, that the pros they are getting out of their job, such as their salary and bonus, are benefits. The more they feel that they are getting something extra out of it, the more they are likely to work and spend that extra mile.

Day 3: Instilling a Sense of Accomplishment

Because of the position, they have the unique opportunity to motivate their employees to do things that not everyone else can. That means, as a leader, it is your job to make sure that your team feels like the they have done something worth doing. How? Well, the best way to get them to do these things is not by simply asking them to or providing them with incentives but by creating a sense of achievement.

A good way to do this is to start focusing on setting up attainable realistic goals for your employees. This is particularly helpful when the job you're doing is too big to take on individually. By breaking down your task into smaller, more workable goals, you are giving your employees a fighting chance.

Sample Exercise

For instance, you are in charge of a sales team. You have 30 employees who are reporting to you. For this business quarter, the company has set you a $300,0000 goal. Now, it may sound like it's impossible to achieve, but if you break it down, it's not that bad. You're looking at 100,000 per business quarter per individual employee or literally just $25,000 a month. Odds are, the amount that each of your employees rake in through sales is already very close to this number. The only thing it's seeking to instill here is consistency. Once you can break the goal down into smaller target goals for your team, you will find that they are less threatened and less negatively reactive. Furthermore, try to keep in mind that employee-centric opportunities give individuals a chance to grow and develop. Not everyone is equally good at their tasks. In addition to breaking down the walls, you can put your employees in the positions where they can achieve the most and do their best. What you are doing is ensuring that your team isn't just competent; it is comfortably placed as well. If you send a quarterback out to play 90 minutes of soccer, for instance, no matter how good your player is, you won't get the same result that you would have if you were able to send out Ronaldo. Keep that in mind while you are setting goals for your team to achieve.

Day 4: Using Visualization Tools

Leadership is not merely about emotional manipulation, though. In fact, leadership is also about harnessing the power of your mind, as well as when and where the minds of your employees and team send it on a specific path with a goal to meet. Inspirational leaders know how to use this power of visualization to protect and create a future, which is not only mutually beneficial but also generally altruistic in some manner or way.

Think about it; if your mental future is one where you are making a ton of money and enjoying exotic locations in Bali and the Fiji Islands, it's unlikely that your vision or mission is speaking to another person who has no investment in your life. On the contrary, you can look at leaders whose dreams or visions have transcended not only in their own homes and abilities but also in the age they have lived in. Starting from John F. Kennedy's vision to put a man on the moon to Steve Job's wish to build a company with the motto "a computer for the rest of us," all of these leaders have begun their journey by tapping into an impossible dream through visualization.

Your words have the power to create.

Sample Scenario

A great example of leaders who help a team succeed using visualization is the 1983 Americas Cup. The Americas Cup was a sailing trophy that American savers had been winning with the past 132 years. In fact, it had gotten to the point where other teams had begun to believe that the Americans simply could not be beaten. So, what changed?

That same year, the Australian team brought in a sports psychologist whose job was to block the bad vibes from the American team and replace it with improved positive vibes so that the Australian team would be in a better mental position. However, that's not all they did. The Australian culture itself decided that in addition to not being afraid of American team, the Australian team needed to be prepared to win. The only way that the psychologist thought they would be prepared to win was if they practiced winning. So, the Australian College Mary did a recording of how they visualized the Australian team Australia II winning the race against America's Liberty. Every day, that same recording was played twice to every single member of the team so that by the time the actual day of the race arrived, the Australian team had already defeated the American team thousands of times. This visualization was so strongly embedded into their minds; it was inconceivable to the Australian team that they would not win. As such, by the end of the race, they did just that.

Day 5: Building a Community

As a leader, it is critical to invest time to cultivate, encourage, and nurture the relationships that surround a community. In a world that is increasingly losing its inherent sense of community, community building at work has become increasingly important. For decades, communities have been the very backbone of any society; even today, support groups such as Weight Watchers and Alcoholics Anonymous remain effective due to their string of community support.

Unfortunately, due to increasing pressure at work and a disastrous economy, not many people have not been able to cultivate personal support groups or personal community ties. As a business leader, you have the opportunity to change that. Not only can you go out and make friends, but you can also start encouraging relationships in the workplace itself. By bolstering communication among team members in the office, you'll be addressing issues that you have no idea ever existed: workplace isolation. So many people come to work feeling like they are going to jail or facing off bullies in high-school, to the point that the workplace mood is already horrible. But it doesn't have to be that way.

Take Twitter as an example. The multi-billion-dollar platform that happens to be POTUS's favorite social media app probably tells you a lot about the President's personal life. Believe it or not, that is exactly how and why the platform has been created. Twitter cofounders Jack Dorsey and Noah Glass were literally just lonely. Noah was going through a divorce and felt like he was losing all his friends, while Jack had mentioned how good it would be to perhaps update your current status and connect with all your friends at the same time. One thing led to another, and Twitter was born with one goal in mind: to create a community.

There are dozens of ways to increase a team's sense of community that sounds prominent and effective, including the facilitation of community activities like workshops, team-building excursions, and active listening.

Day 6: Validating Mental Parking

Validation may sound like a silly thing; however, in reality, the need for validation drives a lot of employees in more ways than you can imagine. Think for a second that you are a jury member who is responsible for deciding if the man brought to court is indeed guilty of the murder that rocked the nation last week or if he is as innocent as he has been claiming consistently. What can help you make up your mind? Proof, right? Evidence, witness testimonies, etc. Despite that, who has to bring the proof to you? Is it enough for the man on the stand to give witness testimony? No! You need more; you need someone else, someone trustworthy, to come in and tell you that what he's saying is true. What you need is validation.

Interestingly, validation is just as important at work as it is in a courtroom, especially if you are dealing with teams. As a leader, it is your job to breakdown and showcase how important each member is and how everything they contribute to the team adds up and acts as a crucial cog in running the company. It cannot run well without the people who are holding it up on their own backs; that isn't just something you say. It needs to be something you believe in, something you remind your employees of. Give them the data, numbers, as well as innovative ideas that they have come up with that have shaped the company into what it is today, and the person who comes in to work tomorrow isn't just another worker bee. Instead, it will be an empowered worker who knows their own worth and is motivated to be even better. If you can get that much done as a team leader, you can be rest assured that you've been doing your job.

Day 7: Words and Actions Matter

How else can you effectively use emotional intelligence to control and develop your team? Well, author Angeles Arrien has four principles that are thought to perfectly complement the application of EQ as we know it. Arrien believes that they will not only enable us to heal ourselves but also promote and cultivate emotional intelligence and positive thoughts in the people around us.

For starters, Arrien recommends that leaders make a habit of *showing up and choosing to be present.* Being active and present is like a King being at the forefront of his forces as they enter into war. It may sound silly and illogical to do since the King is also the chief strategist, but the immense loyalty and respect that he gains is easily worth it. Next, the author recommends that the leader practices *empathetic and active listening* so that he can act as a healer for his team. Taking part in active listening also allows the King to understand and evaluate the situation without blame or judgement and lets him lay a *vision* of the future he hopes to instill. Finally, the leader will also make sure that they are open to the outcome but not attached to it. Emotional attachment to an outcome can narrow the scope of the journey, and no one wants that. Be open to other options and be willing to listen.

As you finish off this week, make sure that you have properly thought about each of the given topics and tried to incorporate what you have learned in your daily actions.

Week 3: Observation

> *"We are being judged by a new yardstick; not just how smart we are, or by our training and expertise, but also how well*

we handle ourselves and each other." – Daniel Goleman

While Week 1 was more understanding-based and Week 2 was more inspiration-based, we've now made our way down to Week 3, which is the observation part of your journey into emotional awareness. Here, we will work on helping you to not just recognize and understand how a good leader acts but also walk you through specific situations and scenarios where you can apply your understanding techniques and use your inspiration to figure out how you can tackle the situation best.

To do so, we'll be using five ideas to deal with workplace emotions, as well as two positive emotions so that you have a balanced idea of how to deal with both types of reaction.

Day 1: Frustration

Because work environments in today's world tend to be extremely interactive, it is critical for every individual team member to know how to and be willing to step up and help the company address its needs. But when the burden falls to one person or when a specific team member is constantly refusing to meet the bar, others feel the load and are forced to work harder than ever to cover what's missing. Frustration also arises from a lack of sufficient resources. Since they are necessary for task, they are supposed to be provided by the company. Otherwise, this insufficient behavior can work against its employees.

As a leader, your job is to be able to understand and assess the feelings that your employees are emoting, then zero in on the exact reason why they react in that specific manner.

Sample Exercise

Imagine that you are a junior manager at an accounting firm

for two years now. Generally, the firm tends to promote junior managers to full managerial position in a year, but the boss had a work with you about six months ago when you brought this up and mentioned that, despite your stellar performance, the company couldn't afford to raise your pay and position right now. Nevertheless, they would definitely do so at the first opportunity. Suddenly, two months later, the company unnecessarily splurges on an office vacation for the whole team and hires 3 new junior managers who are being paid as much as you. Now, how would you feel? How do you think you would act out?

In the same scenario, imagine that you are the boss. Let's say there was no malicious intent and that you honestly forgot about the pay raise and promotion. Suddenly, your star junior manager is acting out, refusing to fulfill targets. Your automatic reaction would be perhaps to get mad, but an emotionally intelligent version of you wouldn't do that. They would calmly reason through the actions. Are there any obstacles to meeting the targets? Is there anything that may have upset them? What do they want? How can you fix this?

Remember that limited promotion opportunities, lack of pay raise, and resource problems are not the issues. The real problem is your ability or lack thereof when it comes to dealing with the emotions that your employee is showcasing. Your job as a leader isn't to fix the company; it's to lead it. So, start here and now.

Day 2: Worry or Insecurity

What else do you think can cause an employee to react badly? Since there are many people who seem to indicate that one of the most difficult emotions that plagues the workforce is a sense of worry or insecurity. Why are your employees worried?

Well, honestly, it can be just about anything, starting from a rogue downsizing rumor to a restructuring team going in to change the way they have been working. It doesn't even have to be that major; something as simple as being assigned to a new project or given a new responsibility can be a cause for concern. For instance, an economic crisis impacts the entire industry.

The question shouldn't be the cause of your worry but the cause of worry in my team or specific employee since these emotions are so subjective in nature.

Sample Exercise

Imagine that you're back in the era of the Wall Street crash, and the entire economy is in a downward spiral. You work in the housing market, and a crashing economy means that the number of prospective homeowners is going to take a nosedive. It means sales will be tight, as well as commissions. At one point, the company will have to start making cuts. How will you survive the cut? How will you ensure that you aren't jobless in the next two months? What if you can't stop it? What is your back up? How do you feed your kids? Do you feel the absolute panic racing through your veins?

Stop. Breathe.

Now, switch places. Imagine that you are the boss of that real-estate company. Because you deal mostly with low-end houses, you already know that the market crash is more likely to increase sales for you than decrease them, considering you will have the whole middle-class market to tap into now that they need to save money. You're basically not very worried, but for some strange reason, one of your best agents has been acting extremely erratic over the past week. Ever since the news broke, she's been so panicked about every sale, to the point that her desperation to make a sale is making prospective owners worry about the quality of the house, and you're feeling particularly annoyed because you have trained her personally and feel that she's just being lazy.

Now, do you remember what the Ability Model told us to do? First, try to recognize and perceive the emotion that is being used before you manage it. So, before you get annoyed and react to your employee, ask yourself how they feel and why they are feeling that way. As in this particular case, a simple conversation can help clear the air, teach you to be a bit more communicative, and be able to anticipate employee concerns better.

Day 3: Anger

Anger is another important emotion. Fortunately, it is a lot easier to spot. The only problem is that it's a lot harder to figure out what cause the emotion to arise. Frankly speaking, anger can arise from just about anything. For instance, your employee may be dealing with a manager who' being excessively critical or someone in the workforce has been bullying them. It may also be that the employee is being dismissed constantly, and so he feels demeaned by the co-workers. Maybe someone is also sarcastic, and they take offense to that. Alternatively, they may be victims of malicious office behavior, and someone tries to make them look bad.

Sample Exercise

Let's say that you work for a software coding company. You have developed a code that not only meets the requirements set out by the client but also exceeds them. In your excitement, you decide to share this with a fellow teammate, who then steals your idea and presents it to the team leader as their own. You are extremely angry and have constantly been dissing him at team meetings for the past week. Your reactions have been noted by the leader, and other members of the team seem to think that you are being jealous, which only makes you even angrier.

Now, it is time to switch roles. You are now the boss, and you have been noticing your employee's seemingly inexplicable anger towards their colleague for a while now. Since you had no logical reason to think that they had been wronged, you chalked their actions up to jealousy and were ready to send them to HR for get reprimanded.

What did you do wrong?

You totally forgot to apply any empathy to the situation. What would have happened if you tried to understand and put yourself in your employee's shoes?

If you had done so, not only would you be aware that actual facts are in their favor and that the employee is at fault. You would also have been able to take immediate steps to address and deal with the situation. Remember, you're not just another employee; you are the leader. Above anyone else, you have a duty to be responsible, calm, aware, and empathetic.

Day 4: Depression

Another emotion that employees are displaying on an unfortunately regular basis is depression. In fact, the whole notion of "feeling down" has become so common in business atmospheres, to the point that it accounts for more than $51 billion worth of absenteeism, as well as for only the percentage of employees who have been diagnosed with the condition.[4] In

---

[4] Mental Health America. (n.d.). Depression in the workplace. Retrieved

reality, depression accounts for much more of absentee costs and productivity loss. The good news, however, is that studies have shown that over 80% of these people show marked improvement with treatment. While we aren't necessarily doctors, every efficient team manager and leader worth their salt owes it to their employees to address and work towards solving their concerns.

Sample Exercise

Imagine that one of your best employees has recently been showing signs of depression. Not only have they had difficulty concentrating and making decisions; there has been a change and inconsistency in their performance and productivity levels. Furthermore, the employee showcases procrastination and oversensitivity when it comes to their work. So, how can you address this as a leader?

The first thing that you need to understand is that your job is not just to make profit. You must lead your team to the best of your ability. To be able to do that, you have to care about them. Don't just see your employees as a number; instead, treat them the way you would treat your friends or how you would want your friend to be treated. Be friendly and open; encourage your workers to speak to you about the things that cause them stress anxiety or depressions; and make sure that you respect their confidentiality. When one of your employees confide in you, remember that it is not bad to support them; it is also important to respect them. When you are supporting them, try to make sure that you are backing up your words with actions. If your employee is depressed, give them flexible working hours or allow them to work shorter hours.

---

from https://www.mentalhealthamerica.net/conditions/depression-workplace

Sometimes, a few days away from work can also bring things back, so encourage them to reduce their load until it becomes manageable and make a point to check up on them periodically.

Day 5: Dislike

The last negative emotion that we'll be dealing with in terms of the business contexts given is dislike. Interestingly, dislike is perhaps the most common negative emotion to find its way into common business situations, particularly when you are working with a team of employees. Because we are all extremely different people, personality-wise, the reason why we like other people also has a tendency to vary widely. Certain individuals tend to describe others for their inability to pull their own weight; the lack of efficiency disturbs them and makes them feel unfairly burdened. Furthermore, other people are more negatively impacted by ruthless or demeaning behavior, which is totally uncalled for. While some people may be okay with the higher-ups treating them as if they are beneath them, not all employees feel the same, and it soon fosters resentment and dislike.

Sample Exercise

Say, you are an employee who works for an extremely demanding boss. Because your boss is a hard worker himself, and he stays at work past office hours and is often on-call on weekends, it is difficult for you to find enough leeway to cultivate your own personal life away from home. Because of this, you have lost touch with almost all of your friends, and you only get to see you family on major holidays. Worse, your boss is openly unapologetic about it. You often tend to feel like you're an indentured labor and have said as much to fellow co-workers when complaining.

Now, imagine you are that boss. First of all, despite the fact that you are feeling all offended, try to identify what you've been doing wrong. Just because you choose to work hours that are beyond your contract, it doesn't mean that the employees in your team should have to make that same choice. Furthermore, when you don't even acknowledge that they have been putting in that time and show no appreciation or gratitude for the effort that they have been making, you not only alienate your employees but create a bad example as well. You need to make sure that you keep in mind that, as a leader, you are meant to guide. You do not control or own them; treating them as such is not in your best interest or the company's. Emotional intelligence doesn't mean you judge everyone by your standards; it entails that you judge them from theirs. Your job is to understand them and what's going on in their lives, as well as act accordingly to avoid making their lives harder. That is not what work should be.

Day 6: Excitement

Today, we won't be looking at negative emotions; instead, we will deal with excitement. Our objective is to understand how happiness or positive emotion can positively impact the workspace and teams working there. So, who's responsible for ensuring that the place is both exciting and efficient? Why, you, of course!

Imagine how much excited your workers will be if they come into the office and say, "I can't wait to see what the boss has planned today" in a positive manner? So, what are you waiting for? Try it out! Plan something positive for your team today and make a habit of doing it often. The goal is to make your employees appreciate the office more than their homes, and the best way to do that is by making the former likeable!

Day 7: Pride

Another positive emotion that usually goes unnoticed is pride. The ability to take pride in your work is crucial to any employee; as a leader, that is the #1 thing you want to instill your employees. A sense of pride not only gives you a sense of achievement; it also gives you as sense of ownership. Frankly speaking, people tend to work harder than ever for things that they believe are theirs.

Keep in mind that disengaged employees cost the US economy over $450 billion a year when it comes to productivity.[5] Unlike other factors, pride isn't something you can force on someone; it has to come from motivation. One of the best ways to ensure that your employees start to take pride in their work is by constantly giving them verbal and tangible reassurances that that their work is being valued. A lot of the employers have also opted to use training to improve specific set skills for their employees. The logic is that the better your employees are at something, the more likely they are to take pride in that activity.

Week 4: How to Respond and Not React

> *"Empathy is one of the most misunderstood yet most powerful tools a leader can use."* – Steven Stein

As we touch upon our last week in the program, it's important

---

[5] Sorenson, S. & Garman, K. (2013). How to tackle U.S. employees' stagnating engagement. Retrieved from https://news.gallup.com/businessjournal/162953/tackle-employees-stagnating-engagement.aspx

that we start taking responsibility for our own actions and reactions and stop blaming circumstances and other people for the things we have done.

The key difference between reactions and responses is the blame factor. Because reactions are immediate and don't generally include time to think, it's easy to basically deflect all the blame and say, "I did this because you did that." But should leaders - true leaders - look for ways to distance themselves from responsibility? No, they shouldn't.

Is it easy to shoulder blame? Of course not, but picking the easy way out isn't what real leaders do. That is exactly why real leaders respond and don't react.

Day 1: Responding vs. Reacting

So, what differs reacting from responding? Think of it like this; you are playing with your child. Suddenly, in a fit of anger, he breaks something like a T.V., toy or whatever object. Still, your reaction needs to stay the same.

When the object breaks, you flinch, and then immediately react by bursting out into a fit of anger as well. You berate the kid for not being more careful and continue to do so until the little boy is in tears. Seeing them in a chair angers you even more because you feel like they are trying to manipulate you. So, frustrated, you get up and leave. How do you think this little interaction has impacted your relationship with your child? Not positively - that's for sure.

Alternatively, think of this approach. If your child breaks something in a fit of anger, the first thing you should do is to recognize that he feels so dissatisfied with something that he has felt the need to grab your attention by acting in extreme method. Breathe in. Decide to check on what's most important first, which is your child. Are they hurt? If he is, your first step is to get them medical attention. If he is not hurt, move your attention to the object that has now been broken. Then, recognize that it is no longer with you and simply let it go.

Ask your child calmly to help you clean the mess. After you've done that, take your child aside and have a conversation about their feelings and why he did what he did.

Now, how do you think that went? Better? Awesome!

Now, you know what it means to respond to a situation instead of reacting to it. You are all set to start applying response techniques to your repertoire!

Day 2: Active Listening Skills in Practice

Active listening is one of the most important skills in a leader's armory. Not only does your ability to listen to instructions allows you to be better at your job; it also actively improve the quality of your relationships with the people around you. Hence, as a leader, it is so crucial. When you start practicing this skill, you have to keep four things in mind:

1. Active listening involves willingness to obtain information.

2. Active listening involves willingness to understand the information provided.

3. Active listening involves willingness to listen for the sake of enjoyment.

4. Active listening involves willingness to listen in order to learn.

Let's say that, as a team leader, you were chosen to mitigate an argument between two coworkers. One of them happens to be your friend; as such, you feel personally biased. A common mistake made by leaders who have interpersonal relationships with their staff, be it platonic or not, is that they fail to understand that there has to be a difference between you as an individual and a leader. When you start listening, therefore, you need to start with a clear mind and without biases.

As you continue to listen, make sure that you are paying attention and obtaining all the relevant information. In order to do so, you are going to want to start off with asking all the right questions. Questions also help show engagement, so the speakers know that you are now listening. Another rookie mistake is to make snap judgments; as a leader, your job is not to judge. In fact, you need to be open to new ideas and perspectives, as well as criticism and opposition. Once you think you understand what the speakers are trying to say, make a point to clarify and reflect on the information. Then, try summarizing the points that both parties have held, show your own opinions, and explain the best way to deal with this particular problem.

Now, was that really so hard?

Day 3: Empathy in the Real World

Moving onto the concept of real-world empathy, we have already spent quite a lot of time talking about how important it is to feel how your staff feels or understand what your employees are thinking of. While both of these factors play a role in establishing empathy, they are not enough.

The problem with empathy is that because of how it is perceived, which is basically as an add-on like sprinkles on top of your sundae, it's not considered important enough to become a requirement like the bananas or other toppings. In business terms, it is not seen as a hard skill but merely as a soft skill that managers and leaders need to master. Fortunately, this opinion is changing as more and more business graduates and owners are coming out and talking about how empathy needs to be embedded into the whole organization in order for it to flourish.

While providing quality services and products used to be enough, this was because most specialized products or services were almost monopolistic in the market. For instance, there was no equal competitor for a FedEx when they started; that's why getting a package from your doorstep to wherever you need it quickly and efficiently was all you care about. This, however, changed when DHL came around and offered the exact same service but with better experience value. Now that you automatically find yourself willing to shift, what do you think that says about empathetic sales? We think it means it's the future, and almost all of the major business founders agree.

Day 4: Dealing With Stress

Because emotional intelligence helps you handle stress, one of the easiest ways to deal with it on the job is by applying basic EQ models.

While the Mixed Model is applicable, the Ability Model is also quite important. In order to start working on your stress factors, the first thing you will want to do is to start cultivating a habit of being aware of how you feel. This way, you can notice when you start becoming stressed and stop it before it expands or gets worse. Once you're aware of how you feel, start to ask questions so that you can identify the source of this emotional reaction. "What is going on?" "Why do you feel this way?" "What is triggering this?"

Once you figure out the reasons, you can respond to the problem by approaching it with empathy. Always remember that the objective of emotional intelligence is to equip you with knowledge to be able to deal with your emotions in such a way that they no longer overwhelm you, just as letters in a book don't scare you because you know how to read.

Day 5: *Hearing out Complaints*

As a business leader, one of the worst parts of the job is to have to deal with constant customer and employee complaints. The fact of the matter is, if your consumer is unhappy with the product that they have received, or if your employee is unhappy with the manner in which they are treated, it is only natural for them to complain. And, honestly, it's really important for them to do this.

When an employee is complaining, they are basically asking for help. They want you to solve their problem, which means that they are still so invested in the product or service, and they aren't looking for a different solution. As long as your consumers and employees are still complaining, they are still invested in your journey. Thus, you need to proactively deal with complaints and learn how to respect them.

This is where unbiased active listening comes into play. When employees begin complaining, they're basically trying to highlight a problem. Whether or not you will recognize that problem is up to you, but the fact that there is a problem on your end or theirs is undisputed.

Day 6: How to Guide Employees Positively

Nevertheless, good leadership isn't just about listening to problems. It's also about making sure that they don't arise from the start. As a business leader, it is extremely important for you to ensure that when you are providing positive communication to your employees, be it to complete specific tasks or otherwise, you always ensure that these directives are given in context. Getting the task without it creates a situation in which an employee cannot always understand the importance of the issue at hand, and that can impact the quality of the work itself.

At the same time, it is extremely important that you are also very specific. Don't just tell them to pick up a bottle; tell them what bottle pick up, what it needs to contain, what size it has to be, and how much liquid should be inside that bottle. The more specific you are, the less your employee will make mistakes. Also, make sure that you are being very respectful. It isn't exactly about being a better person; it's just professionalism and sound business sense, considering it helps avoid unnecessary conflicts.

Day 7: How to Get Mad

A major misconception that a lot of business leaders suffer from is that being angry is bad thing, specifically when you're at work. However, in truth, feeling anger in the right way is an art!

Obviously, this doesn't mean that you should get angry about everything, to the point that you start breaking things around the office. At the same time, it is also important that you aren't so soft, to the extent that even you can't tell that you are angry.

If that's the case, you will not get what you want and end up in a stalemate position. Furthermore, too much anger takes away your credibility. You need to be able to strike the balance between not being taken seriously looking like a nutjob. It's kind of a Goldilocks scenario in which you need to know how much is just right.

When you can't help but get mad, make sure that you have clear, coherent conversations with people. Use 'I' statements to actively discuss and deal with the problems you have on a personal level as well.

Just like that, we are finally done with our four weeks of insanity. It does beg this question, though: what about the extra two days?

Well, those are allocated for practice, but if you want, you can take a break or use them to plan your next four weeks, then start all over again. It's really all up to you!

Conclusion

"I don't want to be at the mercy of my emotions. I want to use them, enjoy them, and dominate them." – Oscar Wilde

And so our journey through *Emotional Intelligence in Business - The Essential Ingredient to Survive and Thrive as a Modern Workplace Leader* ends here.

Leadership - more specifically, good leadership - is intricately involved with good emotional balance. Much like any other field of study, emotional education is the best way to equip yourself with emotional intelligence. The only problem is that, for years, we haven't really had a chance to study and apply the latter to our lives.

Emotional Intelligence in Business - The Essential Ingredient to Survive and Thrive as a Modern Workplace Leader, however, is uniquely positioned to help you overcome these specific difficulties. The five chapters in this book not only cover the main emotional competencies but also provide you with a four-week plan to work your way through the application of emotional intelligence that you may have missed out on.

Nevertheless, all of that is secondary. The primary focus of this program, believe it or not, is what you bring to it. As a leader, the most important thing is to be able to recognize what you are doing wrong, what you are doing right, and what you aren't doing but need to start doing so now. By picking up this book, you have made it clear that you recognize emotional intelligence as something that can change the way leaders and teams work together. You also see that it has the potential to help you become a better and more effective leader. The more you proactively work on these issues, the more equipped you will be to deal with them. Try thinking of the book as a roadmap; the idea here is for you to use it and figure out how to navigate leadership, understand and identify the problem, and then use the techniques highlighted to solve them.

Furthermore, we sincerely hope that *Emotional Intelligence in Business - The Essential Ingredient to Survive and Thrive as a Modern Workplace Leader* has been the solution you've been looking for. When it comes down to it, even though you feel like this is your own journey, for us, it's something that we've been a part of from page 1. As such, we feel deeply invested in it.

Considering this is a joint venture, understanding how much we've been able to help you genuinely matters to us. If you have the time, drop us a line and let us know how you feel about it with a review. We would absolutely love to hear from you!

Stoicism for Business

Ancient stoic wisdom and practical advice for building mental toughness, productivity habits and success in modern management!

Hello fellow stoic,

We live in a stressful and fast-paced business world.

When reading information for the first time, everything seems logical and clear, but when surrounded by distractions at work, we tend to forget quickly and move on as usual.

We forget things, because we have to process a lot of new information every single day and we don´t actively repeat the lessons we have learned.

We have found not 1 but 2 practical and 'stoic' solutions for you.

Quotes

The book is full of quotes from the ancient stoics and from modern day business people. A quote is the ideal medium, to deliver an important story or message in very compact way. <u>Only messages that get repeated will make it to our long-term memory.</u>

3-Month-Self-Evaluation-Journal

It will take time, Self-Awareness and Self-Evaluation to change yourself. A journal is one of the best ways to evaluate and improve yourself and a constant basis. Journaling is used by a lot of successful people to continuously grow and learn.

So my advice is to print the quotes and the ´3-Month-Self-Evaluation Journal´ used in ´Stoicism for Business´. Tape these quotes on your computer screen or on the bathroom mirror. A great way for a daily reminder for your personal road to more success and to hit the next level in your business. Print the Self-Evaluation Journal to help yourself transform in the coming 3 months.

If you want to be productive:

- Go to: https://businessleadershipplatform.com/stoic-quotes-

business-pdf

- Get the 3-Month-Stoic-Self-Evaluation-Journal and the quotes
- print both
- start reading

Enjoy the book.

R. Stevens

Introduction: The Basics of Stoicism

"Stoicism is the wisdom of madness and cynicism, the madness of wisdom." -Bergen Evans

The word 'Stoic' is often misused in today's world, whereas the term would once refer to an almost sacred form of Greek philosophy, the modern-day usage has turned Stoicism into a building block of the composition of an emotionless shell, the opposite of empathy and compassion, a fact which often causes the term to be misconstrued as a negative state of being, much like cynicism.

In other words, this use of the term 'Stoic' is much like the modern-day use of the word 'sick' – what it actually means, and what it is used to refer to are two very different things.

So, what is actual 'Stoicism'?

Why don't we dip into its history a bit, before we answer that question?

Stoicism: A History

The entire concept of Stoicism actually stemmed from the ancient Greek concept of *cynicism*, which ironically, is yet another philosophical doctrine that is greatly misconstrued in modern usage. Historically, *cynicism* was an 'ethical doctrine' which deemed the attainment and adaptation of complete virtue to be the true purpose of life. The idea being that all conventional desires that a person may have in regard to their 'worldly' persona; be it health, wealth, power or fame were all to be rejected as much as possible but for the bare necessities required to sustain natural life. So as to minimize worldly suffering and move towards the ultimate goal of happiness.

Zeno of Citium was a student of Crates of Thebes, one of the most prominent cynical philosophers of all time, was the founder of the notion of Stoicism, and in around 300 B.C. introduced the notion to Athens which at the time was a hub of philosophical discourse.

The school of thought was named 'Stoicism' after the Greek words 'Stoa' and 'Poikile' which were used to refer to the painted Athenian porches from which Zeno of Citium was known to preach.

The Stoic philosophy, as it developed, was built on the correlation of three major tenants – Physics, Logic, and Ethics, the combination of which was thought to help a person attain *eudaimonia* a state of successful happiness or contentment.

The **physics** of Stoicism was simple – all things are tangible, and there is nothing that is not tangible, not God, not logic, or reason, not even thoughts or emotions – their logic was that the concept of a separation of heaven and earth was as impossible as the separation of the body and soul. At the same time, the Stoics promoted the notion of *pneuma* or spirit, which they believed acted as the fuel of all things. This was closely linked with the notion of **logic**, which in Stoicism was thought to stem from verbosity. The idea is that each individual word had a tangible existence, which when spoken in a sentence was what crafted all of the cognitive experiences that a person would have and use to develop their persona and basic behavioral reactions. It was here that the concept of **ethics** would come into play – unlike cynics who deemed human construct such as laws, societies or cultures to be artificial and distinct from nature, Stoics took a much more lax view on the matter and encouraged life in accordance with laws and customs, claiming that such social and communal thoughts in themselves were extensions of nature.

The easiest way to understand this is by looking at Diogenes, the famous Greek philosopher, who was known not only for sassing Alexander the Great but also for eating, masturbating, and even defecating in public – now, Diogenes, a cynic, viewed this as the only way to truly divest oneself of worldly desires. Frankly, that isn't something that would help in modern day to day life and that is where Stoicism comes in. Stoicism is a more mellow form of cynicism, it's not telling you to go thumb your finger at all social norms and laws, but rather teaches followers to accept the world around them, make peace with it, and then to seek virtue and happiness.

Pretty intense, isn't it?

But how does this impact us and why is Stoicism so important in the 21st century?

Take a minute – think of the choices you've been making recently, the discussions you've had, and the fights you've been in. Think of all of those extra emotions; rage, anger, happiness, disappointment, and how often they have lead you to make a decision.

Now, re-evaluate how often these choices have been the right choices.

In our attempt to balance the 'natural world' with the world we live in, we are often prone to deviation – that is to say, we tend to get distracted and end up doing things that aren't logically what is the best choice.

Some people call this following their heart but in truth, it is following an impulse, and the thing about impulses, is the unlike instinct – impulses are reactions to our surroundings which means we are not doing what's best, we are doing what external circumstances make us think we should.

You're essentially being lead around with an imaginary noose.

So, how do you stop letting your emotions rule you?

Hello, Stoicism!

We're not going to be going into a play by play just yet though. First, you need to understand how and why Stoicism came about so that you can then start to explore how to include Stoicism into your own life.

Let's start with the people who are the face of Stoicism, so that you can understand how and where the entire concept stems from, as well as how history's greatest Stoics applied Stoic principles.

Zeno of Citium

Born in 334 B.C. on the island of Cyprus, Zeno of Citium is considered by many to be the Father of Stoicism. Born to Mnaseas, a Phoenician businessman, and a businessman himself Zeno seemed as if he would lead an atypical Greek life. But even as a merchant, Zeno had felt an intense need to be successful. In an effort to find out what he could do to better himself, he sought counsel with an oracle, who told him to 'take on the complexion of the dead'. After having thought about the statement, Zeno took it to mean that he was being told to study ancient authors or scholars and proceeded to do so.

Interestingly, just as he turned thirty, Zeno was shipwrecked on a journey from Phoenicia to Peiraeus. Stranded off the coast of Greece, Zeno began to walk around and soon found himself in an Athenian bookstore. There he came across Xenophon's *Memorabilia*, which held a collection of Socratic writings compiled by one of his students.

Zeno was enthralled and found himself asking the shopkeeper where he could find a man like Socrates, and as luck would have it Crates of Thebes was passing by at that very moment. The shopkeeper pointed to Crates and Zeno, from that moment on, became his pupil. Crates of Thebes was a cynic and for Zeno, who was from a relatively more conservative upbringing, these teachings were often too 'shameless' for him to emulate. From this, Zeno's Stoicism was born.

Stoicism, for Zeno, meant conforming to the divine or natural way of things and as such, Stoicism is said to lead to true happiness or content. Zeno went on to live in accordance with what was natural or what nature destined. So much so, that later on in 262 B.C., when he one day tripped and fell as he left his school he took this to mean that nature intended for him to die and promptly strangled himself to death.

Slightly misguided, we admit, but hold on for a minute and imagine how liberating it must be to literally want for nothing, the way he did. Zeno feared nothing, not even death and as such nothing controlled him, nothing held him back – can you claim the same?

Seneca

But, there is more, Stoicism did not die with Zeno, in fact, it flourished – even in Rome itself. Here in the hands of Seneca the Younger, or as you may better know him Nero's mentor, came in as a Roman Stoic. He not only lived and embodied affluent Stoicism, but he also worked extensively on developing the more humane sides of Stoic philosophy, like the relationship between Stoicism and compassion, or self-awareness. Even though his own life was rife with drama, the man had an affair with Nero's sister, after all, Seneca wrote and studied Stoicism almost in its exclusivity. This fact made him one of the most influential Stoics of all time, influencing Francis Bacon, Pascal, and even Erasmus. Pretty impressive, eh?

Gaius Musonius Rufus

The real 'Roman Socrates' however, wasn't Seneca but Rufus. Unlike his predecessor who was the topic of much scrutiny for the hypocritical bent of his own wealth and choices, Rufus was the Stoic to live up to, with his life mirroring his philosophy perfectly. Interestingly, it wasn't Rufus who made it to the list of the top three Stoic philosophers of his time but his student Epictetus.

However, regardless of that, Rufus was and will remain perhaps the most perfect Stoic in history. He did not let anything waver his stance, not even his own fear or ego. Where other Stoics when banished, chose death over banishment to ease their pride. Musonius Rufus boldly asked, *"If you choose death because it is the greater evil, what sense is there in that? Or if you choose it as the lesser-evil, remember who gave you the choice. Why not try coming to terms with what you have been given?"*. It was for these reasons that he was and continues to be so revered. Like Muddy Waters to the Rolling Stones, Musonius stood out and inspired the most iconic Stoics of history, and his worth and value was visible and stood out to those who knew what to value.

Epictetus

Of all of the Stoic scholars, one of the reasons Epictetus stands out was because of his sheer perseverance. Born as a slave to a wealthy household in modern-day Turkey, Epictetus studied under Musonius Rufus. Soon after the death of Emperor Nero, he became a freeman who taught all that he had learned to the Roman masses for a quarter century until Rome banished philosophers entirely.

Unlike his mentor, who prized ethics above almost everything, Epictetus was known for having a religious tone to his teachings. Even going on to state, 'God has entrusted me with myself,' and it is this that made Stoicism so popular among many Christian scholars, who found his two maxims preaching acceptance of events which were directed by a higher power to be appealing and in line with their own beliefs.

Marcus Aurelius

And finally, the legendary Roman Emperor, Marcus Aurelius is our last Stoic on the list. With his book *Meditations* being one of the most read books of all time and almost religiously studied by numerous world leaders and iconic successes, such as Bill Clinton and J. K. Rowling. Marcus' own take on Stoic philosophy had much to do with endurance and was what many believe to be a primitive form of cognitive behavior therapy – in fact, the emperor was known not only for his fortitude but also for his immense strength of mind. Yet despite all of this, Marcus was an extremely compassionate leader, his ability to navigate the emotional pull of sorrow and joy flawlessly despite the intense pressure he faced as an emperor and a warrior was and remains a commendable feat. Perhaps his most base lesson being that it was important that people as individuals learn how to be happy with who they were, and more importantly, that they accepted and cherish themselves to the point where they were not longing to be someone else. At the same time, it was equally important that people did not love their lives so much that they were in constant fear of losing it, while the conversely shouldn't be so hurt and troubled by it that they choose to end it. In a word, he preached and practiced fortitude, and so much of it that he remains to this day an icon of it.

Now, that's a pretty deep dive am I right?

But other than learning about a bunch of old guys, what are we taking away from this?

Context.

We're taking context and adding that into our understanding of Stoic practicalities. What understanding, you may ask – the one you're about to get!

The Three Practicalities of Stoicism

Stoic philosophy isn't just about a bunch of old dudes being virtuous. It's actually deeply rooted in the concepts of happiness and contentment in human lifetimes and how a specific set of practices can help people find peace, despite any circumstantial issues that may arise. In short, it's a cheat code for the human race, a way for us to find joy without having to fight and claw for it.

So, what are the three most important lessons that we are about to take from Stoicism and implement directly into our own lives?

Why don't you keep reading to find out?

1. *Time is Treasure* –

Despite time being the most precious of commodities, we have a tendency to not only give time away freely but also to somehow disregard its value. We tend to think that there will always be a tomorrow waiting, to do all the good things or all the important things and as we do this; we lose today, tomorrow, and all our tomorrows.

As Stoic philosopher Marcus Aurelius says, *'Don't behave as if you are destined to live forever. What's fated hangs over you. As long as you live and while you can, become good. Now.'*

Or as we say now, stop procrastinating!

2. *Controlling Your Feelings* –

The one thing that Stoicism is perhaps best known for, is controlling emotions. While it is often mistakenly thought to mean that one should erase their emotions. In reality, Stoic focus is on three things – *apatheia, ataraxis,* and *autarkeis*. *Apatheia* is the ability to be free from emotional constraints such as pain, anxiety, or suffering and, on the other hand, *autarkeis* is the ability to conserve this freedom and to ensure that it sustains. *Ataraxis,* on the other hand, is a state of being usually encountered when *apatheia* and *auarkeis* are achieved. Here, your emotions themselves become fortified so that they cannot be wavered by external feelings such as fear or stress.

As the Roman Emperor says,

'Choose not to be harmed – and you won't feel harmed. Don't feel harmed – and you haven't' been.'

3. Be Virtuous –

You'll find that throughout this book, at numerous points, we talk about making choices that are right or choices that are virtuous. This is because virtue or the pursuit of goodness is a core tenant of the subject. As we move forward with life, we tend to see the same; life is worthy when you do what is right. The one thing we should prioritize above all others is goodness; such as honesty over lies, modesty over shamefulness, and values over hypocrisy.

Understanding the Book You Hold

Now, all this must seem like it's pretty heavy reading – and what are you supposed to do with all of this information anyway, right?

Well, as for what you're supposed to do with it – that's simple, you're expected to use it just as Warren Buffet, Bill Clinton, Elon Musk, and Jeff Bezos have, to develop their lives and their companies into something bigger than themselves.

How you're supposed to do so is pretty simple too!

Start by going through every Chapter one at a time. As you come to the end of each chapter, take a week off and try to apply all that you have learned from the chapter in your actual day to day dealings. Practice each lesson until it becomes second nature. Remember Stoicism is a lifestyle, not a fad.

If all goes well, seven Chapters and seven weeks later, you will not only find an amazing sense of balance and peace in your life – you'll also be able to use that balance to promote positivity in the things you do and develop a more productive lifestyle.

So, what do you think? Are you ready to become the best version of you?

Chapter 1: Introspection: Know Thyself

'Look within. Within is a fountain of good, and it will ever bubble up if thou wilt ever dig.' – Marcus Aurelius

If there is one major curse that our generation is besieged with, it would be the senseless FOMO trend that seems to have captivated all of us. Long gone are the days when one would take the time to look at or even maybe deliberate on one's actions – instead nowadays our emotions and memories dictate our actions.

Why did we do something? Because we *felt* like it.

That in itself is possibly the most childish approach to life in existence. Yet for years, we have been justifying it claiming we don't know which day is our last and that we need to live for the moment.

But, what we never asked ourselves was, why does what we feel have to be at odds with what is right?

Why can't we want what is right?

And if we aren't longing for what is 'right' – why aren't we? What is biasing us, what is controlling us and worse, what is influencing us, without us realizing?

These are the questions we as a generation have forgotten how to ask, and worse, the same questions we have failed to answer.

But it's never too late to begin.

Take a minute.

Think back to the quote we started with.

'Look within'.

Ask yourself, why does Stoicism encourage us to look within? Why are we encouraged to understand ourselves? The answer is in the very next line, 'within is a fountain of good and it will ever bubble up if thou wilt ever dig.'

Because at our core, we are good. We are prudent, we are just, we have fortitude, and we are temperate. Stoicism knows this, Stoicism just wants you to recognize it for yourself, within yourself.

Do you think you're ready to understand why it's so important and how you can practice it?

Well, to do so – the first thing you need to understand is that true introspection is based on four fundamental principles – Self-Esteem, Self Confidence, Self-Awareness, and Emotional Control. Now, while we will go into each of the principles in depth, in a moment, let's first focus on the commonalities and differences of the four.

Self Esteem and Self Confidence, for instance, are often seen to be interchangeable. We claim that one lacks confidence or self-esteem – what then is the difference? Simply put, self-esteem is the perception you have of your own being, who you are, how you feel about yourself, and what value do you put upon yourself. In short – what are you worth, in your own eyes?

Self Confidence, on the other hand, is different. Here you are dealing with another weighing in of sorts, not on yourself but rather on a certain skill at a certain time, this is why self-confidence is so subjective. While you may not be very confident about your cooking skills, you could be super confident about how well you speak or play the guitar. It is, as you can see, entirely dependent on the situation and the context in which your skill is being judged.

Self-Awareness is similar but a bit more distinct. hereas, Self Confidence and Self- Esteem deal with your biased perception of your own strengths or weaknesses, Self-Awareness, on the other hand, deals with the same things but in an unbiased way. Who you are, what you are seen to be by your peers, or (if you're dealing with businesses) who you come off as to clients or prospective employees, is key.

Emotional Control, however, is the only clearly distinct issue you'll find yourself confronting – which is interesting because it is also arguably the most important. Whereas, the trifecta of Self-Esteem, Self-Confidence, and Self-Awareness seem to be dealing with your notion of self and the various perceptions of it. Emotional Control is like the key to the lock, it opens up the issue of why and how your perceptions come about and what you can do to liberate them from petty matters such as pride or fear.

Sounds pretty intense, doesn't it? Time to hit the ground running!

Remember, you've got this.

Take a deep breath, steady yourself, and here we go!

Self-Esteem

> *'Everything we hear is an opinion, not a fact. Everything we see is a perspective, not the truth.'* – Marcus Aurelius

You are the sum of your thoughts.

That is to say, everything you choose to hear and choose to see is based on how you choose to see the world. Or rather how your self-esteem has allowed you to. As Marcus Aurelius says, all that we hear is in truth an opinion and all that we see is simply one side of the story, one perspective, a perspective which stems from our biased view of the world as opposed to the actual facts of the matter.

You see, your self-esteem is part of a cycle – you are the sum of your thoughts.

If we see ourselves as valuable, we then value our time and what we do with it, which in turn means we try to engage in activities that have value and add value. Whereas, if we fail to see the worth in ourselves, we continue down that spiral by not valuing our time or our actions, and so it goes on.

This is where Stoicism comes in, Stoics realize that self-esteem is a state of mind, as opposed to a universal truth. In fact, one of Stoicism core tenants is to act on logic or ethics as opposed to emotion or feeling. Which is why it is critical to Stoic principles for one to be able to build a sense of self that is distinct from their judgment and perception of specific events.

Stoicism, therefore, preaches a more tolerant positive approach to thought processing, almost as if we are using a form of mental and emotional hygiene to cleanse our perception.

So, what then, are the ABC's of Self-Esteem? Three things -

1. Controlled Judgement

2. Positive Productivity and

3. Self-Dependency

Controlled judgment is the central issue here, after all, it is your judgment of a situation that sets the tone for how your mind will perceive it. It is here that we need to start to introduce a more compassionate, as opposed to a more critical, view of self. When we are upset with ourselves, when we consider ourselves to have underperformed, or feel like we haven't lived up to the expectations we had of ourselves we begin to launch into a critical self-monologue. For many this is a defense mechanism, we say ugly, horrible things in the hopes that others will see that we are already chastising ourselves and will refrain from doing so themselves. While hoping that our own criticisms will help us build a thicker skin, and as such protect us from other people and what they will think or say. For others though, self-critique is a default mechanism if something has gone wrong, we must have done something to cause it, we are quick to assign and accept blame because we see explanations to be weaknesses and we are afraid of weakness above all.

So, what is the alternate option – what can we do instead of giving in to this negative landslide? Meet – Self-Compassion.

Despite the fact that we often give ourselves a hefty dose of criticism or judgment, much more than what we would deliver upon any random passerby, we oddly seem to find it hard to give ourselves even an ounce of the same compassion that we would afford even to a stranger. Odd, isn't it?

Let's change that – or at the least let's take conscious steps to try to.

So, what do we do? Let's start by having you teach yourself that it is okay to be imperfect, in fact, every time you pick out a flaw in yourself, balance it out by naming something you love about yourself. This positive balance will force you to acknowledge that there is more good to you than you care to admit. And this is the next step, stop feeling shame in admitting the good things about yourself, remember embarrassment is not a Stoic characteristic.

Don't believe it?

Remember Zeno of Citium? Yeah, the founder of Stoicism. Well, do you remember how we mentioned that his first mentor was Crates of Thebes? Crates of Theebes was a notorious cynic, in fact, he was well known for throwing off many of the social norms associated with 'civilized society'. He would eat, defecate, and even masturbate in public – all of which were considered severe breaches of decorum in ancient Greece. Now, Zeno was never really able to fully adopt Crates' shamelessness, he grew up on a small island off the coast of Cyprus, and had a more conservative upbringing that Crates, or even than most other Athenians. Crates recognized this in Zeno, and to him, it was a flaw. His logic was simple, if you feel enough to feel shame or embarrassment for your own harmless actions, you are not distancing yourself from man's artificial constructs of society well enough. And as such he decided to teach young Zeno a lesson. Crates gave Zeno a pot of lentil soup to carry through the town, embarrassed Zeno attempted to hide and disguise the pot as he carried it. As carrying food through open spaces such as Crates had bidden was considered unseemly. Crates refused to allow Zeno to wallow in self-pity, which stemmed from self-shame and struck the pot with a stick so that the pot broke and the soup covered Zeno, forcing Zeno to now continue with food all over his being and not just himself.

The lesson Crates had sought to teach Zeno was simple – embarrassment is a useless emotion and only serves to keep you from properly completing your task. Today, you need to learn the same. Allowing shame to build in you, so that it can be used to control you with negativity is unproductive. Instead of constantly shaming yourself and critiquing yourself, afford yourself the courtesy of kindness just as you would a small child – you will find that a positive sense of self, in the long run, is much better than living with a person you detest.

This brings us to Positive Productivity, a major reason why we lack self-esteem or why we end up losing it, is because we keep on biting off more than we can handle. Taking on tasks that are beyond our ability and then faulting ourselves for not being able to keep up is a major issue. Instead, try to focus on tasks that you do well and slowly build on those skills.

It's important to be able to identify your true skills here because often we go after things we are just not meant to do. Even if you are trained to be an accountant, if you don't have an affinity for numbers your job may be burdensome and hard to excel in. Find your true calling by experimenting with what works for you, the better you are able to understand your own skills and weaknesses the better you will be able to build a strong business foundation. Remember, you are not defined by your weaknesses. You are defined by your choices and that is why perception is so important.

When asked what advice they would want to impart on their younger selves, if they could go back in time, billionaire influencers such as Bill Gates and Mark Zuckerberg both talked about the perception of 'intelligence' and how there is no 'right' way to be smart. Because society has imprinted on our minds that intelligence is a one-dimensional subject that can be measured by specific metrics such as IQ tests, we have a tendency to hold a variety of people and minds to the same standard.

Einstein once famously said that everyone is a genius, but if we judged fish by how well they climbed trees we'd always believe them to be stupid. Keep this in mind when you're struggling with your self-esteem and instead of allowing negativity to flood your mind, try to face your self-esteem issues head-on.

If your self-esteem is tattered, work on it. Be self-dependent. If you have a weakness, don't' expect to be magically good at it one fine morning, try to fix it and at the same time try to see if there is a better alternative for you. It may take time and it will most definitely take patience, but to be able to persevere against the odds is a key component of true Stoicism.

So, keep your chin up, and keep going!

Self-Confidence

'You can tell the character of every man when you see how he gives and receives praise.' – Seneca

As you slowly start to rebuild your sense of self, you will soon find that you also need to start working on how you perceive your abilities. After all, it isn't always just ourselves that we pass harsh judgments on, our skills and talents go through the same unfortunate process. Stoic philosophy knows this and points it out, as does Seneca, as he talks about how people react to praise, noting that our dependence on it is what defines our own self-confidence. We speak as we fear we are viewed and we accept the views that we think we deserve, as such our own judgment of what we are worth, and what we are capable of is critical, to our understanding of self.

So, how do we move forward?

To begin, you'll need to first recognize the power of your thoughts. You see, your thoughts are more than your view or perception of any one thing, they are what set the tone for every thought you will have thereafter and how you will perceive every action you see. If you continue to tell yourself that you are 'worthless' or 'beyond saving', your actions slowly start to reflect those notions. So, watch not just what you say, but also how you think. Remember, compassion trumps cruelty.

The next thing you need to remember to do is to be focused. Remember, confidence is built on actions. So, in order to be able to truly be confident in your own abilities, you need to work on having a plan – in truth though, in terms of modern-day businesses we seem to be drowning in plans. We call for meeting after meeting and console ourselves with the thought we are making plans and taking actions – but when asked what actions we have taken, the answer is that we've planned to take actions. It's like a dog chasing his tail.

We keep going round and round in circles, not realizing that we need to break away and move forward in order to truly achieve anything. Stop.

Billionaire Bill Gates once famously said that if there was one thing that helped him build Microsoft, it was the fact that from a very young age he had confidence in his own self and his abilities. Confidence gives you courage, and it is this courage that later becomes the fuel you burn when you work on overcoming obstacles and going further in life.

When Gates and his college friend Paul Allen, first reached out to the maker of Altair claiming they had a programming language that could run on their computers, they didn't even have an Altair to test it on much less an actual language – but they were confident they could make it. And when Altair's president asked to see them, they spent weeks creating the language which they typed into Altair's own computer system in Albuquerque for the first time – and like magic, it worked.

What guarantees did they have? None.

What got them through? Confidence.

What use are plans or genius ideas if you don't do anything to achieve them. At a point, your actions are all that matter. So, if you want to get away from a bad boss and try your hand at writing that novel you think could be the next *Harry Potter*, what use is it to talk about it if you haven't done anything. Stop thinking, stop planning, just do what you've been saying you will do. Your actions will speak louder than any 'research' or 'preparation' – so stop planning, take hold of your thoughts, take responsibility for them and just get up and act.

Now, as we move forward with our actions, you'll find that our successes are often tempered by failures.

We make mistakes.

We do things wrong.

We all do – none of us are perfect, and that's fine, failure is inevitable when it comes to life. The true test of our character is what we choose to do with our failures.

For most people, failures are the end of the line. We fail and then we run away as if running far enough or fast enough will keep our failures from staining our pride. We forget, rather conveniently, that failure is part of the learning process. Our ability to do something right stems from our ability to accept failure, and even look forward to it. As Thomas Alva Edison once famously said, 'I have not failed 10,000 times. I have successfully found 10,000 ways that will not work.'. The ability to look beyond failure and to allow it to simply pass you by, as opposed to allowing it to define you, is a critical part of Stoicism. Take this opportunity to think back on a recent mistake you have made, and ask yourself – what did you learn from it?

Once you determine what it is you have learned, say thank you. It may sound like an odd thing to do, but thankfulness is actually one of the most important building blocks when it comes to self-confidence. By being thankful, you are acknowledging the good in another person, or at times yourself, and this acknowledgment helps you promote positive thinking. A famous South Korean Pop Band, by the name BTS, recently began taking over music charts in the US. During one of their initial visits, an American passerby called out to the band telling them they would never make it in America. A year later, they were AMA winning, Grammy nominees taking over the world.

Any idea what Jung Hoseok, the band member who heard, said in response? 'Thank you for your concern.' Not only did his acknowledgment take away any power the words were intended to have over the band, but his response by focusing on the good, allowed him to sidestep all the negativity the words would have carried with them.

So, the next time someone says something to you that is designed to perhaps undercut your confidence, take the sting out of it and find a way to be thankful for it.

And the final bit?

Expectations.

If there is one silent enemy that our self-confidence has a tough time facing head-on, it is expectation. What are expectations though? Is it an expectation to assume you'll do well on a test that you studied for, or that you'd get a promotion you worked hard for? Well, to be honest – both are. Now, I know what you're thinking, but how is that fair, I worked hard for those things and they are what I deserve.

That very thought right there is an expectation. The entitlement you have for the future and its effect on your present. Now, Stoicism isn't telling you to just suck it up all the time, Stoicism is about action, remember. When something wrong is happening, address it – make a plan and act on it. But when it comes to the little things, the things that are ruining your present, like you worrying about a long term relationship with a person you literally just matched with on Tinder – yeah, those have got to go. As Gates says, try new things, this allows you to find out what works for you and what doesn't, as opposed to just sitting around and making assumptions.

Don't daydream about things that may or may not ever happen – focus on the task at hand, not only will this help you be more productive, but it'll also keep you from allowing your confidence to fade in the face of trials and tribulations that may never come to pass. Remember, when you transform your ability to be a strong, productive member of society, you are in turn adding value to your skills and helping boost your confidence.

Self-Awareness

> *'These reasoning are unconnected: "I am richer than you, therefore I am better"; "I am more eloquent than you, therefore I am better." The connection is rather this: "I am richer than you, therefore my property is greater than yours" But you, after all, are neither property nor style.'* – Epictetus (Enchiridion)

Self-Awareness is the last of the self-imposed measures poised to not only determine but help grow a clearer sense of self. The concept of self-awareness is actually a very common soft-skill taught around the world to business leaders and business graduates – understand who you are in isolation and work towards improving yourself.

The concept, however, was coined first by Stoic philosophers such as Epictetus and Marcus Aurelius who encouraged people to view themselves separately from what they had in terms of material riches, or what they had achieved in terms of power or success.

The real question is who you are and whether or not *you* are being the best possible version of yourself both internally and externally.

In truth, there is no one better placed to properly test out if you are living up to your potential and principles, then you are. Epictetus used to use a specific word '*dokimazo*' – to refer to this testing. He would encourage, as did many philosophers before him, that you brutally test your own perceptions and opinions, and that you do the opposite for others or rather seek to see the best in them.

There were two reasons for this – one was to avoid self-deception, which was viewed to be disease like in nature and would prevent self-growth and learning. The other was to promote positive thinking and at the same time to keep us from thinking too highly of ourselves.

Self-awareness is critical when dealing with businesses and business choices, not just because it gives you a more realistic view of what's going on- but also because it ensures that you are more in tune with your own inner voice. Billionaires such as tech giant Steve Jobs and media mogul Oprah Winfrey have both discussed this at length.

Oprah Winfrey, who was once an upcoming journalist demoted from co-anchor position and later went on to host the highest-rated talk show in Chicago for over 25 years, explains that unless one takes the time to actually know who they are and why they are here, they will continue to struggle.

In her own words, 'I've come to believe that each of us has a personal calling that's as unique as a fingerprint – and that the best way to succeed is to discover what you love and then find a way to offer it to others in the form of service, working hard, and also allowing the energy of the universe to lead you.'

So, before you move on to do anything else – stop.

Figure out what it is that you want to achieve in life.

Who do you want to be?

What works for you?

What is it that you love?

How can you give this to others?

Once you've got that down pat – we can move on to the last

level of introspection.

Ready?

Emotional Control

> *'It does not matter what you bear, but how you bear it.' - Seneca*

Emotional control is the key to any fruitful application of self-applied introspection. Imagine you have evaluated your self-confidence, your self-esteem, and your self-awareness – none of this will amount to anything if while doing your testing or evaluating you were biased, or if after testing you were biased towards the results.

Now, generally speaking, Stoicism in its 'common' definition is thought to refer to the expulsion of all emotional or passion-driven reactions that swell up within our consciousness. This, however, is not the case, Stoics have never advocated the suppression of emotions. They have merely sought for individuals to cultivate such consciousness that they can control the manner in which such emotions arise so that they can better avoid negative emotions and bask in the positive ones.

The term 'emotional control' itself is a bit tricky – it seems to suggest that we would be able to control our emotions before they arise, and control them in a manner that only some would come forth, but in actuality what you are doing is controlling them *as* they come forth. Your emotions are what you feel and while, like fear when in a life or death situation, you can't control that emotion coming forward, you can control how you act in regard to that emotion. Hence, Seneca claiming that what you bear isn't important, instead how you bear it is of more consequence.

This is because as a rule when you are reacting, your reactions are to another person's action and to a certain extent are senseless and ergo outside of your control. This lack of control is the problem.

So how do you cultivate emotional control?

Well, for most professionals the rule is to play poker. You see, in order to succeed in poker, a critical rule is to respond and not react to the cards you are dealt. Much like life, you have little to no control over what you are dealing with and there is not logic or reason to the events that can and will surround you.

The trick here is to follow four cardinal rules. School your mind to understand these four things, to believe in them, and to apply them and you are set to face the world.

The first rule is that 'There is No Perfection'. As a human, the life that you live is outside your control. Even in the things that are in your control, there will always be things that escape you, these things in layman terms are called 'mistakes' and are a natural, inevitable part of life. You will never be perfect, nothing you ever do will be perfect. There will always be room for improvement and there will always be a better way, that is okay. Accept this as a part of life and move on instead of wallowing in self-pity. There are bigger things to focus on. So, do it.

The second rule of thumb is that you must 'Say No to Temptation' – as you move forward with ideas or project it's very easy to get side-tracked by something that seems like a newer, shinier object. Stay true to your goal, understand that all that glitters is not gold and that willpower is an important component of Stoic success. While a steady 9-5 job may seem to appeal to you over a small startup, know that if you have started something you owe it to the project to see it through; do not waver and do not falter. If you don't work for your own dreams now, you will work to serve another's dreams forever – so which is it going to be?

Thirdly 'Say No to Messes' – no matter what you do, you need to ensure that you are not only being strategic and organized, you must also be transparent and tactical so that you can curb your impulses and follow the plan, as opposed to jumping the gun on a hunch. Remember your instincts are good, but your clarity of mind is better.

Which of course brings us to the final factor, 'Say No to What If's' – one of the biggest threats to emotional stability is the notion of 'what if' – not only do statements like this aggravate the mind and trigger despair and stress, they result in the loss of valuable time and resources. Don't waste your time on if's, but's, or maybe's work on what you have, with what you have and you'll actually achieve *something*.

Chapter 2: Productivity

> *'If a person doesn't know to which port they sail, no wind is favorable.'* – Seneca

One of the core tenants of Stoic philosophy is the constant issuance of mental self-awareness reminders. Imagine if every time you did something, there was an actual voice in your head that holds you accountable.

What are you doing?

Who are you doing it for?

Is it virtuous?

Is it in line with the natural order of justice?

By holding your mind accountable, Stoicism as a practice forces people to reflect daily on their thoughts and actions. By curating your actions and thoughts so that all of your actions come from purposed thoughts, you find yourself creating physiological programming of sorts where your brain hardwires you to both commit to and expect achievement. You are basically talking yourself into being 'efficient' and 'productive' in your thoughts and actions, which just happen to be the two most important words in the Stoic dictionary.

By forcing individuals to create mental roadmaps to deal with issues, Stoicism allows people to bypass the 'niceties' of polite society and move ahead and deal with the actual happenings.

Sounds like something we all need in our lives, doesn't it?

Why don't we simplify it a bit for you and help you figure out exactly how to be a more productive, efficient, and balanced person; both in your personal and professional life?

Sound good?

Awesome!

Here we go!

Actions versus Doubts

> *'Progress daily in your own uncertainty. Live in awareness of the questions.'* – Bremer Acosta

As we move forward with Stoicism, we will soon find that the central point of any lifestyle is not necessarily the principles that it is built on but rather how those principals are invoked. For Stoicism it is the same, the more eye-catching issue is not necessarily what Stoicism is about but rather, how it impacts our actions.

Any form of action, even inaction itself, stems from a decision.

You have decided to act. Or alternatively, you have decided not to act.

This form of decision-making when in the hands of a Stoic comes across a series of questions. Before we go into them however, let's quickly review what Stoic principles teach us – in Stoicism the one thing that supersedes all others is virtue. The ultimate goal of Stoicism is after all to be a virtuous being.

So, does that mean you get to recklessly do whatever you want in the name of looking out for the greater good? Like if you turned down a well-paying job at a cigarette company, because cigarettes are harmful, when you have young children to feed and clothe.

No.

Stoicism may be based on virtue, but it also holds you accountable for your actions.

So how do you know, when you are supposed to act and when you are supposed to restrain yourself?

Start by asking yourself a question, as Acosta says, you must live in awareness of the questions. Ask yourself, is the matter at hand in your control?

If it is not, there is no point in you fussing or worrying about it, as there is nothing you can do to change it. For instance, if you are dealing with an important tender and you know that there is going to be a critical 2nd bidder making a bid today, is it helpful for you to go into a panic and worry about it? Will your worrying about it cause the second bidder not to bid? No! And as such, any action undertaken at this moment is pointless and should mean nothing to you.

On the other hand, if you are perhaps partially in control, it is important for you to then distinguish over which part of the matter is within your control – the effort or the outcome. If the outcome is not within your control, stop fussing about it and again recognize that this is not your concern. If it is, you would deal with it in accordance with Stoic virtues.

If on the other hand, only the attempt is under your control, you must focus on the attempt and as you do so, ask whether the attempt is virtuous. Your colleague Bob is about to be fired, can you stop him from being fired? No. Can you make an attempt? Yes, but then you must ask of the attempt is virtuous – is Bob a good worker, did he have a valid reason for doing whatever he did? If he did, trying to save his job would be virtuous or good and you as a Stoic should take actions to help in the interest of wisdom, justice, and temperance. If he isn't though, and trying to save his job would be in conflict with those principles, taking actions would not be preferred.

So, all you really have to do is ask yourself a few questions, but as Bremer says, you also need to be aware of your uncertainty so that you *do* ask the questions.

The problem when it comes to the applicability of these factors, however, is that human beings don't react well to change, so we don't know what to do with uncertainty. In fact, the doubt-avoidance tendency that is second nature to us has been at the forefront of many corporate failures. Billionaire Charlie Munger, who was Warren Buffett's right-hand man, has described the situation by explaining how hard the brain works to avoid working to learn something new, which to us are presented in the form of doubts. The solution as advocated by Munger is to cultivate *worldly wisdom*, something that he refers to as a form of multi-disciplinary knowledge that helps approach understanding on a whole as part of a more cohesive framework, kind of like understanding that a business is dependent on both people and systems and that both channels have different reactions, different foundations and as such must be dealt with in different manners.

Make sense?

Productivity

> *'If you accomplish something good with hard work, the labor passes quickly, but the good endures; if you do something shameful in pursuit of pleasure, the pleasure passes quickly, but the shame endures.'* – Gaius Musonius Rufus

As we move on to the element of productivity in its micro sense, you will find that you are faced not only with a large never-ending list of to-do's, you are also faced with limited time and somehow the two don't quite add up.

Now, before we start worrying about the imbalance in terms of your time and work ratio (we'll get to that in just a minute, don't worry!), why don't we take a moment to look a little closer at the 'tasks' or jobs you need to get through to be productive – because that's what productivity is all about right? Getting more done in less time?

Buzz!

Nope. Wrong answer!

Productivity in Stoicism is underpinned by two things. One the value or worth of the task, as we discussed earlier – does the task have value in virtue, if yes than it is an appropriate task, if not, it is not.

On the other hand, the importance of the task and its balance against urgency is also super important and is a great way to figure out what is actually necessary. So, who used to use these methods, try Eisenhower, yup, *that* Eisenhower, POTUS 34, the man behind NASA, and the internet and all of that fancy stuff.

So how did he do it?

Eisenhower used to use something he referred to as the box, basically, it was his way of using Stoic principles to sort through the stuff he needed to do. There were four major categories; Important, Not Important, Urgent, and Not Urgent. When it came to deciding what he had to do, POTUS 34 would identify which things were both urgent and important, aka they had virtue, and got to them straight away. As Musonius Rufus, yet another famous Stoic, puts it if you are doing something good by working hard, it may have required a little powering through but the benefits continued. As for the stuff that wasn't important or urgent, like scrolling your newsfeed or drawing up a prettier version of your daily routine so that it looks better – Eisenhower would simply scrap them. If it wasn't important and it wasn't urgent, he just wouldn't do it.

What about when something was urgent, as in it had to be done by this week, but it wasn't a super important task? For instance, if you're a lawyer and your case list for the next week needs to be updated, it needs to be done by next week but it doesn't necessarily need a managing partner looking into it – simple, you delegate! Pass the buck on to someone who has less on their plate and give yourself a little room, you'll need it! Especially since, when it comes to non-urgent tasks that *are* important, you need to schedule in some time and get cracking. It may not be something you particularly want to but you need to get it done, so why procrastinate?

All in all, the key to productivity isn't working more or working harder – it's working smarter! Instead of doing a million things, figure out the things you need to do *right now* and do them. Then make a list and schedule in the other things that you need to do ultimately in the future. Everything else that can survive without you, you delegate or you let go completely and just like that your work burden has been halved as have your stress levels!

Now all that's left is for you to do the things that need to be done, in an efficient manner!

Efficiency

> 'So in the majority of other things, we address circumstances not in accordance with the right assumptions, but mostly by following wretched habit.' - Gaius Musonius Rufus

While processing through our task list, and filtering out what we need versus what we don't need, is a major part of our workload which we've managed to deal with a little more productively. We won't be productive as a whole, if we fail to address the *way* in which we approach these individual tasks.

What are we doing? Why are we doing it? How are we doing it? Is this the best way to do it?

These may seem like simple questions but they are actually super important, not just because they help you re-evaluate how and why you are doing what you are doing, but also because they help you evaluate if the way in which you are getting the task done is the best possible way to do it.

Think about companies like Google and Amazon, efficiency is key here and the only reason they are big, and they are staying big, is because they are constantly adapting to fit the market needs. As a company and an employee, unlike when you are a student, you have to keep in mind that in the real-world, routine and habits actually detract from efficiency. Just think of how much Google has changed and adapted from its early days and how the OG internet browser Explorer seems to have fallen behind – why do you think that is?

Let's be honest, it wasn't like the browser got worse,\ as the years went by, it just didn't get any better and in a constantly evolving world, stagnation is the worst thing that can happen.

If you aren't getting better at your job, you are becoming redundant because somewhere someone is willing to do your job, and for less. Your time has to be an investment that makes you better at what you do, not just something you allow to pass you by.

Which is exactly why it is *so* important to break away from routine. If you feel like what you're doing has become repetitive, that means your mind is settling into a pattern and it's time for you to change things up.

Stop.

Re-evaluate your goal, and then take a hard look at your process – what are you doing, how are you doing it, and what is a better way to achieve the same or better results?

Once you've done that, try adding in those things to your regular routine or better yet throw your routine out altogether and make yourself a new road-map. Remember the goal is to succeed, and sometimes you need to step away from what you know to find another way!

A great tool that you can use, in addition to the Eisenhower Box, is to simply break down your major goals into smaller more manageable goals. So, once you have your final list of the things you need to do, pick any one item off that list and break it down into ten or more tiny tasks that you can get started on. As you go through each of the tasks, tick it off your list. Your mind may be telling you that you haven't done much, but the paper in front of you will testify otherwise. Smaller tasks make larger issues easier to tackle and make them seem less daunting, which helps us get more done!

Pretty cool, eh?

Why don't you grab a piece of paper and break down your task list a little before you move on to the next bit here?

Go on, we'll wait.

Responsibility for the Outcome

> *"The chief task in life is simply this: to identify and separate matters so that I can say clearly to myself which are externals not under my control, and which have to do with the choices I actually control. Where then do I look for good and evil? Not to uncontrollable externals, but within myself to the choices that are my own…" – Epictetus*

Okay, so you have your task plan and you know how to go through it in the most effective manner possible – all good things, but say you try and something doesn't go your way.

What do you do now?

Do you wallow in guilt or do you push the blame off on someone else and say it wasn't your fault?

How about – No.

A key principle of Stoicism is the notion of virtue ethics, a direct contrast to the general consequential ethics. The idea is that if you do not have control over the outcome or the results you aren't completely responsible for them. For instance, if your colleague is being ineffective and irresponsible at work and you complain about it and he gets fired – it's not totally your fault.

Now, what about the partial bit though – doesn't that indicate it's our fault a little bit?

Well, when it comes to Stoicism, what it really means is that it *might* be your fault. While generally speaking, outcomes shouldn't be something you worry about but the scenario changes when you are dealing with non-virtuous actions. So why did you complain about your colleague? Were you being malicious? Or were you asked by a superior, as part of your job, to assess the team?

If it's the latter, what you did was a virtuous act and part of your responsibility, and as such, was how you were meant to act. Any subsequent reaction or result of your action, be it positive or negative, has nothing to do with you because you are not in control. You are only in control if you did something out of a malicious intention, where your goal was not virtuous but rather to see your colleague fired.

But that's for others, when it comes to yourself the same rules apply.

Stoicism doesn't just mean you have to have a stiff upper lip and pretend nothing affects you. It's more about understanding and being able to distinguish what is in your control and what is outside of it. As Epictetus says in his quote, being able to identify what is in your control and what is beyond your control is important so that you can also understand which acts you actually need to worry about.

Case in point? Your own personal development.

When you take responsibility for yourself, you are in effect shedding any crumbs of a victim mentality. When it comes to your own progress you are not dealing with an external control – you have control and you have the power to decide what will happen to you. Everything that happens to you is something you are allowing to happen.

Why?

Because nature has equipped us with all the necessary tools to deal with life and its obstacles head-on. Stoicism teaches us that in order to improve our chances of leading a happy life, which is the ultimate goal, we have to step up and forcefully take back our own destiny. Have a bad boss? Don't let it ruin your life, be proactive and do something about it. Either go over his head or look actively for another job. Your boss being an ass isn't what is ruining your day, your refusal to take yourself out of that toxic environment is.

Canadian-American CEO and motivational speaker Brian Tracy, has touched upon this issue directly and drawn heavily on Stoic principles as when he talks about superior leaders. In Tracy's opinion, superior leaders are those who are willing to admit to their mistakes and cut their losses instead of stubbornly following through when they know they are dealing with a sinking ship. If you are making a mistake, if you made a mistake, the mistake is not what is going to matter in ten weeks, it's how you dealt with the mistake.

Remember, you are the master of your own fate and as such if you are suffering, *you* are also the one with the solution.

Energy Control

> *'To achieve freedom and happiness, you need to grasp this basic truth: some things in life are under your control, and others are not. Within your control are your own opinions, aspirations, desires, and the things that repel you. We always have a choice about the content and characters of our inner lives. Not within your control is literally everything else. You must remember, that these things are externals and are none of your concern.'* –
> Epictetus (Enchiridion)

As we begin to better grasp the basics of Stoicism, we also begin to realize that Stoic productivity relies heavily on efficiency and how we are responsible for certain but not all outcomes. But one thing that a lot of people, particularly in this generation, seem to forget is that not only are we not responsible for the things outside of our control, we also have a duty *not* to worry about them.

Imagine you're a corporate sales manager, in a massive pharmaceutical company, that produces a product called Kanax. Kanax does all the things Xanax does and is a very effective medicine, but it just happens to cost five bucks more than a Xanax. As a sales manager, you have brought up the fact that Kanax isn't likely to be welcomed by consumers and is likely to cause your company a loss, but your boss refuses to listen.

What should you do?

Worry about it, or just do as you're told and try your best to sell the product?

What if I told you, you were asking the wrong question?

Everything you are surrounded with and everything you deal with falls into one of two categories – (a) something you have control over or, (b) something you don't have control over, and both of these are stressors for the mind.

When faced with the former, anxiety or stress can actually cause you to be more ineffective. After all, if you are misusing your energy by worrying over or panicking over an issue, you are in effect wasting time and energy. Worrying about something doesn't change anything, in fact, all it really does is cloud your focus and rob you of clarity of mind and peacefulness. If anything, anxiety and stress make you make bad choices, like that cigarette you smoke to calm down, or that extra donut you had to cope with all the work stress you're under.

But take a minute and think about it – what have you achieved by being worried? What have you achieved by stressing out? Other than an extra kilo and bad lungs, probably nothing. This is because stressing out or worrying over things you can control basically just keeps you from doing what you need to do. If you *can* do something, do it! Why are you wasting your time worrying, when you can be making a game plan to deal with the issue head on?

Makes you wonder, doesn't it?

Now, let's take a look at the flip side, if you are dealing with the latter and you don't have control over the issue at hand, your anxiety or stress is again just another way of you wasting your time and energy. This time because no matter how much you worry you can't do anything. Now, if the matter at hand is not something you can influence or impact, how does your worrying about it help?

281

The solution?

Well, the Stoic solution is to get a grip on your emotions and stop letting them get the better of you. Treat your emotions the way you would children, you humor them but you don't let them run wild. Worry and stress lead to you feeling emotionally drained, tired, and worst of all they tend to suck all the positivity out of you. Instead, be proactive and do something about whatever it is that you are dealing with. Remember doing, not stressing, is what saves the day!

Balance

> 'When you see anyone weeping for grief, either that his son has gone abroad or that he has suffered in his affairs, take care not to be overcome by the apparent evil, but discriminate and be ready to say, 'What hurts this man is not this occurrence itself – for another man might not be hurt by it – but the view he chooses to take of it.' As far as conversation goes, however, do not disdain to accommodate yourself to him and, if need be to groan with him. Take heed, however, not to groan inwardly, too.' – Epictetus (Enchiridion)

If efficiency and productivity are the two most important words in the Stoic's dictionary, the third most important word must be 'balance'. More often than not, Stoics get a bad rep for being detached or unemotional – but in truth, Stoic philosophy isn't about not being humane or not being emotional, it's about knowing how to draw a line and not cross it.

Ergo, balance.

Stoicism refers to two major forms of balance, one of emotional balance and the other of actions. The general idea being that productivity, as a Stoic, would depend on what extent you as an individual are allowing your emotions to fill you and subsequently on how you act on those emotions.

Think of it like this, say you are a doctor who works with Doctors without Borders. You go to Palestine and there, as you are working as a general surgeon, you come across so many hopeless cases that you realize that you are unable to maintain your focus and are sobbing into your pillow every night because there is nothing that you can do to stop the steady influx of literally 'war torn' victims on your operating table.

This is where you must detach yourself from your emotions internally and move forward. The fact that you care is commendable and an important part of living up to the Stoic principles of compassion and love, but that is for you to express externally perhaps to the loved ones of the victim. But when you are dealing with the victim, if you are envisioning him as a laughing five-year-old with a gap tooth, you aren't going to be able to save their lives – extreme attachment is the exact reason why doctors aren't allowed to operate on their loved ones.

Take the time to understand and feel, but do not allow your feelings to undermine your actions. It helps to realize that what you are doing is important and worthy. Remember Stoicism is, in ways, about catering to something bigger than yourself. As a doctor dealing with patients who are being created by selfish nations playing petty games, you are doing something that makes a difference to those individual lives and that difference is what you are achieving through balance.

When you are following proper Stoic values, your actual ability to do good is amplified. So instead of allowing yourself to be faulted for not being more humane, move to seek more balance, both in your thoughts and your actions, so that you can be both more effective and more productive in what you do.

Time Management

> *'It is not that we have a short time to live, but that we waste a lot of it.'* - Seneca

One of the most important things in Stoic philosophy, that we tend to ignore in real life, is the value of time. Now, oddly enough, we've been taught the value of material things and money almost from our infancy – don't waste food, don't break toys, don't lose your lunch money, you name it.

The logic is always very simple – the things in question are valuable and as such deserve to be treated like the precious commodities they are.

But what about our time?

How often has your time been treated with an inch of the same deference?

You wouldn't go out and randomly start handing random people dollar bills, hell you think twice before dropping spare change in a charity tin, and yet when it comes to your time, you are happy to treat it like we do disposable tissue paper.

Why?

Because, honestly speaking, it's never really occurred to you that your time on earth is limited. Yes, you know that you're going to die at some point of time but you feel like that point of time is so far in the future that it's not something you want to deal with right now, at this given point. In Seneca's words, loss of time came in many different forms, some time was forced away from us, like the endless hours you spend in traffic, other bits have merely slipped away, like the hour your spent-on Facebook earlier, or hour before that when you were procrastinating about something you should have done a week ago.

This is where the importance of time management comes in, Stoics like Seneca, make it clear that time is the most precious of commodities and is to be revered above all other material things. Stoic entrepreneurs feel the same. In fact, multiple billionaires such as Mark Cuban, owner of the Dallas Mavericks and Magnolia Pictures, as well as Apple's Steve Jobs and Twitter CEO Jack Dorsey all take little steps to save time such as cutting out meetings. Mark Cuban has even been noted to state that he never does meetings unless someone is writing a check. Other tactics include avoiding multitasking or having themed days such as the 'No-Meeting Wednesday' trend promoted by Facebook's Dustin Moskovitz.

Whatever you do and however you do it, make a point to remember that a true Stoic makes the most of every little bit of time that they are afforded – and so should you. Be it by planning, apps, personal calendars; make sure that you are using your time in the most efficient manner with the most important people for the things you value the most and which are considered virtuous.

Chapter 3: Motivation and Discipline

"What would have become of Hercules do you think if there had been no lion, no hydra, stag, or boar - and no savage criminals to rid the world of? What would he have done in the absence of such challenges?

Obviously, he would have just rolled over in bed and gone back to sleep. So, by snoring his life away in luxury and comfort he never would have developed into the mighty Hercules.

And even if he had, what good would it have done him? What would have been the use of those arms, that physique, and that noble soul, without crises or conditions to stir him into action?"

The truth of the matter is we aren't all mythological heroes with a greater calling determining our role in life – of course, Hercules had bigger better reasons to be proactive; he was going to save the world multiple times, also the chick he liked was kinda hot.

But why us?

What do we have to look forward to – we're not extraordinary people and we don't lead extraordinary lives. What is so wrong with ordinary people giving in to petty, ordinary luxuries?

Do you really need to drag yourself out of bed to help grow your little home-brand into a massive conglomerate, just because it has potential? Why can't you just sell newspapers, and busk and be content, right?

Well, for one, we are forgetting that Stoics don't live life by a 'what do I get out of it' policy. As a Stoic, while you are free from the societal expectations of constantly doing more and doing better, you aren't free from the natural rule which is to live life virtuously, meaning you owe a debt to society. If you are growing your economic growth, that's not just beneficial to you, it helps you employ other people in your orbit and help give back to society. It's not about whether you can afford tickets to Cabo, it's about acting to the best of your ability so that you can give Collin, Carol, and Casey a job.

The challenges you face make you who you are. After all, being Stoic about how you control your emotions or how you think isn't going to make you a true Stoic, unless you are also working on your self-discipline and your motivation.

Why?

Because you don't get to pick and choose which Stoic virtues are convenient for you and claim you are being Stoic. Stoicism is a lifestyle, that only works when you take it all in, kind of like a fitness plan.

So, are you ready to take a walk through your steady mental diet for the week?

Here we go!

Motivation

> *'Let us prepare our minds as if we'd come to the very end of life. Let us postpone nothing. Let us balance life's books each day…The one who puts the finishing touches on their life each day is never short of time'* – Marcus Aurelius

Don't procrastinate.

If one had to sum up everything that Stoicism has preached in regard to motivation in just two words, those would be the words.

In the modern world, the whole wave of millennial thoughts has led to this tendency to prioritize emotions and how we feel over whatever it is that we need to or should do. Even when it comes down to something we are supposed to do or something we need to get done, we wait for 'motivation' or for a divine feeling that will tell us that we need to or should do whatever it is we need to do.

So how do you get over it?

Simple, you just do.

If you sit around waiting for the right moment or the moment when you 'feel' like doing whatever you need to do, you may very well be waiting around forever. Epictetus has a rather harsh take on this matter and explains in *Discourses* how an individual suffering from a runny nose has two options - we can of course easily cry and wail about how we are in agony, or alternatively, we could just wipe our nose and stop looking for an excuse to be upset.

The truth is, you always have a choice.

You *will* always have a choice.

You can choose to act, or you can choose not to.

But what is propelling you to act?

Well, check out for a bit of story time, yeah?

Once upon a time a court jester by the name Damocles began pandering to his king Dionysius and flattered him claiming that he was a man of wealth and fortune for all that he had. Dionysius, the king, offered to switch places with Damocles, so that he would better experience kingship for a day. Ecstatic Damocles agreed and sat comfortably on the throne enjoying all of the luxuries of kingship, however, it all seemed to be tainted by one thing. Dionysius, in his wisdom, had hung a long-unsheathed sword just a hairsbreadth above the throne, so that it would dangle just above Damocles' neck as a way to represent all the anxieties and dangers he faced as a king.

His lesson here was two-fold, on one hand, he is explaining that with great fortune comes great danger and, at the same time in Cicero's studies, it was also a reference to the importance of virtue in life. We all have our own sword of Damocles hanging over our head. None of us know, when, how, or why we will die and while that is a terrifying thought on its own, it is also a sobering thought.

Everything you do, at every single moment, is a part of the legacy you are about to leave behind.

Think of life as the Truman Show – if everything you are doing is being watched, would you rather be seen to do nothing but laze about like a lump of meat? Or would you rather be a trailblazer, who does everything they put their mind to and open the door for opportunities far and wide both for themselves and others?

You're probably thinking the latter. Now, you may have a little voice in your head that is naysaying this instinct – isn't this simple vanity? – it might ask.

Well, the answer is no. Vanity is a subjective judgment you have placed on an action. You perceive this to be vain but the act itself is not vain. Actions on their own do not have weight in terms of attributes, that is to say, they are neither good or bad nor evil. They simply are.

How then do we know we should do or abstain from an action? Simple, we check to ensure it is in alignment with natural principles. Is it good, is it virtuous? If so, it should also be done with haste, in the now. We are not destined to live forever, as Stoicism teaches us again and again. And as such, we have a responsibility to usher in the good and while we still can – that is the only way our life will have meaning.

So, what motivates Stoics? Redundancy.

Our time on earth, and our ability to be something, and do something all hang by an unraveling thread. None of us know when that thread will break, only that it will. So, if you are to be someone worth being, you must be that person now, while you still can.

Discipline

> *'You must cultivate either your own ruling faculty or externals, and apply yourself either to things within or without you that is, be either a philosophe or one of the vulgar.'* – Epictetus

Now, while motivation to adhere to the Stoic principles or rather the natural principles of life itself can seem hard to come by, there are some things that can make it a little easier on you as a person. The first is the understanding of what you are now seeking. You have developed an understanding of yourself and what is yours by laying the foundations through introspection. You have then used this to cultivate for yourself a course of action that is efficient and balanced and most importantly meets your needs. What you now need is something to get you through your little road map. Something that will give you reason and drive to follow through on your chosen path.

As billionaire co-founder of Groupon Andrew Mason puts it – it isn't being smart but being disciplined that changes the route of success. As Mason describes it, he has on occasion met many people who are more 'traditionally' intelligent than he and who logically, therefore, should be more successful than him.

The reason they aren't is simple, they don't have the self-discipline to be as perseverant as he was, that is to say, they haven't been able to stick to what they should have; and also because they haven't had the self-confidence to see things through.

Ring a bell?

Ever run into a high-school buddy who is doing astoundingly well in life, but literally wasn't half as good as you were in school and wonder what happened?

Well, life happened and by life, we mean the choices you made.

In Mason's own words "I often meet people who seem smarter than me, yet are less capable because they don't have the self-discipline and/or self-confidence to introspect on their ability to do what they think they're going to do and **find ways to iteratively improve**. Amazingly, *it's as simple as that*. It's kind of a sore spot for me because I can't understand why people don't take it more seriously."

So, what do you do? How do you avoid being the type of person Mason seems so peeved about?

And most importantly, how can you be less intelligent and do better? Because let's face it, one of the biggest fears that have consistently held us back year after year has been the fear that we weren't good enough.

Well, start off by forming positive habits, some of the habits that are held by billionaires are actually consciously formed to help promote their productivity and as a result their success.

Start off by focusing on yourself – treat yourself the way you would an expensive blue-chip stock and invest in yourself. Every day, do little things that help you develop, work on learning a new language or make sure you are staying fit. Whatever it is you are doing, make sure you do something for yourself. Why? Because you need to value yourself to be able to discipline yourself. And then next, make sure you are investing time and effort in what you love as well.

Billionaire Elon Musk has talked extensively about having a 100-hour work week. His logic being that if a person in the same position with the same or higher skills is putting in 40 hours a week and you are putting in some 100 hours a week, you are by default going to be ahead of your competitor by at least one business quarter, which is the very definition of a head start in terms of corporate success – so what are you waiting for?

Perseverance

> 'To bear trials with a calm mind robs misfortune of its strength and burden.' – Seneca, Hercules Oetaeus

Have you ever wondered, what it takes, to be successful?

According to most millionaires, you're dealing with just two things – persistence and resilience. In Stoic philosophy, Epictetus advocated something similar when he denounced the concept of *cheimaskesai*, or as he defined it part-time soldiering.

What was he referring to?

Before the advent of modern warfare, armies took a winter break when winter actually came about. There was no North waiting in anticipation of war, people simply called a mutual truce until they felt like they were in the mood to go back to battle. Epictetus, believes this concept of taking breaks is extremely detrimental to the achievement of an ultimate goal, his logic is simple – when you have set a goal, you go after it, now, today, and every day until it is achieved. To do otherwise is to be lazy and weak.

Multiple other successful people have followed the same advice, such as LeBron James NBA star, who despite his talent was known for never taking breaks in the summer. Ted

Turner, an American media mogul and businessman, has also spoken highly of perseverance as a necessary element of success. According to Turner, failure isn't an option, and as such, there is no reason to spend time worrying about it, instead focusing on what you want to do and what you want to achieve is core.

Seneca himself goes on to talk about this by explaining that success was, in fact, accessible to the poorly talented and the low born but was subject to the ability to persevere or to remain unwearied in the face of trials and tribulations. Now, the issue here is that not everyone who is successful or rich is the way they are because they have worked hard and clawed their way to the top through grit and willpower. In fact, some people were born with fortune, while others lucked into it, by lotteries or simply by being at the right place at the right time.

Fortune it seems favors fools.

The problem is, luck or fortune cannot be replicated –which is exactly why envy or jealousy happens to be so pointless. Wishing or wanting something isn't going to make it magically drop in your lap, all you are doing is cultivating negativity to feed on later.

The only 'guarantee' that life can offer is that people who persevere, be it through obstacles and difficulties or through pure adversity, will, in the end, be able to master themselves at the very least.

Do you know what it takes to be world class at something?

10,000 hours of deliberate practice.

Bill Gates before he dropped out of college as a sophomore had 10,000 hours of programming under his belt, fast forward a few years and Microsoft was born. The same goes for the global sensation 'The Beatles', still arguably considered by many to be one of the most iconic bands in history, started out by performing every day of the week in Germany, for over 8 hours each day, and at a point became so in sync with each other that they couldn't help but get better.

As long as you are working hard towards a goal and refusing to give up, you are building in many ways a platform for success. While entrepreneurial ventures also depend largely on what is referred to as the click moment or that moment when everything fits, kind of like seeing a lemonade stand in the middle of a desert. For the most part, business and success in businesses stem from how much effort is consistently being put in to promote success.

So, next time don't focus on the failures or what's not working, instead let your mind accept the failure and move on. In the words of Ryan Holiday,

> *'It's okay to be discouraged. It's not okay to quit. To know you want to quit but to plant your feet and keep inching closer until you take the impenetrable fortress you've decided to lay siege to in your own life – that's persistence.'*

And in our books, persistence and perseverance are just about the same, in terms of the endgame.

Emotional Control

> *'A rational person can find peace by cultivating indifference to things outside their control.'* – Naval Ravikant

And that, of course, brings us all the way back to emotional control.

When it comes to how we act or perceive things, emotional attachment, or emotions; one of the biggest problems is that, more often than we care to admit, we have no idea what we feel, much less how we should deal with it.

The first thing that we need to understand is that despite the fact that Stoics have harped on about emotional control for centuries, what they're saying has an actual footing in modern science as well. As Dr. David Hawkins has proved, there is actual energy that is used when we feel any emotion and these emotions, based on their type, actually promote or destroy cell life. Positive emotions lead to increased energy levels while negative emotions, like rage or scorn, lead to the actual death of cells. Which in turn meant that if we weren't controlling how we felt, how we felt was very literally controlling us, physically.

This is exactly why Marcus Aurelius, in Meditation, goes on to state that we must ensure that the part of our soul that rules us independently aka the brain or the mind, is uninfluenced by the actual actions that happen within your flesh. That is to say, it is able to draw a line between what the body itself and its experiences, such that the experiences do not lead to you attaching some form of judgment, good or bad, to the action that has been visited upon it.

To explain this in the most basic way possible, if you get fired from your job today, or if you fail a job interview – how would you feel about it? What would you think?

Upset? Sad? Angry?

You would think, that something untoward or unwanted had happened and that you were now at a loss because there are loose ends and you don't know what to do next.

This right here is what needs to change.

Being fired is not a bad thing. Being fired from one job as a co-host is what lead Oprah Winfrey to become the most influential female talk show host of her time. Michael Jordan didn't make the cut for his high school basketball team, and Walt Disney was fired from his day job for 'lack of creativity'. And all of these things are what allowed them to become who they became.

The ability to separate how we feel about an action from an action is critical when it comes to balancing mental health and productivity. So how did all these successful people do it?

Well, simply put they made a choice.

When something happens to you, your emotions may rise and you may act in a certain manner, but if you want, you can control your emotion by exerting your will – be scared, but stand your ground; be mad, but don't act in rage; be sad, but don't wallow in self-pity. These are all active choices that are made by an individual to apply the Stoic principle of reason over emotion.

Sounds a little complicated, doesn't it?

Why don't we teach you an easy way?

Have you ever heard of the emotional wheel?

Okay let's backtrack for a moment – at any given moment, research has shown that only about 36% of people know how they feel and are capable of pinpointing their actual emotions. So, if you're anxious, that can mean that you are overwhelmed but it can also mean that you are worried. If you are tired, it can mean that you are feeling actually physically tired and you're sleepy or it could be that you are feeling powerless.

Why is this important?

Well frankly, because it's hard to control how you feel if you don't *know* how you feel.

Enter the emotional wheel.

The emotional wheel allows individuals who perhaps don't have a clear understanding of how and why they feel the way they feel, to explore the broad general emotion they are experiencing and slowly narrow it down step by step. You start by evaluating your thoughts against one of the six broader emotional categories and then slowly narrow it down to understand exactly what it is they feel.

Once we've figured out what we feel, we shut down the emotional core of our brain and log into the reasoning chamber. Say for instance one is feeling critical. Being critical means that one is either skeptical or they are suspicious about something – now the question is not how we feel but what we do with how we feel?

So, if you are feeling skeptical, you can either be defiant and reject the feeling and create a cycle of frustration and anger; or you can accept how you feel, inquire into the cause or your mental chain of thoughts and then build towards creating a new perspective.

Now, interestingly although these feelings are being felt, they are not being acted on and are instead being submitted for a logical review. This allows us to decide how we want to react. Much like the Stoic concept of volition, we are the rock in the sea against which emotional waves rise, but which stands fast in its own truth.

How to Deal with Adversity

'The more you seek the uncomfortable the more you will be comfortable' - Conor McGregor

One of the core tenets of Stoicism is the ability to deal with difficulty and face obstacles without allowing the challenge to control you. In fact, if you turn to history, you'll actually find that Stoicism has always had a foothold in adversity, it arises like a phoenix from the ashes of charred souls and minds as a way out of the constant struggle that besieges you.

As Marcus Aurelius puts it, the art of life is more of a wrestler's art than it is a dancer's. Unlike dance where the beauty and lesson of art is to gracefully glide through life, in wrestling you are taught to stand your ground and prepare your body and mind to accept, process, and deflect unexpected 'onsets', which is basically the basis of Stoicism.

The ability to accept all the problems and obstacles that life will throw your way, to use them as learning curves, and to then take from these instances a clarity and peace of mind that stems directly from your strong sense of self, is the basic goal of Stoic philosophy. In fact, adversity as such is actually anticipated by many Stoic scholars. Seneca once claimed that 'Constant misfortune brings this one blessing; to whom it always assails, it eventually fortifies.'

This is a concept that has actually been the basis for countless success stories, look at the Paralympic gold medalist Marc Zupan. Zupan's ordinary life took a nosedive when a drunk driving accident left the young man not just hurt, but drastically maimed. Zupan lost all four limbs and become a quadriplegic, and life, as he knew, seemed to be taken away from him. When it comes to adversity, it's hard to imagine a harder obstacle to overcome. And yet he did, not only did Zupan win the gold medal for wheelchair rugby, but he also went on to star in the Oscar-nominated movie *Murderball,* and was even invited to the White House for his amazing achievements. Now, ask yourself, how would Zupan have done any of that if the accident hadn't happened.

Does this make the accident desirable? Does it mean it was a blessing in disguise?

Absolutely not. The accident wasn't a good thing, the exact same way in which it wasn't a bad thing.

There are no attributes of good or evil, that endure when you are dealing with an event. An event is just that, a happenstance.

The question lies in how you will either react or respond to the issue.

When the billionaire owner of Facebook Mark Zuckerberg, began to develop and seek investments for his company, he faced a seemingly insurmountable obstacle. He was working with a product that basically had no prior business model and therefore, made no sense to investors. An affluent Harvard student, Zuckerberg, could easily have chosen the path of least resistance and gotten a typical job in software development. Instead, he pursued his passion. When it comes to applying Stoicism in business, you will often find that passion becomes the deciding factor – an interesting thought, because any extreme emotion seems to be outside of the Stoic rulebook. But is it really?

Seneca, one of the most iconic Stoic philosophers, has said repeatedly that the means are the only thing that are real and that it is the means that define the end. Here if the goal was the development of Facebook, what were the means?

The simple answer? Action. Persistent action in the face of constant opposition was the way in which Facebook was achieved. Now, yes, the action may have been triggered by passion, but the action itself is a very Stoic notion.

Adversity, when properly approached, is an amazing opportunity. It's like an instant system reboot. The way you face and approach these issues is what is going to not only hone our skills, it is also going to make sure we are equipped to face reality.

The CEO of Goldman Sachs' once famously stated that he simply did not understand individuals who gave up in the face of adversity. To him if one failed, even if they failed miserably, the only thing that made sense was for them to move on and try again because no matter how badly they failed, it wasn't going to be the end of the world and the only way to get past these roadblocks was to work harder.

So, how does that apply to you?

What have you given up on recently? What about not so recently? Why did you do it? What did you learn from it? How can you do it better?

That's a lot of questions, but don't worry, we'll wait. Figure out what your problems were and face them head-on. Remember, direct confrontation is the only way to make Stoicism count.

Chapter 4: Adjusting to the Outside

I have often wondered how it is that every man loves himself more than all the rest of men, but yet sets less value on his own opinion of himself than on the opinion of others.' – Marcus Aurelius

As odd as it may seem, given the fact that Stoicism preaches the isolation of thought and action, the ability to adjust to the outside world is an important cornerstone of Stoic philosophy.

Why?

Well, what do you think separates Stoicism from cynicism?

The acknowledgment and adjustment we make to fit in with our societies and cultures. Stoicism recognizes that we need to work toward making our surroundings a better place, and any good business *must* do the same.

Extrospection: Understanding Others

"When we are no longer able to change a situation, we are challenged to change ourselves." – Viktor E. Frankel

Let's then start with extrospection – first of all, what does 'extrospection' even mean? Is it even a real word?

Well, yes, it is!

Now, we all know what introspection means, right? It means

to look within yourself to find an answer. Extrospection is the opposite, here you are expected to look outside your mind to assess and acknowledge the circumstances that surround you and then identify our role in relation to these external factors to better understand our own place and our own reactions.

Think about it like this, every time you deal with someone other than yourself and keep in mind that doesn't just mean every time you speak to someone else, it means every time you hear voice, watch a movie, listen to a song, or even read a book that is not written by you – you are opening yourself up to another person and their thoughts. These thoughts, actions, and even just the presence can influence how a person views what they are doing.

Think about how self-conscious you feel answering test questions when your teacher is standing over your shoulder. This is the definition of extrospection – your surroundings influence you, and you understanding how and why is what extrospection is all about!

So, what are the things you need to understand about your surroundings? Three things - Impact, triggers and support.

Well, for one, you need to understand how the external environment is impacting you. If for instance, you start working at a place where the people around you are low in spirits, don't have good productivity, and are generally negatively minded – when it comes to your own productivity levels, you'll soon find that you are mirroring your co-workers. You will act as you see the people around you act and this is why measuring impact is so important. The more you understand how your surroundings are causing you to behave, be it positive or negative – the more you know what to expect and the better you can plan.

Measuring impact is a more generalized form of extrospection, there is a lot of stuff that happens around us that causes more direct, more specific reactions, which are called triggers. Whereas impact refers to the general circumstances that influence us by default. Triggers are a reference to the more individually targeted actions such as someone telling you that you look good and that comment causing you to feel a surge of happiness and self-confidence take over, that comment has acted as a trigger and made you feel a certain way.

The third thing that you need to check for when you are extrospecting is the nature of the circumstance, how has this been making you feel? Did you feel happy or sad? Were you encouraged or discouraged? Figuring out if you feel supported and more productive is a great way to evaluate the value levels of the external factors that you are dealing with. Even though Stoicism teaches us to focus on our own actions and reactions, aka introspect, a little bit of extrospection goes a long way in terms of business. It puts you in the customer's shoes and gives you a bird's eye view of what is going on around you and how you can better deal with your surroundings.

Long story short, understanding what is driving your thought process is as important as trying to put a leash on your emotions and emotional outbursts and in fact, is actually more important. Since with the right kind of balance, you can use your extrospection to put yourself in situations where you won't be emotionally triggered at all! Win-win!

Emotional Control: The How-to Manual

> *"Today I escaped anxiety. Or no, I discarded it, because it was within me, in my own perceptions — not outside."* — Marcus Aurelius, Meditations

Now, while we've spoken extensively about what emotional control is, what we haven't quite covered is how we are supposed to implement this emotional control system. This is critical, particularly when dealing with other people because our outward expressions of our emotions are what determine much of our character. That is to say, being extremely upset on the inside and happy on the outside creates a kind of Stoic vortex, where you are physically acting in accordance with the philosophy but not mentally taming your mind.

Similarly, when we deal with other people, it is their external expressions of emotions that lead us to assess and react in a specific way.

So, how do we develop emotional control like the Stoics?

Why don't we give you a cheat sheet?

1. Admit, and Acknowledge

For starters, admit that how you feel is an internalized emotion, a thought rather than a reality. By doing this, what you are doing is you pulling out of the blame game you were playing up till this point. You see, most of us have a tendency of assigning blame to objects or people outside of ourselves. But in truth doing so is just your mind's way of making excuses for itself.

Let's use an example. Donald is a serial abuser, for over 5 years, he has been abusing his wife Kelly, when he comes home drunk. Every time Donald does so, the next day when he is sober, he claims that the entire incident was Kelly's fault and tells her that she needs to stop making him mad.

Let's translate, what do you think Donald is really saying?

I didn't do it willingly. I was forced to. It's not my fault.

It's the exact same thing you are saying when you are saying you couldn't meet a deadline because of X, Y, and Z or when you are justifying getting upset with another external reason. Take a minute, breathe – and be honest. Isn't the real reason you failed to do it because you prioritized something else. Similarly, the real reason that your emotions are getting the better of you is that you are allowing them to. By admitting this, not only are you admitting that you need to fix something that you're doing, but you're also taking control and accepting the fact that you are capable of taking responsibility and therefore that you are your own master. We do not feel things out of our control, rather we feel things that we teach and allow ourselves to feel.

2. *Find Your Own Compass*

Once you've taken responsibility, your next job is to figure out a way to hold yourself accountable. Back in the old days, it was easier for Stoics because they had little Stoic 'clubs' where they could hold each other accountable – but what do you do now?

Well, you find your own compass. Find out what you need to do, define what is right, and stick to it. It's not always easy and you won't always be able to do it, but what's important is that even if you do stray, you always come back and try again.

Seneca, in Letters from a Stoic, suggested that individuals find models or icons to look up to and that they measure themselves against such. If you are a writer facing rejection, look at J.K. Rowling, tell yourself that this woman failed over fifty times before becoming the world's first billionaire author. Remind yourself that every time she was rejected, she worked harder and harder until she got where she is now and use that respect as motivation to keep your impulsive tendency to give up in check. Emotional control is 90% willpower and 10% strategy, ensuring you keep to your true north is all about you staying true to your path, remember that and more importantly act on it.

3. Work On It

Are you a temperamental person? Do you find it hard to keep your temper in check?

Now that you know that, what steps have you taken to address it?

When your emotions hijack your mind and body – the first thing you need to work on is understanding what is triggering you and then you can focus on working on that trigger. So, is your husband telling you that your dress is a little skimpy the problem, or have you been feeling this way for a while based on things he has said before this? Where are your feelings coming from? Can you do anything to change it?

If it is a conflict between people that is leading to your emotional imbalance try talking things out, understand why they said or did what they did and then allow yourself to understand why you are reacting the way you're reacting. Figure out the problem and work on it, and don't stop working on it until it is perfect. Perfection is key. Steve Jobs was often called heartless, but friends have often denied this claim stating that it wasn't that Jobs was heartless, it was merely that the man was a perfectionist and he couldn't stand when people made mistakes.

Emotional outbursts come from a combination of *internal factors* but they all boil down to one thing – we do what we do because we are thinking along specific lines. It is these thoughts that need to change. If your reactions are stemming from fear of failure, counsel yourself on loss aversion. Recognize that failure is not the end of the road and instead challenge yourself to understand your failure – what happened, why didn't it work? Your failures are opportunities, so use them!

Motivation and Inspiration

> *'How long are you going to wait before you demand the best for yourself?" – Epictetus*

And we are back to motivation, but this time we're not just dealing with what motivates us, we are also dealing with what inspires us. Now mankind, in general, is influenced by a myriad of things, starting from the factors we discussed during our bout with extrospection, to other things such as perception and directed inferences but what motivates us and more importantly what teaches us to deal with the world around us?

Well, according to Stoics, motivation is nothing but an impulse and is one of the main areas that Epictetus repeatedly recommends that we train, in order to improve our productivity and more importantly to follow through with our Stoic duty, which is to act deliberately not mindlessly for good reasons.

Sounds pretty complicated, huh?

Let's look at this factor from the point of view of Jack Ma, the Founder and CEO of AliBaba and AliExpress. Jack Ma has gone around for years explaining that he doesn't run a company, he runs an ecosystem and this was because Jack was a firm believer that he *had* to.

Why? Why did he have to? What was his motivation? Patriotism. Jack Ma firmly believed that if he didn't do what he did with his company, in terms of e-commerce, the Chinese economy would have collapsed and as such, he felt compelled to start AliPay, which was a part of the then unsteady financing sector. Ma did this in spite of people repeatedly warning him that he could end up facing jail time if things went south, and regardless, Ma kept moving forward. Ma's logic was simple, it needed to be done, and it was a virtuous act – who does that remind you of?

So, for starters, we are going to work on developing Stoic motivation, like Ma, and in order to do that, we need to train our perception to avoid negative or positive concepts and instead focus on the notion of natural good.

How do we do that?

Well, let's go old school and use a little checklist again – ready?

1. *Train Perception to Avoid Good and Bad*

> *"We are more often frightened than hurt, and we suffer more from imagination than from reality.' – Seneca*

What Seneca is actually trying to say here, is that we have a tendency to feel what we think we're going to feel and kind of build that up in our head. A modern-day psycho-therapist is known for actually using Seneca's letters as an exercise for his students and a particular incident with one of his patients is actually the most amazing way to really establish the power of perceptive thought.

When Dubois was explaining to one of his patients how Stoic philosophy could help them with their ability to cope with the illness they were dealing with, the patient cut him off and told him that he understood and even offered to explain it to him. Intrigued Dubois sat back and listened, as his patient took out a piece of paper and drew a massive black spot on it and then began to explain himself. The young man pointing to the black spot claimed that the spot was the illness that he was suffering from. He then proceeded to draw a line along the edge of the first circle and said, this is what happens when he focuses on this spot, the spot becomes larger Then if he continues to affirm and obsesses over it, the pain becomes greater still as does the circle.

His point was simple, if you leave pain alone, you don't exacerbate it –in fact, it remains what it is, no more no less. And on the other hand, if you put it in focus, your pain becomes central and everything else begins to rotate around it. The solution here is simple, don't focus on attributes given to actions – actions are stand-alone facts, there is no good to them and there is no evil. Your perception is what adds emotional value to these things and as such, this is what must be controlled.

2. Reflect on Your Own Attention

> *"A key point to bear in mind: The value of attentiveness varies in proportion to its object. You're better off not giving the small things more time than they deserve." — Marcus Aurelius, Meditations*

You know how your parents have told you numerous times not to engage bullies and just to ignore them?

Well, negative emotions are mental bullies – so when you allow yourself to wallow in them, be it in rage, in pity, or even in sorrow, what you are doing is you are adding value to something that deserves none. Think about the sheer amount of crimes that are committed due to the fact that the perpetrators want attention – it's the grown-up equivalent to the boy in class with a crush on you pulling your pigtails. Now imagine, if instead of focusing on the perps, the media coverage focused solely on the victims – what has gained value, the bad or the good?

You need to train your mind, the way you wish the global media had been trained. Reflect on the things you are paying the most attention to; is it gossip, or is it an idea that could help change lives? Remember, the attention you give determines the value you are assigning it. Spend your time wisely, it is precious and deserves to be respected.

3. Don't procrastinate

Now it may seem hard, but if you are to work on your self-motivation, you are going to have to start by not being a procrastinator.

Marcus Aurelius discusses this issue in depth and even provides in his personal journal an extremely inspiring conversation he had with himself, that helped him to find purpose and to use that purpose to expel lethargy and laziness from his own subconscious.

For individuals who suffer from procrastination most of all, in terms of how much they can control their minds, the excerpt is a powerful piece of Stoic purpose that is a great way to start your day, to help train yourself to at least aspire to be better.

The Emperor writes -

"At dawn, when you have trouble getting out of bed, tell yourself: 'I have to go to work—as a human being. What do I have to complain of, if I'm going to do what I was born for—the things I was brought into the world to do? Or is this what I was created for? To huddle under the blankets and stay warm?

—But it's nicer here…

So, you were born to feel 'nice'? Instead of doing things and experiencing them? Don't you see the plants, the birds, the ants and spiders and bees going about their individual tasks, putting the world in order, as best they can? And you're not willing to do your job as a human being? Why aren't you running to do what your nature demands?

—But we have to sleep sometime…

Agreed. But nature set a limit on that—as it did on eating and drinking. And you're over the limit. You've had more than enough of that. But not of working. There you're still below your quota. You don't love yourself enough. Or you'd love your nature too, and what it demands of you. People who love what they do wear themselves down doing it, they even forget to wash or eat. Do you have less respect for your own nature than the engraver does for engraving, the dancer for dance, the miser for money or the social climber for status? When they're really possessed by what they do, they'd rather stop eating and sleeping than give up practicing their arts."

How to Deal with Disappointment

"It is in times of security that the spirit should be preparing itself for difficult times; while fortune is bestowing favors on it is then is the time for it to be strengthened against her rebuffs."
- Seneca

Stoicism is about more than just motivation and staying away from negative emotions though, it also helps teach you how to deal with the influx of emotions that you face on a day to day basis. In fact, one of the most iconic Stoic practices is the concept of 'negative schooling' – the idea being that you can actually train your brain to be so well prepared for the worst-case scenario, that you will no longer fear it. One of Seneca's personal ideas was to practice your fears. He recommended that for a set number of days each month one should practice what they feared most, such as poverty or starvation. The idea being that by living through these difficulties in a controlled manner you would be prepared to face it, and therefore wouldn't fear. His theory was basically the same as the philosophical version of guerilla training – by preparing for the worst, you overcame the worst.

So, the next time you feel like you are being controlled by fear, allow yourself to experience it. If your fear is failure, accept failure and allow yourself to fail; failure is never permanent, all you have to do is get back up again. Teach your employees to do the same. Remember the bigger the failure the bigger the effort, which means you are not just overcoming your fear, you are overcoming your inability to get past it!

Rage

> 'Anybody can become angry – that is easy, but to be angry with the right person and to the right degree and at the right time and for the right purpose, and in the right way – that is not within everybody's power and is not easy.'
> - Aristotle

And finally, you have rage – considered by most Stoic philosophers as the most damaging and worthless emotion in the book. One of the best examples of the damage rage can cause was when Alexander the Great, once engaged in a drunken rage-filled brawl with his best friend Cletius. Unfortunately, Alexander in a fit of rage ended up murdering Cletius and it was only after the act that he realized what he had done.

But by then it was too late. This story is almost the same as any rage induced outburst ever – think about how many times you did or said something in a fit of rage and then later realized you couldn't take it back. Once you put something out in the universe it is there forever. So when you speak, when you act, and even when you are merely thinking to yourself; if you aren't careful and if you aren't free from 'passion' you risk becoming Alexander, perhaps you won't have lost a life but a relationship, or an opportunity – but you will lose.

Your willpower to focus your thoughts must be unbendable. Every event that you face and every trigger you meet must be an opponent in a judo match, where your job is to sidestep and deftly use the aggression of your attacker against themselves and it is thus that you take back control. Pretty powerful, isn't it?

Chapter 5: Stoicism in the Business World

> *'Don't dismiss people, don't be a dick, and don't rush. Play the long game.'*
> Tim Ferris

Now, we've gone through a lot of logic and philosophy, but what we haven't had a chance to do is figure out how any of that affects the whole business end of the deal. Sure, we've seen leaders like Obama, Warren Buffett and the founder of Ikea embody numerous Stoic principles in their own lives and we've seen it work for them, but how do we replicate that?

How do we get Stoicism to work for us and our companies?

Well, for starters, looking at the basics of Stoicism helps to focus on the rational side of issues. The philosophy helps blend the clarity of perspective with pure logic, and that helps entrepreneurs stay grounded and self-aware. The awareness, in turn, causes them to develop clear goals and follow them through with the discipline that is preached through it. Simply put Stoicism acts like a personal anti-virus in our mind's personal operating system, every time a virus, be it social or physical, attacks us; Stoicism is there to protect, deflect, and to clean up the mess left behind.

So, why don't we go through a few common issues that business owners face and address them with Stoic principles? Sound good?

Without further ado then – here we go!

What to do when Employees Underperform

So, you've been working your way from the ground up and now currently find yourself in charge of an actual team. This in itself would be awesome but unfortunately, the team happens to have one tiny little problem. One certain member of the team is seriously underperforming, to the extent where it has caught the eye of higher management, and now you've been told to take a look into the issue and fix the problem – what do you do and more importantly where do you start?

Why don't we give a checklist?

Here you go!

1. Practice Active Listening:

> 'I begin to speak only when I'm certain what I'll say isn't better left unsaid."
> – Cato the Younger

Even though it may feel counter-intuitive, the first thing you need to 'do' is absolutely nothing. There is always more than one side to a story and if you don't have all the facts right, not only do you risk blaming someone who could be reacting to a negative stimulator in the group, like a bad team leader perhaps. But you could also, worst case scenario, be putting yourself in some real legal trouble. Wrongful termination is a big deal and you don't want that on your hands or reputation.

Instead, go in with the intent to listen. This keeps you away from the 'bad boss tag' which is important because remember, you have hundreds of other employees who are watching what's happening. f they see you go in fully charged firing first and asking questions later, they are going to decide that this is what you would do to them too. No one wants to work in a work environment that is negative. Not only does it scare them, but it makes them feel unsafe. This is why in specific professions there are actually built-in safety nets, for instance firing a doctor for medical negligence is actually pretty hard – this is because the law believes that if doctors go into operations scared that they are going to make a mistake and then get fired, they are less likely to go into surgeries and even less likely to go an extra mile to save lives.

Instead, go in with the intention of observing and listening. This not only gives you the information you need, it gives it to you from various perspectives, so you can understand the impact as well as your employee's needs.

2. Ask Yourself Questions

> *'Do not explain your philosophy, embody it.' –*
> *Epictetus*

So, you've done your active listening, is it time for you to start talking?

Well, not quite.

Now that you know how and why they are underperforming, you need to take a long hard look at yourself, and at the team – and ask yourself how have you failed them?

While ideally, employees are expected to meet all your set expectations, one thing that is often forgotten, is to check to see if those employees knew what those expectations were. Were they explicitly told and made aware of repercussions?

Even if they were, did you train them accordingly? Be honest, did you ensure that your trainees were equipped to deal with or meet your expectations? Did they even understand them?

If you are faltering when it comes to answering any of these issues, the root issue here is not the lack of performance, but the lack of knowledge and that is what needs to be fortified first. As a Stoic, you cannot assign blame to a person without introspection. Remember, actions are actions, they are not good or bad. Once you take away that element of judgment it is easier to see them for what they are, the result of a sum of other things. Try to understand what this underperformance is a result of and identify which of your own personal actions influenced it.

3. Give Feedback

> 'Use only the appropriate actions of pursuit and avoidance; and even these lightly, and with gentleness and reservation.'

Once you've seen through listening and self-introspection, you are now ready to deal with the issues that relate solely to the employee in question. As the manager, you now have a duty to explain the issues and the expectations in a manner that is honest, but perhaps a little empathetic as well.

Remember, a little compassion goes a long way when it comes to dealing with people, in fact, being kind is a critical component of Stoicism as well. Zeno once said that you should not only be kind and compassionate as you allow people to tell you their problems, but you should also commiserate with them, to the extent that if they are groaning in pain, you should groan too, but only outwardly.

So, keep that in mind as you start talking to your employee, don't be 'blunt' and 'confrontational' – being a bully doesn't make you cool and that is exactly what it would be if you wanted to flex your muscles. Be clear and consistent, but also be nice about it. Tell your employee exactly what is going on, how the company is suffering, how their incomplete task load came to the forefront, and how you and the company have certain expectations of them and what they are.

Furthermore, try not to have the conversation alone – you don't want to be cornering them. Bring in their immediate superior or their line manager and an HR representative, so that they feel the situation is balanced. Remember your job is not to scare them, it is to explain to them what you need and how you need it done by them.

4. Document Everything

> *'Don't demand that things happen as you wish, but wish that they happen as they do happen, and you will go on well.'*

The next step goes beyond just the boardroom discussion you're about to have. Let's start with the discussion you are having with the employee in question. Keep in mind that documentation or writing things down during the meeting is important because it creates a clear sense of consciousness – not only will your employee clearly hear what you are saying, they'll be able to visualize it and clarify anything they are unclear on.

But documentation is more than a meeting technique, in fact, it is critical for post-intervention follow-ups. So, if you are having problems with the employee, even if you are speaking to them face-to-face, make sure there is documented proof of this; send an email, or a memo containing all the major points and ensure that this is sent to and received by the employee in question.

Basically, think like a lawyer. Ensure that you have proof every step of the way. This doesn't make you strict, this makes you smart. By being thoroughly documented, you are sending a message that says, you are going to be holding them accountable and you are also prepared to do what is necessary to do that. Ideally, you will never need the documents and the scare tactic will be enough, but in case it isn't you at least have what you need to deal with the employee in accordance with company directives.

5. Find Positive Ways to Help instead of Berate

> *'When we are no longer able to change a situation, we are challenged to change ourselves.' – Viktor Frankl*

As you proceed as a leader, it is important to understand that you are dealing with people from a point of power and they are already intimidated by you. A good leader knows that fear is the worst of motivators, instead try using positive reinforcement techniques, like reminding them of how good they used to be or talking to them about the potential they have and use that to show them that they can if they want chose to be better.

It is also important to show them how good performances can and will benefit them. Remember, even though Stoic principles are important, it is also important to learn to adapt them to fit in with the context. Give them a broad goal that helps and benefits the world, but also give them small goals to help motivate them on small scale levels, such as promotions or pay raises.

6. Stick to What You Say

> *'Other people's mistakes? Leave them to their makers.'* – Marcus Aurelius

In many ways, being a boss is a lot like being a parent and you need to play bad cop sometimes. Even though docking someone's pay because they are late, may seem petty to you, it can be a necessary measure – remember you can't be giving one employee leeway to come in late every day, while other people have to come in on time – that is discrimination and it will lead to massive tension in the group.

Start laying out and enforcing clear consequences – don't just go up and say, you need to come in on time or there will be problems. Call a meeting and clarify that now for every 3 days an employee is late to work, without a valid medical cause or emergency as approved by their line manager, they will be written up and or fired!

Do the same for larger issues as well, if you need a specific task to come in by a specific date, go and talk to the employee in question and explain to them, kindly that you don't want to do this, but if they don't meet the deadline the will be facing a fine, or they won't be eligible for a promotion or whatever else you need to do to keep them in line.

It's great to have compassion for your employees and while that may make you reluctant to actually take proactive steps, you have to remember that other people's mistakes are theirs and they need to face them You can't intervene everywhere and more importantly, you shouldn't.

7. Avoid Trigger Based Self-talk

> *'The universe is change; our life is what our thoughts make it.'*
> *– Marcus Aurelius*

Remember how we talked about rage earlier and how it was considered to be a roadblock, and clearly against Stoic principles – another thing that is clearly against Stoic principles is dosing yourself with negativity. Remember no actions have attributes, which means nothing is good or bad, things simply are.

As such when you are dealing with your problem employee, if you keep dosing yourself with negative back talk – by saying stuff like 'He's so dumb', 'He's doing this on purpose', you are in effect creating a mental context for the actions – you are in a word 'villainizing' your employee, which will make it hard for you later to see their actions from a neutral point of view. So, if you are looking at a missed deadline and thinking 'She's such a lazy person', you are preparing yourself to see only the worst in that particular employee. At the same time, you don't want to be overly optimistic, that's problematic as well.

As a manager, you'll find that you're facing a bit of Goldilocks paradox – you can't be too negative or too positive and need to find a productive mid-way. But it's a bit of a conundrum, how do you do that?

Try adopting a neutral stance – be unbiased. Don't change, 'She's so lazy' to 'She's the most hardworking person I know', change it to 'I don't know enough about her work ethic, but based on this missed deadline I feel she needs to work harder.'. This allows you to acknowledge your own perception, so that you don't get carried away with your thoughts and stay accountable for them. Remember, when you deal with one employee you are actually dealing with a whole team. If you are being too positive and giving them too much leeway you risk demoralizing other employees. While if you are too negative, you risk upsetting and scaring the other employees. You have to find your sweet spot.

Once you do, a great way to reinforce this is to engage your employees by opening them up to their individual performance targets. Explain the problems you are dealing with and without getting excited or upset, talk about how they can and need to improve. Keep in mind that it's always better to do this by using 'we' statements, since drawing yourself into the mix helps prevent your employee from running scared. Remember this isn't cynicism you're dealing with it's Stoicism. The objective is to get the message across in the most compassionate way possible, not just vent your anger and dissatisfaction.

8. Do What You Have to Do

> *'First say to yourself what you would be; and then do what you have to do.'*
>
> *– Epictetus*

And finally, let's come down to the dirty ground work. Sometimes, leaders also need to know when to cut their losses. If you have put ample support and effort into maintaining and cultivating an employee to the highest standard and your employee unable or unwilling to give you a return on those investments, you need to know when to give up hope and do what you have to.

Firing someone can being an unpleasant experience and, as such, is something that many managers and leaders tend to put off. But think of your employees as an extension of yourself. If you contract gangrene, as badly as you may want to keep your hands or legs, it is critical that in the interest of saving yourself, or in this case the rest of your team, you are courageous enough to step up and make the decisions that are necessary. Remember there is a statute of limitations on everything, even second-chances.

The Nuances of Negotiations and Sales

> *"What's left to be prized? This, I think--to limit our action or inaction to only what's in keeping with the needs of our own preparation... by having some self-respect for your own mind and prizing it, you will please yourself and be in better harmony with your fellow human beings, and more in tune with the gods--praising everything they have set in order and allotted you."*
>
> --- Marcus Aurelius

Because the principles of Stoicism: perception, action, and persistence mirror good business ideals with such fervor it is in fact very beneficial to look at business issues from the eyes of a Stoic philosopher.

Stoicism, at its core, aspires to logic and rationality while acknowledging the presence of normal human emotions such as anger, grief, or happiness. Because it sets *logos* as a goal, it allows businesses and owners to do the same. When in business you seek the bigger picture, it is important that you look at things logically and rationally, not with fear or anxiety or even with optimism. By infusing our business acumen with a little bit of Stoic philosophy we are opening ourselves up to a rational world where we act like the wisest of men, with reason instead of emotion and as such work more consciously and consistently to a greater good.

Sounds pretty fancy, doesn't it?

Why don't we take a look at how we can do that?

1. *Business Partners*

> *"There's nothing worse than a wolf befriending sheep. Avoid false friendship at all costs. If you are good, straightforward, and well-meaning it should show in your eyes and not escape notice."*
>
> —Marcus Aurelius

One of the most important things you'll find yourself dealing with when it comes to your business is of course, the people you choose to go into business with. So, who should you go into business with?

Well, that's a rather subjective question, however, why don't you try asking what type of people you should go into a partnership with? The answer to that is fairly simple, people who share the same philosophy and vision. Always remember that your business partners are like your spouse but in a corporate sense.

While dealing with business partners can be a bit tricky, there are actually three cardinal rules to picking a good business partner and they are all based on Stoic principles – why don't you see if they make sense to you and can help you figure who would be a better fit for you and your company?

a. **Pick Ambition not Greed**

There is a saying that pigs get fat, while hogs get slaughtered – the same goes for people, when you are dealing with business partners you want to pick someone who is ambitious and will always help move the company forward. Picking someone who is greedy can actually harm the company in the long run, not only do you not want that but you'll have a hard time making any negotiations with someone who only sees the money, which will make taking risks harder. While that may sound like a good thing, it's actually a really bad thing because it will almost definitely cause your company to stagnate. So, the next time you are picking business partners, ask questions that help you get a feel of what their main goal is, what are they in it for – the money or the product.

b. **Be Teammates not opponents**

The next thing you need to do is ensure that the person you are partnering up with is someone who you can go into an actual team relationship with. Once you become a partner you need to be able to play together, so someone with drastically different morals or ideas will be hard to accommodate when it comes to making delicate company decisions.

c. **See the Big Picture**

Next up is your ability to see the big picture. Is this someone you can see yourself running the company within 10 or 20 years? Don't just pick someone who would fit in the short-term, you can hire consultants for that. In a partnership, this needs to be someone who would do for you as they would for themselves and you need to do the same – try to go for an even 50-50 split, so that the partnership isn't just benefiting one side and has the emotional investment from both ends.

2. Clients

> *"Crimes often return to their teacher."*
>
> —Seneca

Negotiating with clients can be tricky, particularly since in order to keep the business up and running it's hard to be willing to lose a client. Playing hardball, therefore, is a particularly sore point, especially in this economy. Regardless, there are a number of things you need to know and a bunch of principles you need to hold true to or else you're going to end up running your business into the ground.

Remember when it comes to negotiating, emotion running loose is emotion that is going to cost you. Start by making sure you have your priorities in order, what are you willing to negotiate on, and what is an absolute no go for you? Identify them and list them so that you don't get caught up in the moment and do something untoward. Once you've figured out what you're willing to compromise on, also work on how much you are willing to compromise, what is your hard limit and what is your soft limit. If you can't meet at least one of these, you need to walk away. Giving away more now is not the solution, there will always be other opportunities. Another tip is to never be over-invested. Don't look at any client as your only hope, if they stay they stay but you can't compromise on your business to keep them. This is not only detrimental to the company in the long run, but it can also lead to you giving out unreciprocated concessions that will cost you in the short-term as well.

Do exactly how much you can afford to continue to do, in fact under promise and over deliver. Word of mouth promotion is much better than any other form of PR.

3. Employees

> *"For I believe a good king is from the outset and by necessity a philosopher, and the philosopher is from the outset a kingly person."*
>
> —*Musonius Rufus*

And finally, you are back to employees. this time though, you aren't dealing with the problem child, you're dealing with the star kid who you want to keep on the team. Now, just as it's important to know how to deal with underperforming staff, it's even more important to know how to deal with good staff. After all, staff retention is a huge part of boosting company productivity.

So, what to do you do?

Start by figuring out what they want, remember, preferences need to be assessed carefully so that you not only know what your employees are thinking but also what they want and why. The best way to do this is to have a clear discussion that promotes integrative negotiation so that you can both walk away feeling like you've won something. Also try to keep your employees happy, remember a happy employee is an efficient employee. If you need to invest in training or perhaps talk about job facilities that can help promote happiness, that is exactly where you need to start.

Stress and Anxiety

> *"When I see an anxious person, I ask myself, what do they want? For if a person wasn't wanting something outside of their own control, why would they be stricken by anxiety?"*
>
> *—Epictetus*

Management and strategies aside though, Stoic philosophy's biggest role in terms of business and in particular modern day entrepreneurial businesses is its ability to not only mitigate but actually deal with and address the immense stress and anxiety that comes along with creating something with no safety net.

Stoicism helps people not only seek and find value, but it also teaches them to acknowledge and adapt to the surroundings they are in, which helps us constantly move forward. At the same time, it helps us stay grounded in thought and actions, so that we can ensure we are doing things for all the right reasons and aren't running after things that are either unfeasible or unworthy.

Striking Balance – Find Personal Value

> *"Don't be bounced around, but submit every impulse to the claims of justice, and protect your clear convictison in every appearance."*
>
> *—Marcus Aurelius*

When you are dealing with a new venture, it is natural that not everyone will see what you see, and not everyone will believe in your project as you do. As a person and as a business leader, you need to be able to accept and understand every other opinion you come across without reacting like a four-year-old throwing a temper tantrum. At the same time, you also need to not waver with every negative opinion so much so that you can't hold on to your own convictions.

Stand strong and steady. Jeff Bezos of Amazon, once noted that a good businessman knew when to stand firm in their convictions and at the same time knew how and when to be flexible on the little things such as details. He used the example of his own company, stating that while the company's overarching vision never changed, the intricate details did, vastly. This was particularly due to the fact that for many of the smaller things, the way he had thought things would work, just didn't pan out and that they had to change all of that keeping the big picture in mind. The bottom line is that you need to listen to opinions as they will help you grow and stabilize, but they are a dime a dozen, so you don't necessarily have to follow them.

Everything Ends

> *"Many are harmed by fear itself, and many may have come to their fate while dreading fate."*
>
> *—Seneca*

What else do you need to keep in mind?

That nothing is constant and nothing is forever.

Running a business can be a time-consuming venture. Not only that, but it can also be overwhelming. How many other people do you know who have let their job or their business take over their whole life, while health and relationships got shot to hell?

Probably more than you care to mention. But the truth is that life ends, everything does frankly. Your life, your business, your legacy, all of it will come to an end at some point. So why are you giving it all up?

What is the purpose?

Stoics believe that the purpose of all things is happiness – and as such, happiness is both the end goal and the purpose of the journey. Keep that in mind the next time you look at your venture. Don't moan about not becoming a multi-billion-dollar outfit, be thankful and happy that you have encountered great profits in your first year and that you are still sustaining and growing. You can't always figure out where you are going to be in a year, but you can always be thankful for where you are today.

Accept What You Cannot Control

> *"I don't agree with those who plunge headlong into the middle of the flood and who, accepting a turbulent life, struggle daily in great spirit with difficult circumstances. The wise person will endure that, but won't choose it—choosing to be at peace, rather than at war."*
>
> *—Seneca*

Another important lesson is acceptance. We have an unfortunate tendency to stress out and get all anxious about a million and one things that we usually don't have a whole lot of control over. Think about product market viability, let's say you have a product that is perfect for the market and consumer base – but just days before the launch, your investor pulls out or a corporate spy takes your idea and sells it to another company. All that effort all that energy and it's all gone to waste.

Sucks doesn't it – makes you want to go crawl into a hole in the wall and stay there forever.

You know what Stoicism says though? – Go with the flow.

If it happens, it happens. It's not something to be over the moon about. It is an advantage and treat it like one, but don't treat it like it's the only opportunity you'll ever have because that makes it harder to let go. It means that on the off chance that things don't work out and you don't win that tender or secure that investor, it sucks, but it's not the end of the world. Life lesson? Dial down the drama in your head and you'll find the drama in your life will take a nosedive as well.

Be Compassion Driven

> *"The soul becomes dyed with the color of its thoughts.'*
>
> *–Seneca*

You become who you emulate. And because this is true, it is super important to ensure that the business you run or the focus you hold is not to be the most successful person in the world, no matter what – that would make you Donald Trump, detestable and unpalatable by society at large. Instead, try the opposite. Be kind and compassionate wherever there is an opportunity to be so – be it in the way you run your company, your behavior towards your company, your attitude towards your consumer base, or even your attitude towards nature.

Wherever it is and whatever it is you do – you need to start with compassion, so that you can end there as well.

Obstacles are Opportunities

> *"Once you start learning from your problems, you stop wishing for a life without problems."*
>
> — Mokokoma Mokhonoana

The last but perhaps most important lesson that you will find in Stoic business philosophy is the Stoic view on obstacles. When it comes to building a company, you will find that you are faced with numerous challenges on a daily basis. It could be something as simple as an unhappy customer or a bad employee, it could even be a technical problem like an issue with the product line.

But if there is one certainty, it is that there will be *some* sort of a problem. In the moment, that problem may seem like a curse and you'll be exasperated or even discouraged, you'll feel helpless and you won't see the point of all your hard work. But that is the short run.

In the long run, you will find that every single one of these problems was a blessing – they taught you an important lesson about customer service, or product management, or even team building. Whatever it is, whatever you learned, you learned thanks to that obstacle. So the next time you see a problem coming your way, welcome it with open arms. Your product is about to get that much better and your company that much more efficient, which is perhaps the very definition of a blessing in disguise.

Chapter 6: Stoicism in the Real World

> *"Your potential, the absolute best you're capable of — that's the metric to measure yourself against. Your standards are. Winning is not enough. People can get lucky and win. People can be assholes and win. Anyone can win. But not everyone is the best possible version of themselves."*
>
> *— Ryan Holiday*

And finally, let's come down to the real world. Stoicism has been giving us a lot of information about what we can do in terms of our mental and philosophical growth, particularly in terms of who we want to be and how to get there as a business leader and as an individual.

But how do we do really get this started?

Knowing *why* we should do it and that we *should* do it is different than creating an actual roadmap.

So, why don't we start there – with an actual road-map a 90-day plan to get you to be your Stoic best!

What do you think? Sound exciting?

Why don't you grab yourself a pen and a piece of paper and we'll get right to it!

Go on, we'll wait!

Back?

So, there are just two main things you are going to need to focus on in order to get your Stoic mojo going. The first is to plan like Stoic master and the second is to give your planning a little human spin by putting it into a structure that you are used to. We'll start by showing you how to use Stoic planning, Stoic analytics, and developmental Stoicism specifically to help you create a clear outline for your days. Then we'll take all that and dump it into a Stoic style journal so that you have your Stoic road map for the next three months all planned out – how does that sound?

Well, then without further ado!

We are *off*!

Stoic Planning and Stratagems

The best way to deal with Stoicism and its practice is by thinking of Stoicism as a habit instead of a task – if you tell yourself it is a task, you will find it hard to deal with and more importantly you will find it hard to use as a tool. Instead, recognize that Stoic principles are like lanterns guiding a midnight walker – all you have to do is allow them to light the way.

Three key Stoic actions are to reflect, to evaluate, and to consciously attempt to implement logos in the world around you. By shedding the burden of emotional baggage you are preparing your mind and your soul for the endless possibilities that surround it.

Keep this in mind.

You are powerful.

You are capable.

And most importantly you are willing.

Now, why don't we take all that will and hard work and direct it to development and maintenance of a Stoic lifestyle through the Stoic form of journaling!

The Importance of Journaling and Maintaining a Schedule

> *"Could bitching and moaning on paper for five minutes each morning change your life? As crazy as it might seem, I believe the answer is yes."*
>
> *– Tim Ferriss*

Journaling is central to Stoic philosophy and has been a part of the lives of all three major Stoics, so much so, that Marcus Aurelius's most famous piece of literary work, *Meditations,* actually comes from his personal journal and was never really meant to be published. All three philosophers, Seneca the Younger, Marcus Aurelius, and Epictetus all had their own ways of journaling. Marcus Aurelius, for instance, preferred to journal in the morning and would use the act as a form of self-meditation to set the tone for the rest of his day. Seneca the Younger, on the other hand, was a night owl and preferred to journal late at night when his wife had gone to sleep. He took his journaling to be an opportunity to look back on his day. A form of introspections and self-reflection that was also seen in Epictetus, who journaled both during the day and at night, advocated the same, stating "Every day and night keep thoughts like these at hand—write them, read them aloud, talk to yourself and others about them."

But how far does this go in terms of modern day practitioners?

Journaling 101

> *'Genuine happiness can only be achieved when we transform our way of life from the unthinking pursuit of pleasure to one committed to enriching our inner lives, when we focus on 'being more' rather than simply having more'*
>
> *– Nassim Nicholas Taleb*

Since journaling is a little on the complicated side, if you really want to involve Stoic philosophy into your daily routine, we're going to go ahead and give you a 90-day road map – meaning every day for ninety days, we are about to chalk out a prompt specific journal entry to help you dig deep and find your inner Stoic.

If you're just listening, you can rewind back to this point and note down the prompt and questions for yourself each day, or alternatively, if you are holding the e-book, you can copy or print out the relevant pages so that you have the perfect format in front of you.

The first 10 days, we are going to work on understanding ourselves and how we feel and see the world. The next ten days, we'll focus on planning the days in advance. The plans will stay constant each month to help you create a sense of routine and will then be followed by the self-reflection. On the final ten days of the month, we'll work on and analyze how our days went and what we learned from them. And then we'll do it all over again for two more months, until journaling becomes a part of our daily lives – so, are you ready?

If you want to be productive:

- Go to:

    https://businessleadershipplatform.com/stoic-quotes-business-pdf

    Or use the QR code

- Get the **3-Month-Stoic-Self-Evaluation-Journal** and the **Stoic Quotes**
- print both

Month One

Daily Self-Evaluation

Day One

Date:
Time:

Quote: 'Be happy for this moment, this moment is your life."- Marcus Aurelius

Questions: What am I grateful for today? What are the things that bring me joy? How have these things impacted my life?

Day Two

Date:
Time:

Quote: 'As long as you live, keep learning how to live.' - Seneca

Questions: What are the things I am doing wrong? What did I do wrong today? How can I avoid doing this tomorrow?

Day Three

Date:
Time:

Quote: 'How much more grievous are the consequences of anger, than the causes of it?' Marcus Aurelius

Questions: When was the last time you dealt with an uncontrollable fit of anger? What was about? How did it benefit you? How did it harm you?

Day Four

Date:
Time:

Quote: 'Keep company with only the people who uplift you.'- Epictetus

Questions: Who are the people who uplift you? How do you feel around them? Who are the people who don't uplift you? Why do you stay near them?

Day Five

Date:
Time:

Quote: 'Curb your desire – don't set your heart on so many things and you will get what you need.' - Epictetus

Questions: What are the things you desire? What are the things you need? Why do you think there is a difference?

Day Six

Date:
Time:

Quote: 'I do not forget any good deed done to me and I do not carry a grudge for a bad one.' Viktor Fankel

Questions: Why do find it hard to forget wrongs done to you? What was the last good deed that was done for you? How would you compare them?

Day Seven

Date:
Time:

Quote: 'To be wronged is nothing, unless you continue to remember it.' - Confucius

Questions: Why do you feel wronged? What was done to you that you feel was unfair? Why do you find it hard to forget?

Day Eight

Date:
Time:

Quote: 'We cannot choose our external circumstance, but we can always choose how we respond to them.' - Epictetus

Questions: What do you choose to perceive differently today? How did you perceive this previously? Is it hard to change your perception?

Day Nine

Date:
Time:

Quote: 'We cannot control the evil tongues of others; but a good life enables us to disregard them.' - Cato

Questions: How do you plan to live a good life? How is this helping you to move past the things that people have said? Why did what they say matter?

Day Ten

Date:
Time:

Quote: 'Life isn't about finding yourself, life is about creating yourself.' – George Bernard Shaw

Questions: Who do you want to be? What are the qualities you want to grow in yourself? Who would you consider your model, and why?

Plan Your Day

Day Eleven

Date:
Time:

Daily Stoic Tasks: Refuse to react in anger, no matter how high the temptation.

Questions: What is the cause of your anger? Why do you feel angry? What did you feel like doing out of anger? What would the consequences of this be?

Day Twelve

Date:
Time:

Daily Stoic Tasks: Refuse to give in to sorrow.

Questions: What is the cause of your sorrow? Why do you feel sad? What leads to you feeling sad? What would being sad accomplish?

Day Thirteen

Date:
Time:

Daily Stoic Tasks: Refuse to feel despair.

Questions: What is the cause of your despair? Why do you feel upset? How did it make you feel? What did you want to do?

Day Fourteen

Date:
Time:

Daily Stoic Tasks: Refuse to feel disgust.

Questions: What is the cause of your disgust? Why do you think it triggered that particular feeling? Why do you disapprove?

Day Fifteen

Date:
Time:

Daily Stoic Tasks: Refuse to anticipate and draw expectations.

Questions: What do you normally expect? How would you feel without it? Why is it important to you?

Day Sixteen

Date:
Time:

Daily Stoic Tasks: Refuse to be overjoyed.

Questions: What is the cause of your joy? Why is it of such high value? What would it feel like to be let down now?

Day Seventeen

Date:
Time:

Daily Stoic Tasks: Refuse to feel shame.

Questions: Why do you think you should be ashamed? Who has deemed this to be shameful? Does this contradict with the Stoic principle of virtue?

Day Eighteen

Date:
Time:

Daily Stoic Tasks: Refuse to envy.

Questions: What is the cause of your jealousy? Why do you feel jealous? What did you wish was yours? What would the value of this be?

Day Nineteen

Date:
Time:

Daily Stoic Tasks: Refuse to be helpless.

Questions: Why do you feel helpless? What holds you back?

What do you need to be powerful?

Day Twenty

Date:
Time:

Daily Stoic Tasks: Refuse to feel contempt.

Questions: What is the cause of your contempt? Who do you feel contempt for? What did they do to make you feel that they are unworthy of consideration?

Daily Reflections

Day Twenty One

Date:
Time:

Daily Stoic Reflection: Who did you interact with today? How did they make you feel?

Day Twenty Two

Date:
Time:

Daily Stoic Reflection: What did you do today? How was it difficult?

Day Twenty Three

Date:
Time:

Daily Stoic Reflection: What should you have done today? Why did you not?

Day Twenty Four

Date:
Time:

Daily Stoic Reflection: How was your day? What could have made it better?

Day Twenty Five

Date:
Time:

Daily Stoic Reflection: When was the best time of your day? What made it special?

Day Twenty Six

Date:
Time:

Daily Stoic Reflection: Who did you think of today? Why were they on your mind?

Day Twenty Seven

Date:
Time:

Daily Stoic Reflection: What is a concern you faced today? What do you think you can do about it?

Day Twenty Eight

Date:
Time:

Daily Stoic Reflection: What is a positive thing you did today? How do you think that will help people?

Day Twenty Nine

Date:
Time:

Daily Stoic Reflection: When is it hard for you to get through the day? What do you have to do to keep going?

Day Thirty

Date:
Time:

Daily Stoic Reflection: What healthy choices did you make today? What could you have done to improve them?

Month Two

Daily Self-Evaluation

Day One

Date:
Time:

Quote: 'Adapt yourself to the life you have been given; and truly love the people with whom destiny has surrounded you.'- Marcus Aurelius

Questions: What adaptations do you think you need to make? Why is it hard for you to make them? Who are the people around you? What makes it hard to love them?

Day Two

Date:
Time:

Quote: 'One of the most beautiful qualities of friendship is to understand and to be understood.' - Seneca

Questions: What are the things you are grateful for in your friendships? Who is this friend? How do they make you feel?

Day Three

Date:
Time:

Quote: 'Is a world without pain possible? Then don't ask the impossible.' Marcus Aurelius

Questions: What is making you feel pain? How does this pain feel? Why is it able to hurt you? What does it make you think of?

Day Four

Date:
Time:

Quote: 'The more we value things outside our control, the less control we have.'- Epictetus

Questions: What is outside of your control? Why do you hold it in a position of value? Why does this take away control from you?

Day Five

Date:
Time:

Quote: 'A ship should not ride on a single anchor nor life on a single hope.' - Epictetus

Questions: What is something you hope for? How would you

feel if you don't get it? How can you overcome not having it?

Day Six

Date:
Time:

Quote: 'Not to assume it's impossible because you find it hard. But to recognize that if it's humanly possible, you can do it too.'

Questions: Why do you think certain things seem impossible to you? What are they? How do you think you can overcome these problems?

Day Seven

Date:
Time:

Quote: 'If it is not right do not do it, if it is not true do not say it.' – Marcus Aurelius

Questions: What wrong things have you done in life? How does it feel to lie? How often do you lie to yourself? What do you lie about?

Day Eight

Date:
Time:

Quote: 'Hold, unhappy man, be not swept along with your impression! Great is the struggle, divine the task; the prize is a kingdom, freedom, serenity, peace.' - Epictetus

Questions: What do you think Epictetus is talking about here? What impressions do you have? What struggles do you face?

What would be your kingdom?

Day Nine

Date:
Time:

Quote: 'It is a rough road that leads to the heights of greatness.' - Seneca

Questions: What difficulties have you faced when trying to succeed? What has been your biggest obstacle? How did you overcome it?

Day Ten

Date:
Time:

Quote: 'Waste no more time arguing what a good man should be. Be one.' – Marcus Aurelius.

Questions: Who do you consider to be a good man? What defines good for you? How would you aspire to be a good person?

Plan Your Day

Day Eleven

Date:
Time:

Daily Stoic Tasks: Refuse to react in anger, no matter how high the temptation.

Questions: What is the cause of your anger? Why do you feel angry? What did you feel like doing out of anger? What would the consequences of this be?

Day Twelve

Date:
Time:

Daily Stoic Tasks: Refuse to give in to sorrow.

Questions: What is the cause of your sorrow? Why do you feel sad? What lead to you feeling sad? What would being sad accomplish?

Day Thirteen

Date:
Time:

Daily Stoic Tasks: Refuse to feel despair.

Questions: What is the cause of your despair? Why do you feel upset? How did it make you feel? What did you want to do?

Day Fourteen

Date:
Time:

Daily Stoic Tasks: Refuse to feel disgust.

Questions: What is the cause of your disgust? Why do you think it triggered that particular feeling? Why do you disapprove?

Day Fifteen

Date:
Time:

Daily Stoic Tasks: Refuse to anticipate and draw expectations.

Questions: What do you normally expect? How would you feel without it? Why is it important to you?

Day Sixteen

Date:
Time:

Daily Stoic Tasks: Refuse to be overjoyed.

Questions: What is the cause of your joy? Why is it of such high value? What would it feel like to be let down now?

Day Seventeen

Date:
Time:

Daily Stoic Tasks: Refuse to feel shame.

Questions: Why do you think you should be ashamed? Who has deemed this to be shameful? Does this contradict with the Stoic principle of virtue?

Day Eighteen

Date:
Time:

Daily Stoic Tasks: Refuse to envy.

Questions: What is the cause of your jealousy? Why do you feel jealous? What did you wish was yours? What would the value of this be?

Day Nineteen

Date:
Time:

Daily Stoic Tasks: Refuse to be helpless.

Questions: Why do you feel helpless? What holds you back? What do you need to be powerful?

Day Twenty

Date:
Time:

Daily Stoic Tasks: Refuse to feel contempt.

Questions: What is the cause of your contempt? Who do you feel contempt for? What did they do to make you feel that they are unworthy of consideration?

Daily Reflections

Day Twenty One

Date:
Time:

Daily Stoic Reflection: What did you do today? What did you want to do in addition? Why did you not do it?

Day Twenty Two

Date:
Time:

Daily Stoic Reflection: What is the most positive thing that you saw today? How did it affect your perception?

Day Twenty Three

Date:
Time:

Daily Stoic Reflection: What responsibilities did you carry today? How many did you fulfill? What did you miss?

Day Twenty Four

Date:
Time:

Daily Stoic Reflection: What was the most difficult part of your day today? Why was it difficult? How could you have changed this?

Day Twenty Five

Date:
Time:

Daily Stoic Reflection: When was the worst time of your day? What made it so difficult?

Day Twenty Six

Date:
Time:

Daily Stoic Reflection: What was your strongest emotion today? Why did you feel it? How do you think your feelings were communicated?

Day Twenty Seven

Date:
Time:

Daily Stoic Reflection: What is something that disturbed you today? What did you want to do about it? What did you do about it?

Day Twenty Eight

Date:
Time:

Daily Stoic Reflection: What is a negative thing you did today? How do you think that will harm people? How has it harmed you?

Day Twenty Nine

Date:
Time:

Daily Stoic Reflection: What was a kindness you experienced today? Who was kind to you? What did you do in return?

Day Thirty

Date:
Time:

Daily Stoic Reflection: How calm were you today? On a scale of 1-10, how would you rank your calmness? How did it make you feel?

Month Three

Daily Self-Evaluation

Day One

Date:
Time:

Quote: 'Ask: What is so unbearable about this situation? Why can't you endure it? You will be embarrassed to answer.'- Marcus Aurelius

Questions: What unbearable situation do you feel you are in? Why do you find it to be unbearable? Why are you finding it hard to deal with? Why do you think you would be embarrassed?

Day Two

Date:
Time:

Quote: 'Lives badly who does not know to die well.' - Seneca

Questions: What are the things you do that make you feel that you should live a better life? How can you do that? What do you think about death?

Day Three

Date:
Time:

Quote: 'The first rule is to keep an untroubled spirit, the second is to look things in the face and know them for what they are.' Marcus Aurelius

Questions: What is an untroubled spirit? How do you gain an untroubled spirit? What do you need to look in the face?

Day Four

Date:
Time:

Quote: 'Remain calm in every situation because peace equals power.'- Joyce Meyer

Questions: What is the hardest thing about staying calm? Where do you need to stay calm the most? Why do you think peace is powerful?

Day Five

Date:
Time:

Quote: 'Any person capable of angering you becomes your master; he can anger you only when you permit yourself to be disturbed by him.' - Epictetus

Questions: What is something that angers you? Who causes this anger? Why do you allow this anger to form?

Day Six

Date:
Time:

Quote: 'First learn the meaning of what you say, and then speak.'

Questions: What have you said that you did not understand? What did you say that you wish you had thought of more?

Day Seven

Date:
Time:

Quote: 'You can't calm the storm, so stop trying. What you can do is calm yourself. The storm will pass.' – Timber Hawkeye

Questions: What do you need to do to calm yourself? How have you tried to do so? What was effective? What was not effective?

Day Eight

Date:
Time:

Quote: 'Be strong. Because things will get better. It may be stormy now, but it never rains forever.' – Winston Churchill

Questions: What do you think you should do to stay mentally strong? What is your most difficult moment? Why is it hard to overcome?

Day Nine

Date:
Time:

Quote: 'Learning to ignore things is one of the greatest paths to inner peace.' – Robert J. Sawyer

Questions: What difficulties have you faced when trying to ignore something that bothers you? What has been your biggest hardship? How do you think you can come to terms with it?

Day Ten

Date:
Time:

Quote: 'Never let the future disturb you. You will meet it, if you have to, with the same weapons of reason which today arm you against the present.' – Marcus Aurelius.

Questions: What do you expect of the future? What daunts you? What do you find inspiring?

Plan Your Day

Day Eleven

Date:
Time:

Daily Stoic Tasks: Refuse to react in anger, no matter how high the temptation.

Questions: What is the cause of your anger? Why do you feel angry? What did you feel like doing out of anger? What would the consequences of this be?

Day Twelve

Date:
Time:

Daily Stoic Tasks: Refuse to give in to sorrow.

Questions: What is the cause of your sorrow? Why do you feel sad? What lead to you feeling sad? What would being sad accomplish?

Day Thirteen

Date:
Time:

Daily Stoic Tasks: Refuse to feel despair.

Questions: What is the cause of your despair? Why do you feel upset? How did it make you feel? What did you want to do?

Day Fourteen

Date:
Time:

Daily Stoic Tasks: Refuse to feel disgust.

Questions: What is the cause of your disgust? Why do you

think it triggered that particular feeling? Why do you disapprove?

Day Fifteen

Date:
Time:

Daily Stoic Tasks: Refuse to anticipate and draw expectations.

Questions: What do you normally expect? How would you feel without it? Why is it important to you?

Day Sixteen

Date:
Time:

Daily Stoic Tasks: Refuse to be overjoyed.

Questions: What is the cause of your joy? Why is it of such high value? What would it feel like to be let down now?

Day Seventeen

Date:
Time:

Daily Stoic Tasks: Refuse to feel shame.

Questions: Why do you think you should be ashamed? Who has deemed this to be shameful? Does this contradict with the Stoic principle of virtue?

Day Eighteen

Date:
Time:

Daily Stoic Tasks: Refuse to envy.

Questions: What is the cause of your jealousy? Why do you feel jealous? What did you wish was yours? What would the value of this be?

Day Nineteen

Date:
Time:

Daily Stoic Tasks: Refuse to be helpless.

Questions: Why do you feel helpless? What holds you back? What do you need to be powerful?

Day Twenty

Date:
Time:

Daily Stoic Tasks: Refuse to feel contempt.

Questions: What is the cause of your contempt? Who do you feel contempt for? What did they do to make you feel that they are unworthy of consideration?

Daily Reflections

Day Twenty One

Date:
Time:

Daily Stoic Reflection: What was your greatest temptation today? What did you want to do? Why did you not do it?

Day Twenty Two

Date:

Time:

Daily Stoic Reflection: What is something you find kind and loving, that you experience daily? How does it affect your mood?

Day Twenty Three

Date:
Time:

Daily Stoic Reflection: What responsibilities did you fail to carry out today? How many? Why did you fail? How are you going to make this up?

Day Twenty Four

Date:
Time:

Daily Stoic Reflection: What was the biggest blessing you had today? When did it happen? How thankful do you feel?

Day Twenty Five

Date:
Time:

Daily Stoic Reflection: When was the worst time of your day? What made it so difficult?

Day Twenty Six

Date:
Time:

Daily Stoic Reflection: What was your weakest emotion today? Why do you think it was weak? How do you feel about it?

Day Twenty Seven

Date:
Time:

Daily Stoic Reflection: What is something that inspired you today? How do you wish to emulate it? How are you going to see through this thought?

Day Twenty Eight

Date:
Time:

Daily Stoic Reflection: What is a positive thing that you plan to do tomorrow? How is it positive? Who does it benefit?

Day Twenty Nine

Date:
Time:

Daily Stoic Reflection: How would you define inner peace? What do you think you can do that would help you create inner peace for your own self?

Day Thirty

Date:
Time:

Daily Stoic Reflection: How meaningful did your life feel today? Why do you think this? How can you add more meaning?

And just like that, you are done with 90 whole days of Stoic living. Give yourself a pat on the back! This is gladiator level persistence and you deserve every bit of the mental celebration you have going right now. Just remember, you can't just do ninety days and quit, that's like relapsing after going 90 days sober.

Big no-no.

Instead, why don't you take a quick minute and flip back through the 90 days you have done to see how much your answers have changed from day one to your final Day 30?

Not only will that help you better understand how far you've come, but it'll also help you work on where you want to go from here. Where is your Stoic lifestyle going to take you now? Who are you going to be? How are you going to use these new habits to improve the productivity levels of your life and career?

And most importantly, who are you going to be?

You'll be answering all this, so do you think you're ready?

Conclusion

> *'I have often wondered how it is that every man loves himself more than all the rest of men, but yet sets less value on his own opinion of himself than on the opinion of others.'* – Marcus Aurelius

Whew! That was quite the ride wasn't it – it's been a loooong journey, hasn't it?

Well, to begin though, let us take a moment to thank you for buying "Stoicism for Business - *Ancient stoic wisdom and practical advice for building mental toughness, productivity habits and success in modern management*"- we sincerely hope that the book has been able to help you effectively and systematically develop your ability to deal with emotions and life in general, in a more efficient and productive manner just as our Stoic ancestors did.

Now although we have already made a point to cover all of the relevant Stoic philosophies that can and do impact your life, we've also gone on to illustrate how noted world leaders and successful innovators have been using Stoic philosophy as a tool to build their success! There is a reason we did that! The fact that you picked this book up tells us that even if you haven't already started to establish your own company and have things running, you've been thinking about a business venture for some time now and haven't quite been sure how to prepare. Well, your wait is officially over!

Now with the right kind of effort and support, you could be one of the future Stoic success stories and join the ranks of Mark Zuckerberg and Warren Buffet (imagine that!) – but that's only if you make sure you are actually following the Stoic regimen, of course. Stoic living is almost like a fitness plan, it's a lifestyle choice that you are going to have to stick to if you really want to see results. Not only does Stoic living teach us restraint and perspective, it also teaches us persistence and perseverance both of which are necessary if you are looking to build your empire, and if you're thinking of starting small, this is even more important!

But that's not it, in the words of Marcus Aurelius, 'In your actions don't procrastinate. In your conversations, don't confuse. In your thoughts, don't wander. In your soul, don't be passive or aggressive. In your life, don't be all about business'. The Stoic journey you just finished has an overarching purpose that goes beyond preparing you for a successful career. It's also meant to help you find true happiness and content. Your well-being, your ability to process, your mental peace; all of these are factors that we are deeply invested in – this isn't just your journey, it's *our* journey and we need for you to be happy and content at the end of it.

And we've really gone in depth to show you how – starting from grassroots level Stoic philosophy, the book also deals with practical application techniques and plans that can and will help you cultivate a Stoic mind, if you so choose. But it doesn't end just yet!

If you enjoyed reading this, a few of the other books that you definitely would love to read are Meditations by Marcus Aurelius, The Daily Stoic by Ryan Holiday, Epistulae Morales ad Lucilium by Seneca, A Guide to the Good Life: The Ancient Art of Stoic Joy by William B. Irvine, How to be a Stoic – Ancient wisdom for modern living by Massimo Piglijucci, The Obstacle is the Way – Ryan Holiday, Discourses of Epictetus, The Shortness of Life by Seneca and How to think like a Roman Emperor by Donald Robertson.

That's a whole lot of reading, isn't it?

Don't fret – remember panic isn't becoming of a Stoic influencer instead, focus on the plan. All you have to do is get through this one book at a time. You can actually do this in addition to your journal, as a daily thing, by covering a chapter or two per day. You'll soon find that – the more you read the more you'll find you are amazed and prepared to take on the world.

Which is why on that final note, we wanted to remind you that we are super grateful for your trust in us and hope sincerely that we have been able to provide you with content that has been worth both your time and your effort! We are grateful for your love and support and we can only hope that you feel that we have delivered on our promise – in fact. if you do feel like we've been helpful and think this book was a worthy use of your time, please do take a minute out of your busy schedule (it only takes a minute, promise!) and please leave a review! We'd love to hear back from you!

References

Cialdini, R. B. (2007). *Influence: The psychology of persuasion.* New York: HarperCollins Publishers, Inc.

Levitin, D. (2014). *The organized mind: Thinking straight in the age of information overload.* New York: Dutton Penguin Random House.

Munger, C. (2005). *Poor Charlie's almanac.* Brookfield: The Donning Company.

Academy of Leadership Coaching & NLP. (n.d.). The importance of building self-awareness in leaders. Retrieved from https://nlp-leadership-coaching.com/the-importance-of-building-self-awareness-in-todays-business-leader/

Ask Dr. Universe. (2017). Why do we have feelings? Retrieved from https://askdruniverse.wsu.edu/2017/06/05/feelings/

Babuta, L. (2019). Learn to respond, not react: Zen habits. Retrieved from https://zenhabits.net/respond/

Bariso, J. (2014, October 29). Empathy: The basic quality many leaders keep getting wrong. Retrieved from https://www.inc.com/justin-bariso/empathy-the-basic-quality-many-leaders-keep-getting-wrong.html

Belludi, N. (2017). How to respond to others' emotional situations. Retrieved from http://www.rightattitudes.com/2017/10/25/how-to-respond-to-others-emotional-situations/

Boyd, N. (n.d.) Introspection and self-awareness theory in psychology: Definition & examples [Video File]. Retrieved from https://study.com/academy/lesson/introspection-and-self-awareness-theory-in-psychology-definition-examples.html

Bradt, G. (2016). Disney's best ever example of motivating employees. Retrieved from https://www.forbes.com/sites/georgebradt/2015/05/20/disneys-best-ever-example-of-motivating-employees/#363084c9144b

Brogaard, B. (2018). Basic and complex emotions. Retrieved from https://www.psychologytoday.com/intl/blog/the-superhuman-mind/201806/basic-and-complex-emotions

Casnocha, B. (2019). First step in starting a business: Introspection. Retrieved from https://www.entrepreneur.com/article/63224

Cherry, K. (2012). The purpose of emotions. Retrieved from https://www.verywellmind.com/the-purpose-of-emotions-2795181

Cherry, K. (2017). Understanding body language and facial expressions. Retrieved from https://www.verywellmind.com/understand-body-language-and-facial-expressions-4147228

Cherry, K. (2019). The 6 types of basic emotions and their effect on human behavior. Retrieved from https://www.verywellmind.com/an-overview-of-the-types-of-emotions-4163976

Choi, P. (2012). Self awareness vs. introspection. Retrieved from https://paulchoiblog.wordpress.com/2012/04/18/self-awareness-vs-introspection/

Clark, J. (2010). What are emotions, and why do we have

them? Retrieved from https://science.howstuffworks.com/life/what-are-emotions.htm

Donaldson, M. (2018). Plutchik's wheel of emotions. Retrieved from https://www.6seconds.org/2017/04/27/plutchiks-model-of-emotions/

Fallon, N. (2014). 7 tips for leaders to improve self-awareness. Retrieved from https://www.businessnewsdaily.com/6097-self-awareness-in-leadership.html

Finkelstein, S. (2018). Reading facial expressions as a channel of non-verbal communication. Retrieved from https://medium.com/kinesics/reading-facial-expressions-as-a-channel-of-non-verbal-communication-26f929ba172a

Free Management Books. (n.d.). Ability-based model of emotional intelligence. Retrieved from http://www.free-management-ebooks.com/faqpp/measuring-03.htm

Freed, J. E. (2014). Leaders build community. Retrieved from https://trainingmag.com/trgmag-article/leaders-build-community/

Freedman, J. (2010). The business case for emotional intelligence. Retrieved from https://www.academia.edu/1293046/The_Business_Case_for_Emotional_Intelligence?

Gillespie, S. (2016). Leadership lessons: The power of validation. Retrieved from https://www.firehouse.com/leadership/article/12161639/leadership-lessons-the-power-of-validation

Goleman, D. (2015). Self-regulation: A star leader's secret weapon. Basic emotions, complex emotions, Machiavellian emotions. Royal Institute of Philosophy Supplement, 52, 39–67. doi: https://doi.org/10.1017/s1358246100007888

Golis, C. (2017). A brief history of emotional intelligence. Retrieved from https://www.emotionalintelligencecourse.com/history-of-eq/

Gourguechon, P. (2018). A neglected but essential leadership trait -- Why self-control really matters. Retrieved from https://www.forbes.com/sites/prudygourguechon/2018/04/03/a-neglected-but-essential-leadership-trait-why-self-control-really-matters/#a904eae787af

Innovation Management. (n.d.). The power of outrospection. Retrieved from https://innovationmanagement.se/2013/01/16/the-power-of-outrospection/

Jane. (2014). Learned helplessness and the ABCDE model. Retrieved from https://www.habitsforwellbeing.com/learned-helplessness-and-the-abcde-model/

Juneja, P. (2015). Self motivation at work. Retrieved from https://www.managementstudyguide.com/self-motivation-work.htm

Kiger, D. R. (2013). Curiosity is a key to success for CEOs. Retrieved from https://www.davidrkiger.com/blog/curiosity-is-a-key-to-success-for-ceos/

Kiger, D. (2019). Self-awareness is essential in business leadership. Retrieved from https://www.business2community.com/leadership/self-awareness-is-essential-in-business-leadership-02057971

Krell, K. (2017). Does love have a place in business? Retrieved from https://www.virgin.com/virgin-unite/our-community/does-love-have-place-business

Laserfiche. (n.d.). Why empathy is the most important business skill. Retrieved from https://www.laserfiche.com/ecmblog/why-empathy-is-the-most-important-business-skill/#

Levy, L. (2018). 4 ways HR can leverage positive psychology at work. Retrieved from https://blog.eeihr.com/4-ways-hr-can-leverage-positive-psychology-at-work

Lewis, J. (2011). The disadvantages of impulsive management. Retrieved from https://smallbusiness.chron.com/disadvantages-impulsive-management-36243.html

Lippincott, M. (2018). Effective leadership starts with self-awareness. Retrieved from https://www.td.org/insights/effective-leadership-starts-with-self-awareness

Lofgren, L. (2019). The power of emotional marketing. Retrieved from https://www.quicksprout.com/emotional-marketing/

Macalister, T., Treanor, J., & Farrell, S. (2017). BP shareholders revolt against CEO's £14m pay package. Retrieved from https://www.theguardian.com/business/2016/apr/14/bp-pledge-shareholder-anger-ceo-bob-dudleypay-dea

MacDonald, S. (2019). Customer complaints: Why angry customers are good for business. Retrieved from https://www.superoffice.com/blog/customer-complaints-good-for-business/

Make A Dent Leadership. (n.d.). The power of visualization is used by leaders to change worlds. Retrieved from https://www.makeadentleadership.com/power-of-visualization.html

Markel, G. (2017). Impulsive work/life decisions and their affect on a leader's productivity. Retrieved from http://gerimarkel.com/impulsive-worklife-decisions-and-their-affect-on-a-leaders-productivity/

Martinuzzi, B. (2019). 7 tips to help improve your emotional self-control and leadership. Retrieved from https://www.americanexpress.com/en-us/business/trends-and-insights/articles/emotional-self-control-and-leadership/

Mental Health America. (n.d.). Depression in the workplace. Retrieved from https://www.mentalhealthamerica.net/conditions/depression-workplace

Mind Tools. (2019). Managing your emotions at work - Controlling your feelings... Before they control you. Retrieved from https://www.mindtools.com/pages/article/newCDV_41.htm

Nelson, K. (2018). 7 examples of healthcare: Healthcare companies to model. Retrieved from https://www.wegohealth.com/2017/11/27/examples-of-empathy-healthcare/

Patel, N. (2016). The 7 secrets self-motivated entrepreneurs know. Retrieved from https://www.entrepreneur.com/article/251591

Pennock, S.F. (2019). What is self-esteem? A psychologist explains. Retrieved from https://positivepsychologyprogram.com/self-esteem/

Petrides, K. (n.d.). Ability and trait emotional intelligence history and background [PDF File]. Retrieved from http://www.psychometriclab.com/adminsdata/files/Trait%20EI%20-%20HID.pdf

Petrides, K. (n.d.). Trait emotional intelligence [PDF File]. Retrieved from https://www.thomasinternational.net/getmedia/6bf0569a-8da3-4646-bfc0-ce7e2aed07d5/Trait-EI-Presentation-General-(2016).pdf

Price, K. (2018). Why self-awareness is vital to leadership. Retrieved from https://thriveglobal.com/stories/why-self-awareness-is-vital-to-leadership/

Rathe, R. (n.d.). Responding to emotions (BATHE). Retrieved from https://rathe.medinfo.ufl.edu/responding-to-emotions-bathe/

Razzetti, G. (2018,). How to stop your thoughts from eating you alive. Retrieved from https://blog.liberationist.org/how-to-stop-your-thoughts-from-making-you-foggy-67bfa1fb1721

Razzetti, G. (2019). How to increase self-awareness and be at peace with yourself. Retrieved from https://blog.liberationist.org/how-to-increase-self-awareness-and-be-at-peace-with-yourself-74df445bc26c

Robson, P.K. (2012). The "ABCDE" method for changing your mind – for the better! Retrieved from https://wishfulthinkingworks.com/what-2/the-quotabcdequot-method-for-changing-your-mind-for-the-better/

Ruestow, J. (2008). The Effect of a Leader's Emotional Intelligence on Follower Job Satisfaction and Organizational Commitment: An Exploratory Mixed Methodology Study of

Emotional Intelligence in Public Human Services. Retrieved from https://www.researchgate.net/publication/277997030_The_effect_of_a_leader's_emotional_intelligence_on_follower_job_satisfaction_and_organizational_commitment_An_exploratory_mixed_methodology_study_of_emotional_intelligence_in_public_human_services

Runkel, H. (2018). What's more powerful than fear? Retrieved from http://screamfree.com/whats-more-powerful-than-fear/

Schmitz, T. (2018). Self-esteem: Behavior patterns. Retrieved from https://www.conovercompany.com/self-esteem-behavior-patterns/

Seredich, B. (2018). Lack of impulse control: Is it preventing leaders from engaging with their teams? Retrieved from https://www.achievers.com/blog/lack-of-impulse-control-is-it-preventing-leaders-from-engaging-with-their-team/

Siegling, A. B., Furnham, A., & Petrides, K. V. (2014). Trait emotional intelligence and personality. Journal of Psychoeducational Assessment, 33(1), 57–67. doi: https://doi.org/10.1177/0734282914550385

Sherman, E. (2018). Martin Shkreli's real crime: Stealing from the wrong people. Retrieved from https://www.forbes.com/sites/eriksherman/2018/03/09/martin-shkreli-real-crime-stealing-from-the-wrong-people/#303d572d122c

Shrestha, P. (2017). Trait theory of personality. Retrieved from https://www.psychestudy.com/general/personality/trait-theory

Silverman, S. (2016). Former pharma CEO Martin Shkreli tarnishes the image of his profession. Retrieved from http://silvermanleadership.com/former-pharma-ceo-martin-shkreli-tarnishes-the-image-of-his-profession/

Simons, I. (2009). Why do we have emotions? Retrieved from https://www.psychologytoday.com/intl/blog/the-literary-mind/200911/why-do-we-have-emotions

Small, M. F. (2008). Why humans bother with emotions. Retrieved from https://www.livescience.com/2431-humans-bother-emotions.html

Sorenson, S. & Garman, K. (2013). How to tackle U.S. employees' stagnating engagement. Retrieved from https://news.gallup.com/businessjournal/162953/tackle-employees-stagnating-engagement.aspx

Spodek, J. (2013). The model: Characteristics of emotions. Retrieved from http://joshuaspodek.com/model-characteristics-emotions

Taggart, J. (n.d.). Emotional intelligence - The inner side of leadership [PDF File]. Retrieved from https://changingwinds.files.wordpress.com/2010/10/ei-the-inner-side-of-leadership.pdf

The Rule of Balance -- Logical Mind vs. Emotional Heart. (2019). Retrieved from https://westsidetoastmasters.com/resources/laws_persuasion/chap14.html

Universal Class. (n.d.). Emotional intelligence: Mixed model. Retrieved from https://www.universalclass.com/articles/psychology/emotional-intelligence-mixed-model.htm

Universal Class. (n.d.). Emotional intelligence: The ability model. Retrieved from https://www.universalclass.com/articles/self-help/emotional-intelligence/emotional-intelligence-the-ability-model.htm

Waters, L. (2015). Why happiness is contagious. Retrieved from https://www.weforum.org/agenda/2015/10/why-happiness-is-contagious/

Weir, K. (2012). A complex emotion. Retrieved from www.apa.org website: https://www.apa.org/monitor/2012/11/emotion

Wheeler, W. (2017). Evolution in leadership. Retrieved from https://www.evolutioninleadership.com/blog/2017/7/9/6-steps-for-leaders-on-how-to-deal-with-angry-staff

Ye, L. (2015). 7 outdated sales closing techniques that are flat out terrible. Retrieved from https://blog.hubspot.com/sales/terrible-closing-techniques

Zoller, K. & Preston, K. (2014). The key to self-motivation and employee motivation. Retrieved from https://hiring.monster.com/employer-resources/small-business-hiring/employee-engagement/self-motivation/

Comaford, Christine. "The Secret To Controlling Your Emotions -- Before They Control You." *Forbes*, 29 Mar. 2018, www.forbes.com/sites/christinecomaford/2017/10/15/the-secret-to-controlling-your-emotions-before-they-control-you/#4841d56437de. Accessed 10 Apr. 2019.

"Emotional Self-Control Habits to Make You a Billionaire!" *Gutshot*, 2018, www.gutshotmagazine.com/news/details/emotional-self-control-habits-to-make-you-a-billionaire. Accessed 9 Apr. 2019.

exida.com LLC. "How to Become a World-Class Expert (the

10,000 Hour Rule).” *Exida.Com*, 2016, www.exida.com/Blog/how-to-become-a-world-class-expert-the-10000-hour-rule. Accessed 9 Apr. 2019.

Fors, Kristian R. "COLUMN: Stoicism — A Countermeasure to Stress - The Utah Statesman." *The Utah Statesman*, 21 July 2018, usustatesman.com/column-stoicism-a-countermeasure-to-stress/. Accessed 8 Apr. 2019.

https://www.facebook.com/BusinessAlligators. "How Successful People Control Emotions." *Business Alligators*, 2 May 2017, www.businessalligators.com/how-successful-people-control-emotions/. Accessed 9 Apr. 2019.

Massimo. "Stoic Advice: Is Compassion Possible, or Advisable, for a Stoic?" *How to Be a Stoic*, How to Be a Stoic, 17 June 2017, howtobeastoic.wordpress.com/2017/06/10/stoic-advice-is-compassion-possible-or-advisable-for-a-stoic/. Accessed 8 Apr. 2019.

---. "What Would a Stoic Do? The Stoic's Decision Making Algorithm." *How to Be a Stoic*, How to Be a Stoic, 10 Dec. 2015, howtobeastoic.wordpress.com/2015/12/08/what-would-a-stoic-do-the-stoics-decision-making-algorithm/. Accessed 7 Apr. 2019.

Quora. "I Studied Billionaires and Talked to Neuroscientists, and I've Realized There Are 4 Key Parts to Making Great Decisions." *Business Insider*, 23 Nov. 2017, www.businessinsider.com/ultimate-framework-for-making-better-decisions-based-on-billionaires-2017-11. Accessed 9 Apr. 2019.

RicardoGuaderrama. "Emotion Control." *STOIC ANSWERS*, STOIC ANSWERS, 17 Apr. 2018, stoicanswers.com/2018/03/18/emotion-control/. Accessed 9

Apr. 2019.

Vetter, Amy. "4 Lessons From Greek Philosophy to Improve Your Business and Life." *Inc.Com*, Inc., 6 Feb. 2019, www.inc.com/amy-vetter/4-lessons-from-greek-philosophy-to-improve-your-business-life.html. Accessed 7 Apr. 2019.

Hello,

You live in a stressful and fast-paced business world.

When reading, everything seems logical and clear, but when you´re at work, you tend to forget quickly and move on as usual.

You forget things, because you have to process a lot of new information every single day and you don´t actively repeat the lessons you have learned.

I have found a practical solution for you. One which doesn´t require any mental energy.

Based on the contents of the book you will get access to 4 different programs and summaries:

- Summary of 29 mental models, some used by presidents, billionaires and other successful business people.
- ´The 30-Day Emotional Intelligence Booster Program´ in PDF format
- The stoic quotes in a easy to print format
- 3-Month-Self-Evaluation-Journal

If you want to think, act and behave like a great leader:

- Go to: https://businessleadershipplatform.com/programs-to-be-a-great-leader

  OR Scan the QR Code below

- Get the programs and summary
- print the one you want to work on first
- start reading and initiate the desired change

Tip: **Work on 1 program at the time**

Enjoy the book.

R. Stevens

Business Leadership Platform

www.businessleadershipplatform.com